VEGETABLE GROWING HANDBOOK

VEGETABLE GROWING HANDBOOK

Walter E. Splittstoesser, Ph.D.

Professor of Plant Physiology in Horticulture
University of Illinois
Urbana, Illinois

AVI PUBLISHING COMPANY, INC.
Westport, Connecticut

©Copyright 1979 by
THE AVI PUBLISHING COMPANY, INC.
Westport, Connecticut

*Frontispiece courtesy of Mobay Chemical Corporation,
Kansas City, Missouri*

Library of Congress Cataloging in Publication Data

Splittstoesser, Walter E
   Vegetable growing handbook.

   Includes index.
   1. Vegetable gardening.   I. Title.
SB321.S645   635   79-394
ISBN 0-87055-319-4

Printed in the United States of America
by Eastern Graphics, Inc.
Old Saybrook, CT.

Preface

The key to a successful vegetable garden is the understanding and utililization of the basic principles of crop production. Knowledge and understanding of the planning, planting and procedures for producing vegetables will reward the gardener with an abundant supply of quality vegetables. This book provides the necessary information and is designed for use by the National Junior Horticultural Assoc., 4-H Clubs, Future Farmers of America (FFA) and for use in high schools and in vocational, community or junior colleges; or, for use at a beginning college level. It is designed to serve as a ready reference for county agents or farm advisers and be a reference manual for the astute and informed gardener. It is easily read by those who have not had special courses in agriculture.

The book is divided into sections covering the principles and practices of growing vegetables successfully with biological, chemical, mechanical and organic methods. Successful insect and disease control methods are given along with illustrations of beneficial and harmful insects so that these may be easily identified. The book contains a section on physiological events such as seedstalk formation and describes why these events occur and how to prevent them. The section on soils and plant nutrition gives detailed information on the essential plant elements and describes how these may be obtained from chemical and organic sources or manures as fertilizers. The use of composts and mulches are included.

The harvesting and storage of vegetables is given. Detailed information is given on growing over 60 different vegetables and includes a number of easily grown garden herbs. An appendix lists the addresses of state agricultural experiment stations and seed companies; and the nutritional value of vegetables. As most gardeners have not adopted the metric system, the English system of inches, feet, pounds, etc. is used. (A conversion table is included in the appendix).

This book is an outgrowth of lectures, and greenhouse and field procedures used in the author's course on "Organic and Traditional Vegetable Gardening." Various publications from state agricultural experiment stations and the United States Department of Agriculture have been used to insure that the book can be used in all sections of the country.

The author is indebted to agricultural scientists everywhere for providing the research upon which this book is based; to Shirley Splittstoesser for proof reading and raising questions a novice gardener would want answered; and to Pamela Splittstoesser for typing the manuscript.

It is also a pleasure to acknowledge the encouragement and assistance of my colleague, Dr. Joseph S. Vandemark, Professor, Vegetable Crops, University of Illinois, in this endeavor.

The author also wishes to express his appreciation to Dr. Norman W. Desrosier, Mrs. Shirley DeLuca and the AVI Publishing Company for encouragement and assistances in bringing this book into being.

WALTER E. SPLITTSTOESSER

August, 1978

Contents

1

Planning The Garden

Interest in gardening is at its highest level since World War II (Blackwell 1977). The US Department of Agriculture reported that nearly half of the households surveyed either had a garden or intended to have one. People cited three major reasons for having a garden: 1) a desire for fresh vegetables; 2) as a hobby; and 3) a desire to save money and reduce the amount spent for food.

Many purchased fresh vegetables do not have the taste and flavor of home-grown ones. Asparagus and sweet corn are good examples. Sweet corn loses sugar rapidly upon harvest. Only a home-gardener can have the water boiling before harvesting the sweet corn so it can be eaten a few minutes after picking (Gomez 1974).

The average urban gardener can produce more than $150 worth of fresh vegetables (Vandemark *et al.* 1975). One garden of 150 square feet in Columbus, Ohio, for example, produced enough vegetables to provide a return for labor of $1.08 per hour; and this value was calculated after all expenses, including depreciation on the garden tools, were deducted (Utzinger and Connolly 1978). Few leisure time activities pay you for doing them.

If you are a beginning gardener, be prepared for some problems. Weeds and insects will invade the garden. Weather often does not cooperate and problems with rainfall, drought, early or late frosts or too much sunlight may occur. Gardening requires work. Do not expect to plant the garden and three months later to return for a bountiful harvest. Certain gardening jobs will need to be done at certain times and these may interfere with ones hobbies. If you spend little time at home, limit the size of your garden.

This book is intended to answer the questions of beginning and experienced gardeners alike. It provides the information required to be a successful gardener. This book gives standard "chemical methods" and gives equal treatment to "organic methods." The methods used are the gardener's decision. However, regardless of the method you decide

1

upon, the specific techniques given herein are those that have been researched and that have proven effective.

RECORDS

Keep records about your garden. At the end of the season, these records can be reviewed and methods to improve your specific garden can be determined. A loose-leaf or bound notebook is better than individual notes.

Varieties.—Keep a list of varieties planted and record which ones performed well for you. Record where the seeds or transplants were purchased and how much was purchased and used. By comparing varieties, poor ones may be eliminated and a different variety, which may be an improvement, may be added next year.

Soil fertility.—Record soil test reports and types and amounts of fertilizer used (Marr 1977). It is particularly valuable to record soil pH and how much lime or sulfur was used to adjust the pH. Amounts of organic and natural fertilizer used should be recorded. Most natural deposits release their nutrients slowly and initial rates are high but can be reduced in subsequent years. It is valuable to know which organic fertilizers were used so that different ones can be used in subsequent years. This will help prevent the soil nutrients from becoming out of

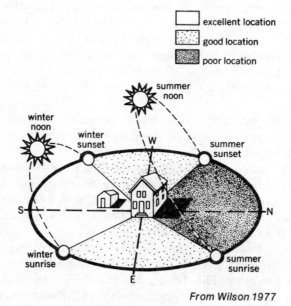

From Wilson 1977

FIG. 1.1. THE BEST LOCATIONS FOR YOUR GARDEN

balance with each other and prevent deficiencies of one nutrient from occurring.

Crop yields.—Record how much was produced by each vegetable; and how much was used fresh and how much was processed. Record when a vegetable was harvested and when harvest was complete. Gardeners can then determine if more or less space will be required next year for each variety to meet your particular needs. Succession planting may be needed to provide vegetables throughout the season. Alternatively some vegetables may be omitted from the garden, if their time of harvest coincided with the gardener's vacation away from home.

Growing conditions.—Record the time of year transplants were started and when they were planted into the garden. Should they have been planted earlier or later? Record when cool-season, warm season and fall plantings were made so timing can be improved. The last frost in the spring and the first frost in the fall should be noted.

Record insect and disease problems, and what, if any, control measures were taken. If no control measures were used, was the quality of the harvested vegetables satisfactory?

GARDEN LOCATION AND ARRANGEMENT

You can grow vegetables successfully in full sunlight, on good soil and away from tree roots. In practice however, gardening locations are a compromise (Wilson 1977). The area you choose should have good soil but soil on many homeowner lots is from the basement or crawl space under the house. This soil can be used if adequate nutrients and organic matter are added but this requires considerable work and effort over several years. The garden needs at least six hours of direct sun each day. Soil receiving direct sun warms up quickly inducing the seeds and plants to grow more rapidly, reducing insect and disease problems. Gardens on the North side that are within six to eight feet of one-story buildings do not receive enough sunlight (Figure 1.1).

Gardens should not be shaded by trees. Trees and shrubs also compete with vegetables for nutrients and water. Various root barriers generally are of little value. The location should be near an abundant water supply for irrigating your garden during dry spells. Plan your garden near your home if possible. Gardeners are more likely to spend time working in the garden and checking for pests if it is nearby.

If the requirements of good soil, adequate light and sufficient water are met, gardens can be located almost anywhere; in backyards (Figure 1.2), in front yards, as mini-gardens, in a community garden (often sponsored by the local park district), in window boxes, patios of high-rise apartments or on the roofs of buildings in large cities.

FIG. 1.2.   A WELL PLANNED GARDEN

Backyard and frontyard gardens.—Most gardens are located in the backyard. However, sometimes the best garden location is in the front yard (Wilson 1977). Front yard gardens need to be neat and should be mulched or planted to a cover crop during winter.

Check local ordinances before beginning a garden in the front yard. Some cities have ordinances against permanent fences in the front. A low temporary fence of chicken wire or snow fence may be used to keep out dogs and unwanted visitors. Some front yards contain rapid-growing trees which provide so much shade that even grass will not grow. If the tree is unattractive or not valuable it should be trimmed or removed before beginning a garden. The branches can be ground and used as a mulch.

Front yard gardens need a flower border with tall annual flowering or foliage plants to screen out the garden and obscure low temporary fences. Lettuce, peas, carrots, beets, potatoes, tomatoes and many other vegetables can be grown in a front yard garden. Melons, however, usually disappear if grown in a front yard.

After selecting the garden location, the arrangement of the vegetables in the garden can be planned. The garden size depends upon the amount and kinds of vegetables desired and the space available (Figure 1.3). The garden should not be so large that it becomes a burden upon the gardener's time and energy and that considerable amounts of unwanted vegetables are produced.

The garden should contain those vegetables that are enjoyed and that

Planting	Row No. and width	30 feet		
1st	1-12"	Early peas (Snap beans late)		
	2-12"	Second early peas (Lettuce and kohlrabi late)		
	3-12"	Spinach (Spinach late)		
	4-12"	Leaf lettuce (Spinach late)	Turnips (Spinach late)	Kohlrabi (Spinach late)
	5-12"	Onion sets (Radishes late)		
	6-12"	Onion seed planted with radishes (Turnips late)		
2d	7-24"	Early cabbage plants		
	8-24"	Carrots planted with radishes		
	9-18"	New Zealand spinach	Beets planted with radishes	
	10-30"	Tomato seed		
	11-24"	Snap beans		
3d	12-24"	Tomato plants		
	13-24"	Snap beans		
4th	14-18"	Lima beans		
	15-24"	Summer squash or peppers	Cucumbers or eggplant	
	18"	(Border strip)		

25 feet

Crops in parentheses can be planted in the indicated rows after the early crops are harvested.

From Vandemark et al. 1977

FIG. 1.3. ARRANGEMENT OF A SMALL INTENSIVE CULTURE GARDEN

can be grown successfully in your area. Give special care to variety selection. Rhubarb, for example, requires cool weather and cannot be grown easily in the South, except in mountain areas.

Some vegetables utilize space better than other vegetable plants. Sweet corn requires more space than most vegetables but it is frequently grown because of its high quality. Fast-maturing crops such as radish, sweet corn, lettuce, peas and green onions can be grown as an early crop. The same or a different vegetable can then be grown in the same area. Perennial crops such as asparagus, rhubarb and some herbs grow in the same location for many years and should be planted on one side of the garden. A large garden will provide a continuous variety of vegetables over the entire season and provide additional vegetables for future use (Figure 1.4).

Minigardens.—A minigarden requires only a small amount of space. These gardens can easily be made a part of the general landscape design. Any small unused area may be used to grow vegetables. The space may be behind the garage or next to the house (Figure 1.5). Plants grown in a minigarden should be supported with stakes, fences, or trellises. The plants should be trained to grow vertically to take advantage of all available space.

Container gardens.—Gardening can still be experienced by people with limited space (Figure 1.6). Apartment dwellers, mobile home residents and homeowners with yards shaded by mature trees can garden

Planting	Row No. and width	120 feet		
1st	1-4′	Asparagus	Rhubarb	Perennial onions
	2-4′	Onion seed planted with radishes		
	3-1½′	Onion sets	Spinach	
	4-3′	Early potatoes		
	5-3′	Early potatoes		
	6-3′	Early potatoes		
	7-3′	Early potatoes		
	8-3′	Leaf lettuce	Early turnips	Kohlrabi
	9-1½′	Peas		
	10-1½′	Peas		
2d	11-2′	Early cabbage seed		Head lettuce plants
	12-2′	Early cabbage plants		New Zealand spinach
	13-2′	Beets	Carrots	Parsley
	14-1½′	Parsnips planted with radishes		Swiss chard
	15-3′	Tomato seed		
3d	16-3′	Early sweet corn	Main-crop sweet corn	Main-crop sweet corn
	17-3′	Early sweet corn	Main-crop sweet corn	Main-crop sweet corn
	18-3′	Early sweet corn	Main-crop sweet corn	Main-crop sweet corn
	19-3′	Snap beans		
4th	20-1½′	Snap beans		
	21-1½′	Carrots		Beets
	22-2′	Peppers Eggplant	Bush lima beans	Bush or pole lima beans
	23-3′	Tomato plants		
	24-5′	Muskmelons		
	25-5′	Squash Cucumbers		
	26-8′	Watermelons		
	27-8′	Winter squash		
	28-8′	Sweet potatoes		
Special*	29-4′	Late cabbage seed		
	4′	(Border strip)		

*The special planting of late cabbage is for fresh use in late fall, sauerkraut, or winter storage.

From Vandemark et al. 1977

FIG. 1.4.   ARRANGEMENT OF A LARGE GARDEN
Distances between rows may be varied according to the equipment used.

From Vandemark et al. 1975

FIG. 1.5.   A MINIGARDEN ALONG THE SOUTH SIDE OF A HOUSE

in containers. The containers can be placed on sidewalks, patios, window boxes, porches or balconies.

Courtesy of T.L. Gettings and
Organic Gardening Magazine

FIG. 1.6. A CONTAINER GARDEN ATOP A NEW YORK BUILDING

Types of containers.—The type of container depends upon the vegetable being grown. As long as there is enough root space, most vegetable plants will thrive. Wooden barrels, decorative boxes, plastic garbage cans, tin cans, plastic laundry baskets (Figure 1.7), and various pots have been used successfully. To reduce frequency of watering, use containers with a four gallon capacity or larger. Small containers dry out quickly and may blow over in the wind. Large containers may be placed on low carts and moved easily. Square, rectangular or circular containers work equally well.

All containers should have holes in the bottom to provide for water drainage. Most vegetables grown in a container need daily watering and ample drainage is a must. If the container does not have drainage holes, the bottom one-fourth of the container can be filled with rocks or pebbles to hold the excess water until it evaporates or is used. Plastic materials are non-porous and retain more water than clay materials (Vandemark and Splittstoesser 1978). Plants grown in plastic containers dry out less rapidly and can be watered less frequently.

Soil mix.—Most container gardens use a commercial potting mix. These mixes are lightweight, fast-draining and free of insects, diseases and weeds. Some commercial mixes are very lightweight. These latter

From Mansour and Baggett 1977

FIG. 1.7.   RADISHES GROWING IN A PLASTIC BUCKET

mixes are good for hanging baskets, window boxes and containers which are moved around. These lightweight mixes are a disadvantage for growing large plants. Sweet corn, staked tomatoes and eggplant may grow large enough to cause the container to tip over.

Some container gardeners make their own soil mix. These mixes can be made from equal amounts of good garden soil, washed coarse sand and organic material such as peat moss, leaf mold or sawdust (Carbonneau 1969). The mix needs to be free of various pests, and this can be accomplished by heating the mix at a low temperature in the oven. For specific times and temperatures your state Agriculture Experiment Station should be contacted (See Appendix for locations).

Varieties for containers.—There are a number of varieties now on the market especially designed for small gardens and container gardens. These varieties do not grow large but still produce good yields (Arthurs 1977). Many traditional varieties of vegetables are also easily grown in containers. Larger growing plants need a larger container size. Most herbs, chives and parsley need a container holding three pints of soil (a standard six inch pot). Beets, lettuce, onions and radishes require a container holding about one gallon of soil mix (Figure 1.7). Chard, pepper and small tomato varieties grow best with two gallons of soil. Large plants such as cucumbers, eggplants, sweet corn and tomatoes grow best in a four gallon container or larger. With proper water and fertilizer most of these plants can be grown in a surprisingly small container. The following varieties have been grown successfully in containers.

Artichoke, variety Green Globe, can be grown in large containers.

Beans of all types can be grown. Bush types are best but pole beans can be grown if poles or trellises are used for support. (The author's youngest daughter picked 249 pods from a single container grown, staked, lima bean plant over one season). Snap beans such as Bush Blue Lake, Bush Romano, Green Crop and Tender Crop grow well. A purple pod variety is Royalty. For lima beans, try Henderson Bush or Jackson Wonder Bush.

Beets need to be grown in containers about one foot deep. Early Red Ball, Little Egypt and Ruby Queen have been grown.

Brussels sprouts need cool weather and a large container. Jade Cross and Long Island Improved have been recommended.

Cabbage varieties usually grow too large for containers. The early maturing varieties Dwarf Morden and Earliana can be used.

Carrots need containers at least one foot deep and to prevent deformed roots, should not be grown in soil mixes containing compost. The small varieties, Danvers Half Long, Little Finger, Short & Sweet and Tiny Sweet grow well.

Chard requires a container about two feet deep. Any standard variety grows well.

Chinese cabbage is a good crop to grow in containers. Burpee Hybrid and Michihli are two varieties.

Collards can be grown for a continuous supply of greens. If the outer leaves are routinely harvested, a small container can be used. The standard variety Vates is a compact type.

Cucumbers need a large container and some type of trellis support. Cherokee 7, Little Minnie, Tiny Dill and Spartan Dawn are standard varieties with small vines. Two varieties which were developed for container growing are Patio Pik and Pot Luck. These can also be used in hanging baskets.

Eggplant needs warm conditions and a large container for best growth. Most standard varieties grow well but two small plant types are Morden Midget and Slim Jim.

Herbs can easily be grown in containers. Many of them can be grown in window boxes or pots. These can be taken into the house or apartment in cold weather and grown during the winter for fresh herbs.

Endive can be grown in containers. Most varieties are satisfactory.

Kale can be grown in a large container. By continuous harvesting of the outer leaves, a smaller container may be used.

Kohlrabi is fast growing and can be grown in small containers. Any variety is satisfactory.

Lettuce is a cool season crop that can be grown in partial shade or full sunlight. Any variety can be used. The red variety, Ruby can be grown indoors in the winter months.

Melons do not grow very satisfactorily in containers. They require a large container and their vines use a large amount of space. Several varieties of small cantaloupes and watermelons are available but these are best grown in minigardens.

Mustard can be easily grown for greens in a container.

Okra is easily grown in a large container. Those which produce well are Clemson Spineless, Dwarf Green Long Pod and Red River.

Onions, particularly green onions, can be grown easily in containers.

Peas do not grow well in containers. They need a large container, require staking or trellises and produce a low yield. The edible podded varieties produce a better yield and are mentally more satisfying to grow than standard varieties.

Radishes are easy to grow in a container (Figure 1.7). All varieties are acceptable but try Champion in a container placed in a South window during the winter. This variety is more adapted to low light conditions.

Rhubarb can be grown in a tub or large container. If taken care of, the plants will grow for many years.

Spinach is a cool season crop. Both regular spinach and New Zealand spinach, which is not a true spinach, can be grown in containers.

Sweet corn is somewhat difficult to grow in containers. It requires a large container, must be cross-pollinated, and produces a low yield. However many container gardens grow good quality sweet corn. At least four stalks of sweet corn are needed for pollination and these should be planted near each other. Dwarf varieties, such as Golden Cross Bantam, Golden Midget or Midget Hybrid should be tried.

Squash is usually not a good crop to grow in containers. However the bush types of summer squash can be grown in a bushel basket containing eight gallons of soil.

Tomatoes can be grown in containers of all types. Standard varieties need to be staked and be grown in large containers. The small dwarfed tomato plants usually produce cherry tomatoes (about the size of a cherry). Varieties which grow well in containers include Pixie, Patio, Patio Hybrid, Salad Top, Small Fry, Stakeless, Presto, Sugar Lump, Sweet 100, Tiny Tim, and Toy Boy. Tumbling Tom is often recommended for hanging baskets.

General care.—Plants growing in containers should not be crowded. The number of plants per container must be limited, often to one per container. Root crops and greens should be planted on the basis of the

Courtesy of Harris Seeds

FIG. 1.8. PRESTO TOMATOES GROWING IN A PATIO CONTAINER

space they need when mature, not as seedlings. The containers should be thinned to allow ample growing space for the plants. Seedlings should be removed by cutting the unwanted seedling's stem at the soil line. If the seedling is pulled out, roots of the remaining seedlings are frequently damaged, particularly when they are growing in soil mixes.

Container grown plants need frequent watering and fertilizer. Plants receiving too much water develop root rots, and with too little, wilt and die. Once the edible part (fruit, root, or leaf) is produced, the plants will need more water and fertilizer.

Plants should be watered with cool, not hot, water from a hose, at moderate water pressure. At high pressure, the water will make holes in the soil mix and damage the roots. If plants are watered in the morning, they will be dry by evening and help prevent disease. However, as containers dry out rapidly, plants grown in warm climates may need a second watering in the afternoon. As a general rule, it is better to keep the containers a little dry rather than too wet. This is particularly important for containers without drainage holes.

Containers placed near reflective surfaces warm up rapidly and lose more water than plants placed on black surfaces such as blacktop. Plants growing in containers placed on walks, drives and concrete patios will require more water.

TABLE 1.1.   SPACING OF VEGETABLES GROWING IN CONTAINERS.

Vegetable	Approximate number of plants per square foot
Beans	3–4
Beets	25 [1]
Broccoli	3
Brussels sprouts	2
Cabbage	2
Carrots	100 [2]
Cauliflower	2
Chard, Swiss	9
Corn (dwarf)	4
Cucumber (standard)	1 [3]
(dwarf)	2 [3]
Dandelion	6
Eggplant	1
Endive	4
Garlic	36
Kale	4
Kohlrabi	4
Leeks	64
Lettuce (head)	4
(leaf & semi-head)	6
Muskmelon	1 [3]
Mustard greens	9
Onions (cooking)	16
(hamburger)	9
(green bunching)	100 [4]
Parsley	16
Parsnips	25
Peanuts	4
Peas	25 [3]
Peppers	4
Potatoes	1
Sweet potatoes	1
Radishes	144 [5]
Rutabaga	5
Spinach	4
Summer squash (bush)	1
Winter squash (bush)	1
Tomato (regular)	1 [3]
(dwarf)	2
Husk tomato (Physalis)	2
Watermelon (dwarf)	1 [3]

[1] Thin at 1-inch diameter for "greens" and let remainder grow.
[2] Thin every other one when "fingerlings" and let others grow.
[3] Train on trellis.
[4] Can thin to eat and let others grow into cooking onions.
[5] Thin small ones to eat and let others grow.

SOURCE: Abraham and Abraham (1977).

Many commercial soil mixes contain few plant nutrients and weekly use of fertilizer is needed. The containers are watered daily and many added plant nutrients are also removed from the container. Various water soluble fertilizers may be used. Timed-release fertilizers are often used. These materials release a small amount of fertilizer each time the container is watered and need to be added only once each season. Natural gardeners should make up their own soil mix (see soil mix above). The organic matter can be replaced with fish emulsion, dried blood or soybean meal to supply nitrogen. The coarse sand in the mix can be replaced with equal parts of greensand and rock phosphate to supply potassium and phosphorus. The containers can routinely receive organic materials as a fertilizer.

Plants growing in containers need adequate sunlight and must be spaced sufficiently apart. If large containers are used the plants must be spaced further apart than in a full size back yard garden. Table 1.1 gives the number of vegetable plants a square foot of container space will support. Vegetable plants need at least six hours of sunlight each day. If the plants are growing in an area where less than this occurs, reflected light may be used. Aluminum foil, mirrors, chrome reflectors, white gravel and white buildings reflect light. If this reflected light is of high enough intensity, many vegetable crops can be grown. Lettuce, peppers and tomatoes have been grown with only three hours of direct sunlight and reflected light the remainder of the day (Abraham and Abraham 1977). Containers may also be placed on wheels and moved to take advantage of the available sunlight.

Container grown vegetables can be spaced so that, with the exception of sweet corn, no two plants of the same variety are near each other. This will reduce insect problems. However, insect problems usually develop. Since the containers are watered each day, most insects will be noticed and can be handpicked or other mechanical or cultural methods used (See Section 4).

Plant arrangement within the garden.—Perennials such as rhubarb and asparagus should be planted in one section of the garden. They should not be disturbed when the rest of the garden is prepared for annual plants.

The soil composition and drainage of the garden should be considered when planning where to plant individual types of vegetables. Crops such as celery, onions and late cucumbers can be planted in low moist areas. Crops such as squash, pumpkins and early season vegetables can be planted in high areas which are warm and dry. Tall crops such as sweet corn, sunflowers and pole beans should be planted together. Tall crops should be planted on the north side of the garden so they will not shade low-growing vegetables.

It does not appear to make much difference as to whether or not the garden rows are laid out in a north and south direction or an east and west direction. On gardens planted on a slope, the rows should extend across the slope at right angles to reduce erosion.

Many gardeners use intercropping to utilize the space more efficiently. This technique is discussed under cropping systems in this section.

GARDEN TOOLS AND SUPPLIES

Gardening does not require a lot of tools or supplies. The amount purchased depends upon the size of the garden, the types of jobs to be done and the amount of money the gardener wishes to spend.

Tools

It is best to select good quality tools that can be used for many years rather than poorly designed or cheaply made tools. A small garden only needs a hoe, rake, shovel or spade, stakes and string and a means to water plants during dry weather. Larger gardens can effectively use some types of power equipment.

After each use, the tools should be cleaned and then stored in a clean, dry place. A light film of oil on shovels, hoes and trowels will provide rust protection. At the end of the season, the tools should be sharpened and any repairs made. Power tools with engines should be winterized according to the manufacturers recommendations.

Hand tools can be stored in the garage, basement, barn or storage shed. If there is not storage available for power tools, they should be covered during winter to protect them.

Hoe.—A hoe is needed for weed control and to cover seeds after planting. It can also be used to make a small trench into which seeds can be planted.

Irrigation equipment.—If water is available, irrigation equipment is desirable in nearly all gardens. Furrow irrigation requires careful planning of the garden and precise handling of the soil to insure even water distribution. Trickle irrigation is used in many gardens and this equipment can be purchased during the winter. Most gardeners will use a garden hose with or without a sprinkler to provide water to their garden. (For a discussion of plant water and the systems used to supply it, see Section on soils and plant nutrition).

Rake.—A rake is used to smooth out the soil and to prepare the seedbed. It can also be used to loosen the crust which forms on some soils after a heavy rain.

Shovel or spade.—A spade or shovel is needed to turn the soil over and incorporate organic material into the soil. A shovel can also be used to harvest large root crops such as potatoes and sweet potatoes.

Trowel.—An inexpensive trowel is very handy in the garden. It can be used to dig holes for transplants, for cleaning equipment free of soil, and loosening soil around plants, such as onions, for easier harvest.

String, stakes and measuring stick.—These can be used to lay out evenly spaced rows in straight lines. String is also needed to help train plants, such as cucumbers, onto a trellis or as a guide for pole beans. When the garden is planted, each row should have a stake labeled with the vegetable that was planted.

Sprayer or duster.—Some method of insect and disease control is needed. For most small gardens, the use of the spray or dust in an aerosol can or a self-contained duster is the most economical and convenient method of applying pesticides. In large gardens, an inexpensive sprayer or duster can be used. Both are effective. When finished with the sprayer, it should be rinsed in the garden area, placed upside down and allowed to completely dry.

Hand cultivator.—A hand-held or wheel-supported cultivator saves time and effort in weed control in large gardens. It can also be used to loosen the soil crust so water can penetrate some soils more easily. A hand cultivator is useful to dig a deep trench for planting of some crops such as potatoes.

Seeder.—For large gardens, some type of seeder will take the backache out of planting. Some seeders open the furrow, plant, cover the seed, and then pack the soil in one operation. Most seeders are adaptable to various sized seed.

Fertilizer spreader.—Fertilizer is easily applied by hand in a small garden. For a large garden a spreader will make the job quicker, easier and provide a more uniform application. It is particularly useful for organic gardeners who apply large amounts of various natural deposits.

Rotary tiller.—There are a number of rotary tillers adapted for large gardens. They can plow the garden and prepare it for planting or be adjusted to cultivate shallow for weed control. If a tiller is to be used, the garden rows need to be wide enough to easily operate the tiller between rows. Common tillers need 16-30 inches between rows of large gardens.

There are two general types of tillers available. The common and least expensive type uses the rotating tiller shaft to provide forward motion. The engine weight helps provide penetration into the soil.

The second type of tiller is more expensive but easier to use. The engine provides the power to the rotating tiller shaft and the wheels separately. The tiller speed may be regulated and is not greatly affected if stones are encountered. These tillers frequently have a reverse gear which allows the gardener to work in cramped areas.

Chipper-shredder.—A chipper-shredder is extremely valuable for all gardens. It is particularly useful for homeowners and organic gardeners. Although expensive, a machine which will grind two or three inch limbs and used Christmas trees is best. Most rotary mowers can be used to chop leaves and succulent branches. A chipper-shredder will grind garden debris for compost, prepare and mix material for soil mixes and grind leaves, newspapers, and material pruned from trees and shrubs for use as a mulch. These mulches can be used not only in the garden, but around trees and shrubs as well.

Chemicals and Fertilizer

Supplies.—Various gardening supplies should be purchased during the winter and early spring. The materials will then be available when they are needed.

Chemicals.—Various insect and disease control chemicals should be ordered in advance. This is particularly important if botanical insecticides are used. Some botanical and biological control agents are readily available but must be ordered from seed catalogues. All pesticides should be stored in a locked box or cabinet to keep them away from pets and children.

Fertilizer.—Fertilizer can be purchased in the spring and easily stored in a dry place. Many fertilizers become solid when exposed to wet conditions. Various organic fertilizers and natural deposits should be ordered early. The natural deposits should be added at the end of the growing season rather than in the spring. Many garden centers only stock these items in the spring however.

Mulch.—Many gardeners use a mulch to control weeds, conserve moisture and keep the fruits clean. Organic materials such as peat moss, leaves, wood chips or straw should be on hand. Leaves can be collected in the fall, and straw is also available. The grass in a lawn can be allowed to grow quite tall and then mowed but not collected. The lawn clippings are allowed to dry, raked up and used as a mulch. Organic mulches are normally added after the plants are established.

Various non-organic types of mulches, such as black plastic or aluminum foil need to be on hand before planting. These materials are normally applied to the soil before planting.

Courtesy of Germain's

FIG. 1.9. HOTCAPS ARE OFTEN USED TO PROTECT TENDER CROPS
FROM SPRING FROSTS

Plant growing aids.—Many types of devices are available which allow plants to utilize the vertical space in a garden. Various stakes, bean poles, fencing, tomato cage wire and trellises are often used. Hot caps may be needed in early spring. Various fences to keep out unwanted animals may be required; and nylon or other types of netting may be needed to prevent bird damage.

Seeds and Plants

Good quality seeds and plants are required to produce quality vegetable plants with high yields. The seeds are often ordered from seed catalogues in the winter. Some varieties are frequently sold out by spring. Not all varieties recommended for your area will be available from one seed source. Several seed catalogues should be obtained. (See appendix for a listing of some seed companies). Seeds can also be purchased at garden centers and department stores but they seldom have unusual varieties or many types that are suited for container gardens.

Seeds should be stored in a cool, dry location such as in a glass jar or candy tin container. Frequently, not all the seeds purchased are used and some seeds may be stored for several years (See section on Plant Growth-Seeds). It is sometimes more economical to purchase a large amount of seeds which are viable for several years, than to purchase small amounts yearly.

Transplant supplies.—Some vegetables are better planted in the garden as transplants. To grow transplants, a potting mix or peat pellets will be needed, plus containers to grow the plants in. Plant growing lights and a cold frame or hot bed may also be needed. If transplants are used, the gardener should remember that these plants are started six to eight weeks before they are planted into the garden, and transplant supplies are needed earlier than general garden supplies.

CROPPING SYSTEMS

No one garden plan or arrangement of the plants within the garden will be suitable for all conditions. If space is at a premium, and hand cultivation or mulching is practiced, the distance between rows can be kept to a minimum. The suggestions presented here can be adapted to the specific needs of individual gardeners.

Intercropping.—Many gardeners prefer to mix several types of vegetables rather than plant them in blocks. Sweet corn must be planted in a block for proper pollination, however. Intercropping uses all the garden space efficiently. This technique also reduces insect activity and helps reduce problems with insect pests. Intercropping is the planting of fast-growing and slow-growing vegetables, either, in alternate rows, alternating them within the same row, or planting early maturing crops between the rows of late maturing ones.

An example of intercropping in alternate rows is to plant a row of radishes, then tomatoes, then onions, and then cauliflower. The radishes and onions can be harvested in time to make room for the later maturing crops. Pumpkins, winter squash and gourds are often planted beside an early block of sweet corn. The vines can be trained to grow into the area where the sweet corn is growing. After the early crop of sweet corn is harvested, the stems are cut off about a foot from the soil surface and the vine crops can now utilize this space.

An example of intercropping by alternating different plants within the same row is to plant green onions, radishes or lettuce between caged tomato plants or vine crops (cucumbers, pumpkins, winter squash). The early maturing crops can be harvested before the tomatoes or vine crops require the space.

Several types of vegetables can be intercropped by planting them between rows. Green onions, lettuce, radishes or spinach may be planted between rows of cabbage, peppers, sweet corn and tomatoes. An early maturing sweet corn can be planted in the middle of the growing season between rows of early planted potatoes. The early maturing crops will not interfere with the growth of the late maturing ones.

From Anon 1978

FIG. 1.10. CHINESE CABBAGE GROWING ABOVE A CROP OF EARLY POTATOES

In dry-land areas where moisture is limited, intensive intercropping is generally not feasible. In these areas more space or irrigation water is required.

Succession planting.—Succession planting is the growing of one crop, removing it, and then planting another crop in the same space. Except in dry-land areas, the garden space should be fully utilized throughout the growing season. In order to have a continuous supply of fresh vegetables, successive plants are required. It is better to plant a small area which will yield a small amount that can be used, than to have a large amount produced all at once. Two or three small plantings of leaf lettuce and radishes should be made a week apart during the cool season. Onions can be planted every two weeks to provide for green onions. An early planting of carrots, cabbage and beets can be used fresh and a late planting can be used for freezing or storage.

It is best to follow one crop, not with a similar crop, but with a different one to reduce insect and disease problems. Tomatoes can be planted after harvesting radishes; and cucumbers after spinach. Early peas or beans can be followed by beets, late cabbage, carrots or celery. Early sweet corn or potatoes can be followed by spinach or turnips. Fast-maturing vegetables that can be harvested early and the space used by another crop include: early beets, early carrots, early Chinese cabbage, kohlrabi, leaf lettuce, green onions, peas, radishes and spinach.

In the south, south Atlantic, gulf coast, and some western regions, some vegetables can be grown in the garden every month of the year. In the north, late summer and fall plantings of vegetables should be made. In the extreme north, where the growing season is relatively short, succession plantings of early maturing vegetables only are possible. In the south, the late fall garden is as important as the late summer one. Late plantings of snapbeans, lima beans, spinach, radishes and beets can be grown.

Courtesty of Twilley Seeds

FIG. 1.11. A SALAD TOMATO STAKED TO USE VERTICAL SPACE

Vertical cropping.—Many garden plants can be trained to use some type of support to use the space above the garden. This area is not used and the garden space can be increased without increasing the soil area. This is particularly important for growing plants in minigardens and container gardens. Peas and pole beans will climb naturally but tomatoes, cucumbers, squash, melons and gourds can be trained to climb upward.

Only the gardener's imagination limits the use of various structures to support plants. Wire, fences, poles, trellises and other structures can be used to support plants. Vines can be partially supported by loosely tying them to wooden fences. Tomatoes can be staked or grown in a wire cage. Peas and various pole beans can be grown on a fence made of string and closely spaced stakes. Cucumbers and other vines can be trained to grow into trees and shrubs at the edge of the garden.

It is important that the structures be sturdy enough so they will not tip over in the wind or from the weight of the plants growing on them. The fruit of pumpkins and some varieties of winter squash and melons become very large. These fruits need to be supported to prevent them from breaking off from the vine and falling to the ground. These fruits can be supported by wrapping them with several layers of cheesecloth or other material and tying this to the support.

PLANTING DATES

Temperature and rainfall are the two most important factors which determine when to plant a garden. These two factors are not only important in determining when to plant, but they also affect crop quality and insect and disease problems.

High temperature hastens ripening of fruits (tomato) and reduces quality. These temperatures induce sweet corn to mature so rapidly that the length of the harvest period is reduced and two successive plantings may mature at the same time. Sugar content and color are increased when crops (beets, carrots) mature under sunny, cool, dry conditions. Hot, wet conditions induce the production of fruit that is soft, watery, low in sugar and has poor storage quality.

Warm, wet periods increase diseases such as scab, bacterial wilts, leaf blights, mildew and fruit rots. Cool, dry periods help reduce these problems. Hot, dry conditions increase insect problems while cool, moist periods help suppress these pests.

Cool and warm season crops.—Vegetables differ in their ability to withstand cool and warm temperatures. Cool season crops can withstand light frosts, and asparagus and rhubarb plants (not the edible part) can withstand winter freezing. Cool season crops are planted early in the spring, but they must have time to mature before temperatures become too warm. They can be planted during hot weather if there is a long period of cool temperature in the fall for them to reach edible maturity. Varietal differences exist within crops.

Cool and warm season crops differ by more than their susceptibility to cool temperatures. Seeds of cool season crops germinate at a colder soil temperature. Cool season crops are smaller in size and their root systems are shallower. Therefore, these plants must be irrigated more frequently if rainfall is inadequate. Some cool season crops are biennials, that is, they can produce seedstalks and flowers the second growing season. However, if these biennials, such as celery, beet, cabbage and carrot are exposed to an average temperature of 50°F or lower for several weeks and the plants have enough food reserve, they will produce seedstalks the first year instead of the edible part. The edible portion of cool season crops is not susceptible to chilling injury at temperatures between 32° and 50° F as are some warm season vegetables.

The season of the year in which a vegetable may be grown depends upon the region of production. In southern Florida and Texas, warm season crops can be grown during the winter. During the summer, cool season vegetables can be grown at high elevations. A good rule-of-thumb on planting time is that for every 100 miles distance from south to north, a weeks delay in planting time is required. This generality does not hold if the climate is moderated by large bodies of water.

The food value of a cool season crop is usually higher per pound than for a warm season crop (Sims *et al.* 1977). A vegetative part, such as a root, stem, leaf or flower part is eaten from cool season crops. The edible plant part of a warm season crop is usually an immature or mature fruit or seed.

Very hardy vegetables.—These crops can be planted four to six weeks before the average date of the last frost in the spring. Collards, kale, kohlrabi, lettuce, onions, peas, rutabaga, salsify, spinach and turnip may be planted from seed. Asparagus, broccoli, Brussels sprouts, cabbage and onions may be planted as transplants. Onions may also be planted from sets. Horseradish and rhubarb roots and potato tubers may be planted at this time also.

Frost tolerant vegetables.—These crops are planted two or three weeks before the average date of the last frost in the spring. These include beets, carrots, chard, mustard, parsnip, and radishes planted from seed. Cauliflower and Chinese cabbage may be planted as transplants. Most herbs may be seeded or transplanted on this date.

Tender vegetables.—The tender vegetables should be planted on the average date of the last frost in the spring. These include snap beans, New Zealand spinach, summer squash, sweet corn and tomatoes as transplants.

Warm requiring vegetables.—These crops require the soil to be warm before they will germinate. They should be planted one or two weeks after the average date of the last frost in the spring. These plants are lima beans, cucumber, cantaloupe or muskmelon, okra, pumpkin, Southern peas, winter squash and watermelon. Eggplants, peppers and sweet potatoes can be planted as transplants.

Medium heat tolerant vegetables.—These vegetable crops are good for summer plantings. All beans, including soybean, chard, New Zealand spinach, squash and sweet corn are included here.

Late summer or fall vegetables.—These are hardy plants that can be planted in late summer or fall about six to eight weeks before the average date of the first freeze in the fall. In the extreme north, there is little opportunity for fall plantings. These plants include beets, Brussels sprouts, collards, kale, lettuce, mustard, spinach, and turnip.

The specific planting date.—To determine the specific time for planting each vegetable, the gardener needs to know the average date of the last frost in the spring and the first frost in the fall. Figure 1.12 shows the average dates of the last killing frost for locations in all 50 states. From this figure the planting dates can be determined. Table 1.2 gives planting dates between January 1 and June 30 for spring and early summer crops. This table gives *the earliest time it is safe to plant;* it also gives the spring and early summer dates *beyond which planting usually gives poor results* (Webster 1972).

Opposite each vegetable given in Table 1.2 are a series of columns. No gardener needs to use more than one of these columns. Each column contains two planting dates. The first date is the *earliest safe date* that a specific vegetable can be planted or transplanted by a person using that particular column. The second date is the last satisfactory date for planting that vegetable. All the times between these two are not equally satisfactory. Most of the vegetables grow better and yield more when planted near the earlier date given.

The proper time to plant any vegetable in a non-sheltered location in the spring can be determined as follows: 1) Find the location of the garden in Figure 1.12. Then find the solid line on the map (Figure 1.12) that is closest to it; 2) find the date shown on the solid line. This date is the average date of the last killing frost in the spring. The first number represents the month; the second number represents the day. Thus 4-30 is April 30. Once the gardener has found the date, the map is no longer needed; 3) Now turn to Table 1.2 and find the specific column that has your date over it. This is the only date column that the gardener will need. It can be outlined in ink for ready reference; 4) Find the dates in your column that are on the same line with the vegetable you wish to plant. The dates show the period during which the crop can be planted safely. The best time for planting is on the first date or shortly thereafter.

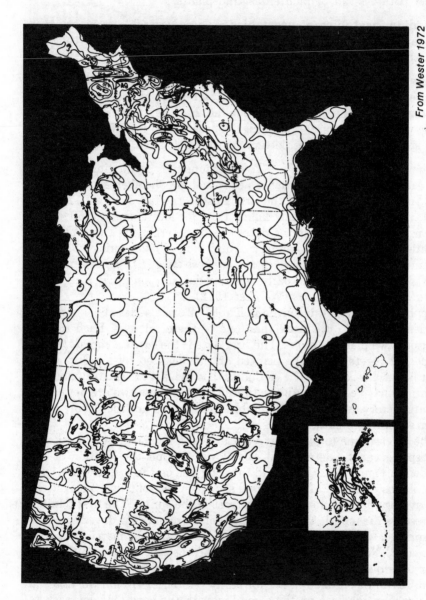

From Wester 1972

FIG. 1.12.   THE AVERAGE DATES OF THE LAST KILLING FROST IN THE SPRING

TABLE 1.2. THE EARLIEST DATES, AND THE RANGE OF DATES FOR SAFE PLANTING OF VEGETABLES IN THE SPRING

Crop	Planting dates for localities in which average date of last freeze is—						
	Jan. 30	Feb. 8	Feb. 18	Feb. 28	Mar. 10	Mar. 20	Mar. 30
Asparagus[1]	Feb. 1-Apr. 15	Feb. 10-May 1	Mar. 1-May 1	Mar. 15-June 1	Jan. 1-Mar. 1	Feb. 1-Mar. 10	Feb. 15-Mar. 20.
Beans, lima	Feb. 1-Apr. 15	Feb. 1-May 1	Mar. 1-May 1	Mar. 15-June 1	Mar. 20-June 1	Apr. 1-June 15	Apr. 15-June 20.
Beans, snap	Jan. 1-Mar. 15	Jan. 10-Mar. 15	Jan. 20-Apr. 1	Feb. 1-Apr. 15	Feb. 15-June	Mar. 15-May 15	Apr. 1-June 1.
Beet	Jan. 1-30	Jan. 1-30	Jan. 15-Feb. 15	Feb. 1-Mar.	Feb. 15-June	Mar. 15-May 15	Mar. 1-June 1.
Broccoli, sprouting[1]	Jan. 1-30	Jan. 1-30	Jan. 15-Feb. 15	Feb. 1-Mar.	Feb. 15-Mar. 15	Feb. 15-Mar. 15	Mar. 1-20.
Brussels sprouts[1]	Jan. 1-15	Jan. 1-Feb. 10	Jan. 15-Feb. 25	Jan. 15-Feb. 25	Jan. 25-Mar. 1	Feb. 15-Mar. 15	Feb. 15-Mar. 10.
Cabbage[1]	(²)	(²)	(²)	(²)	(²)	(²)	(²)
Cabbage, Chinese	---	Feb. 1-Mar. 10	Feb. 1-20	Feb. 15-Mar. 15	Feb. 15-Mar. 15	Feb. 15-Mar. 20	Mar. 1-Apr. 10.
Carrot	Jan. 1-Mar. 1	Jan. 1-Mar. 1	Jan. 15-Mar. 1	Feb. 15-Mar. 1	Feb. 10-Mar. 15	Feb. 15-Mar. 20	Mar. 1-Apr. 10.
Cauliflower[1]	Jan. 1-Feb. 1	Jan. 1-Feb. 1	Jan. 15-Feb. 20	Jan. 20-Feb.	Feb. 1-Mar.	Feb. 1-Mar. 10	Feb. 20-Mar. 20.
Celery and celeriac	Jan. 1-Feb. 1	Jan. 10-Feb.	Jan. 20-Feb. 20	Feb. 1-Mar. 1	Feb. 20-Mar. 20	Mar. 1-Apr. 1	Mar. 15-Apr. 15.
Chard	Jan. 1-Apr. 1	Jan. 10-Apr. 1	Jan. 20-Apr. 15	Feb. 1-May 1	Feb. 15-May 15	Feb. 20-May 15	Mar. 15-Mar. 25.
Chervil and chives	Jan. 1-Feb. 1	Jan. 1-Feb. 1	Jan. 1-Feb. 1	Jan. 15-Feb. 15	Feb. 1-Mar.	Feb. 10-Mar. 10	Feb. 15-Mar. 15.
Chicory, witloof	---	---	---	---	June 1-July 1	June 1-July 1	June 1-July 1.
Collards[1]	Jan. 1-Feb. 15	Jan. 1-Feb. 15	Jan. 1-Mar.	Jan. 15-Mar. 15	Feb. 1-Apr.	Feb. 15-May 1	Mar. 1-June 1.
Cornsalad	Jan. 1-Feb. 15	Jan. 1-Feb. 1	Jan. 1-Mar. 1	Jan. 1-Mar. 15	Jan. 15-Mar. 15	Feb. 1-Apr. 1	Jan. 15-Mar. 15.
Corn, sweet	Feb. 1-Mar.	Feb. 10-Apr. 15	Feb. 20-Apr. 15	Mar. 1-Apr. 15	Mar. 1-Apr. 15	Mar. 20-May 1	Apr. 10-June 1.
Cress, upland	Jan. 1-Feb. 1	Jan. 1-Feb. 15	Jan. 15-Feb. 15	Feb. 1-Mar. 1	Feb. 10-Mar.	Feb. 20-Mar. 15	Mar. 1-May 15.
Cucumber	Feb. 15-Mar. 15	Feb. 15-Apr. 15	Feb. 15-Apr. 15	Mar. 1-Apr. 15	Mar. 10-Apr. 15	Apr. 1-May 1	Apr. 10-May 15.
Eggplant[1]	Feb. 1-Mar. 1	Feb. 10-Mar. 15	Feb. 20-Apr. 1	Mar. 10-Apr. 15	Mar. 15-Apr. 15	Apr. 1-May 1	Apr. 15-May 15.
Endive	Jan. 1-Mar. 1	Jan. 1-Mar. 1	Jan. 15-Mar. 1	Feb. 1-Mar. 1	Feb. 15-Mar. 15	Mar. 1-Apr. 1	Mar. 10-Apr. 10.
Fennel, Florence	Jan. 1-Mar. 1	Jan. 1-Mar. 1	Jan. 15-Mar. 1	Feb. 1-Mar. 1	Feb. 15-Mar. 15	Mar. 1-Apr. 1	Mar. 10-Apr. 10.
Garlic	(²)	(²)	(³)	(²)	(²)	(²)	Feb. 10-Mar. 10.
Horseradish[1]	---	---	---	---	---	---	Mar. 10-Apr. 10.
Kale	Jan. 1-Feb. 1	Jan. 10-Feb. 1	Jan. 20-Feb. 10	Feb. 1-20	Feb. 10-Mar. 1	Mar. 1-20	Mar. 10-Apr. 1.
Kohlrabi	Jan. 1-Feb. 1	Jan. 10-Feb. 1	Jan. 20-Feb.	Feb. 1-20	Feb. 10-Mar.	Mar. 1-Apr. 1	Mar. 10-Apr. 1.
Leek	Jan. 1-Feb. 1	Jan. 1-Feb. 1	Jan. 1-Feb. 15	Jan. 15-Feb.	Jan. 25-Mar. 1	Feb. 1-Mar.	Feb. 15-Apr. 15.
Lettuce, head[1]	Jan. 1-Feb. 1	Jan. 1-Feb. 1	Jan. 1-Feb. 15	Jan. 15-Feb. 15	Jan. 15-Feb.	Feb. 1-Mar. 10	Mar. 1-20.
Lettuce, leaf	Jan. 1-Mar. 1	Jan. 1-Mar. 1	Jan. 1-Mar. 15	Feb. 1-Apr. 1	Feb. 15-Apr.	Feb. 15-Apr. 1	Mar. 15-Apr. 15.
Muskmelon	Feb. 15-Mar. 15	Feb. 15-Apr. 1	Feb. 15-Apr. 15	Mar. 15-Apr. 15	Mar. 15-Apr.	Apr. 1-May 1	Apr. 10-May 15.
Mustard	Jan. 1-Mar. 1	Jan. 1-Mar. 1	Jan. 15-Apr. 1	Feb. 1-Apr. 15	Feb. 10-Apr. 15	Feb. 20-Apr. 15	Mar. 1-Apr. 15.
Okra	Feb. 15-Apr. 1	Feb. 15-Apr. 15	Feb. 15-June 1	Mar. 1-June 1	Mar. 20-June 1	Apr. 1-June 15	Apr. 10-June 15.
Onion[1]	Jan. 1-15	Jan. 1-15	Jan. 1-15	Jan. 1-Feb.	Jan. 15-Feb. 15	Feb. 10-Mar. 10	Feb. 15-Mar. 15.
Onion, seed	Jan. 1-15	Jan. 1-15	Jan. 1-15	Jan. 1-Feb.	Feb. 1-Mar. 15	Feb. 15-Mar. 15	Mar. 1-Apr. 1.
Onion, sets	Jan. 1-15	Jan. 1-15	Jan. 1-Mar. 1	Jan. 1-Feb. 1	Jan. 15-Mar.	Feb. 1-Mar. 20	Feb. 15-Mar. 20.
Parsley	Jan. 1-30	Jan. 1-30	Jan. 1-30	Jan. 1-Mar. 1	Jan. 15-Mar.	Feb. 1-Mar. 15	Feb. 15-Mar. 15.
Parsnip	---	---	---	Jan. 15-Mar. 1	Jan. 15-Mar. 1	Feb. 1-Mar. 15	Mar. 1-Apr. 1.
Peas, garden	Jan. 1-Feb. 15	Jan. 1-Feb. 15	Jan. 1-Mar. 1	Jan. 1-Mar. 15	Jan. 15-Mar. 15	Feb. 1-Mar. 15	Feb. 10-Mar. 20.
Peas, black-eye	Feb. 15-May 15	Feb. 15-May 15	Mar. 1-May 15	Mar. 1-June 15	Mar. 15-July	Apr. 1-July 1	Apr. 15-July 1.
Pepper[1]	Feb. 1-Apr. 1	Feb. 15-Apr. 15	Mar. 1-May 1	Mar. 15-May 1	Apr. 1-June 1	Apr. 15-June 1	Apr. 15-June 1.
Potato	Jan. 1-Feb. 15	Jan. 15-Mar. 1	Jan. 15-Mar. 1	Jan. 15-Mar.	Feb. 1-Mar.	Feb. 10-Mar. 15	Feb. 20-Mar. 20.
Radish[1]	Jan. 1-Apr. 1	Jan. 1-Apr. 1	Jan. 1-Apr. 1	Jan. 1-Apr. 1	Jan. 1-Apr. 15	Feb. 1-May 1	Feb. 15-May 1.
Rhubarb[1]	---	---	---	---	(²)	Jan. 1-Apr. 1	Feb. 15-Mar. 15.
Rutabaga	---	---	---	---	---	---	---
Salsify	Jan. 1-Feb. 1	Jan. 1-Feb. 1	Jan. 15-Feb. 20	Jan. 15-Feb.	Jan. 15-Feb. 15	Jan. 15-Mar. 1	Feb. 1-Mar. 1.
Shallot	Jan. 1-Feb. 1	Jan. 1-Feb. 1	Jan. 1-Mar. 1	Jan. 1-Feb.	Jan. 1-Mar. 1	Jan. 1-Mar. 10	Feb. 1-15.
Sorrel	Jan. 1-Feb. 1	Jan. 1-Mar. 1	Jan. 1-Mar. 1	Jan. 1-Mar. 10	Feb. 1-Mar. 10	Feb. 1-Apr. 1	Feb. 20-May 15.
Soybean	Mar. 1-June 30	Mar. 1-June 30	Mar. 10-June 30	Mar. 20-June 30	Apr. 10-June 30	Apr. 10-June 30	Apr. 20-June 30.
Spinach	Jan. 1-Feb. 15	Jan. 1-Mar. 1	Jan. 1-Mar. 1	Jan. 1-Mar. 1	Jan. 15-Mar.	Jan. 15-Mar. 15	Feb. 1-Mar. 20.
Spinach, New Zealand	Feb. 1-Apr. 15	Feb. 15-Apr. 15	Feb. 15-May 1	Mar. 1-May 15	Mar. 20-May	Apr. 1-May	Apr. 10-June 1.
Squash, summer	Feb. 15-Apr. 15	Feb. 15-Apr. 15	Mar. 1-Apr. 15	Mar. 15-May 15	Mar. 15-May 15	Apr. 10-June	Apr. 10-June 1.
Sweetpotato	Feb. 15-May 15	Mar. 20-May 15	Mar. 20-May 15	Apr. 1-June 1	Apr. 10-June	May 1-June	Apr. 10-June 1.
Tomato	Feb. 1-Apr. 1	Feb. 20-Apr. 10	Mar. 1-Apr. 20	Mar. 10-May	Mar. 20-May 10	Apr. 10-June	Apr. 10-June 1.
Turnip	Jan. 1-Mar. 1	Jan. 1-Mar. 1	Jan. 10-Mar. 1	Jan. 20-Mar. 1	Feb. 1-Mar. 1	Feb. 10-Mar. 20	Apr. 10-June 1.
Watermelon	Feb. 15-Mar. 15	Feb. 15-Apr. 1	Feb. 15-Apr. 15	Mar. 15-Apr. 15	Mar. 15-Apr. 15	Apr. 1-May 1	Apr. 10-May 15.

[1] Plants.
[2] Generally fall-planted

TABLE 1.2. (*Continued*)

Crop	Planting dates for localities in which average date of last freeze is—						
	Apr. 10	Apr. 20	Apr. 30	May 10	May 20	May 30	June 10
Asparagus[1]	Mar. 10-Apr. 10	Mar. 15-Apr. 15	---	---	---	May 1	May 15-June 1.
Beans, lima	Apr. 10-June 30	May 1-June 20	May 15-June 15	Mar. 20-Apr. 30	---	---	---
Beans, snap	Apr. 10-June 30	Apr. 25-June 30	May 10-June 30	May 10-June 30	May 15-June 30	May 25-June 15	---
Beet	Apr. 10-June 1	Mar. 20-June 1	Mar. 10-June 1	May 1-June 15	May 1-June 15	May 1-June 15	May 15-June 15.
Broccoli, sprouting[1]	Mar. 15-Apr. 15	Mar. 25-Apr. 20	Apr. 1-May 1	Apr. 15-June 1	May 1-June 15	May 10-June 10	May 20-June 10.
Brussels sprouts[1]	Mar. 15-Apr. 15	Mar. 25-Apr. 20	Apr. 1-May 1	Apr. 15-June 1	May 1-June 15	May 10-June 10	May 20-June 10.
Cabbage[1]	Mar. 1-Apr. 1	Mar. 15-Apr. 10	Apr. 1-May 15	May 1-May 15	May 1-June 1	May 10-June 15	May 20-June 1.
Cabbage, Chinese	(2)	(2)	(2)	Apr. 1-May 15	May 1-June 15	May 10-June 15	May 20-June 15.
Carrot	Mar. 10-Apr. 20	Mar. 15-Apr. 20	Apr. 1-May 15	Apr. 15-June 1	May 1-June 1	May 10-June 1	May 20-June 1.
Cauliflower[1]	Mar. 1-Mar. 20	Mar. 15-Apr. 20	Apr. 10-May 10	Apr. 15-May 15	May 10-June 15	May 20-June 1	June 1-June 15.
Celery and celeriac	Apr. 1-Apr. 20	Apr. 10-May 1	Apr. 15-June 1	Apr. 20-June 15	May 20-June 15	May 20-June 1	June 1-June 15.
Chard	Mar. 15-June 15	Apr. 1-June 15	Apr. 15-June 15	Apr. 20-June 15	May 10-June 15	May 20-June 1	June 1-June 15.
Chervil and chives	Mar. 1-Apr. 1	Mar. 10-Apr. 10	Mar. 20-Apr. 20	Apr. 1-May 1	Apr. 15-May 15	May 1-June 1	May 15-June 1.
Chicory, witloof	June 10-July 1	June 15-July 1	June 1-July 1	June 1-July 1	June 1-20	June 1-15	June 1-15.
Collards[1]	June 1-July 1	Mar. 10-June 1	Apr. 1-June 1	Apr. 15-June 1	May 1-June 1	May 10-June 1	May 20-June 1.
Cornsalad	Feb. 1-Apr. 1	Feb. 15-Apr. 15	Mar. 1-May 1	Apr. 1-June 1	Apr. 15-June 1	May 1-June 15	May 15-June 15.
Corn, sweet	Apr. 10-June 1	Apr. 25-June 15	May 10-June 15	May 10-June 1	May 15-June 1	May 15-June 1	---
Cress, upland	Mar. 10-Apr. 15	Mar. 20-May 1	Apr. 10-May 10	Apr. 10-June 1	May 10-June 15	June 1	June 1.
Cucumber	Apr. 20-June 1	May 1-June 15	May 15-June 15	May 20-June 15	June 1	June 1-15	---
Eggplant[1]	May 1-June 1	May 10-June 1	May 15-June 10	June 1	June 1-15	June 1-15	---
Endive	Mar. 15-Apr. 15	Mar. 25-Apr. 15	Apr. 1-May 1	Apr. 15-May 15	May 1-30	May 1-30	May 15-June 1.
Fennel, Florence	Mar. 15-Apr. 15	Mar. 25-Apr. 15	Apr. 1-May 1	Apr. 15-May 15	May 1-30	May 1-30	May 15-June 1.
Garlic	Feb. 20-Mar. 20	Mar. 1-Apr. 1	Mar. 15-Apr. 15	Apr. 1-May 1	May 20-May 20	---	May 15-June 1.
Horseradish[1]	Mar. 10-Apr. 10	Mar. 20-Apr. 20	Apr. 1-30	Apr. 15-May 15	May 10-June 1	---	May 15-June 1.
Kale	Mar. 1-Apr. 1	Mar. 10-Apr. 1	Mar. 20-May 1	Apr. 1-May 1	Apr. 15-May 20	May 1-30	May 15-June 1.
Kohlrabi	Mar. 1-Apr. 10	Mar. 10-Apr. 10	Mar. 20-May 1	Apr. 1-May 10	Apr. 10-May 15	May 1-30	May 15-June 1.
Leek	Mar. 1-Apr. 1	Mar. 1-Apr. 1	Mar. 15-Apr. 15	Apr. 1-May 1	Apr. 15-May 15	May 1-June 1	May 1-15.
Lettuce, head[1]	Mar. 1-Apr. 1	Mar. 10-Apr. 1	Mar. 20-Apr. 15	Apr. 1-May 1	Apr. 15-May 15	May 1-30	May 1-15.
Lettuce, leaf	Mar. 15-May 15	Mar. 20-May 15	Apr. 1-June 1	Apr. 1-June 1	Apr. 15-June 1	May 10-June 30	May 20-June 30.
Muskmelon	Apr. 20-June 1	May 1-June 15	May 15-June 15	June 1-June 15	June 1-June 30	May 10-June 30	May 20-June 30.
Mustard	Mar. 1-Apr. 15	Mar. 10-Apr. 20	Mar. 20-May 1	Apr. 1-May 10	Apr. 15-June 1	May 1-June 30	May 20-June 30.
Okra	Apr. 20-June 20	May 1-June 1	May 10-June 1	May 20-June 10	June 1-20	June	May 10-June 10.
Onion[1]	Mar. 1-Apr. 1	Mar. 1-Apr. 10	Mar. 15-Apr. 15	Apr. 1-May 1	Apr. 20-May 15	May	May 10-June 10.
Onion, seed	Mar. 1-Apr. 1	Mar. 1-Apr. 10	Mar. 15-Apr. 15	Apr. 1-May 1	Apr. 20-May 15	May 1-30	May 10-June 10.
Onion, sets	Mar. 1-Apr. 1	Mar. 1-Apr. 10	Mar. 15-Apr. 10	Apr. 1-May 1	Apr. 15-May 15	May 1-30	May 10-June 10.
Parsley	Mar. 1-Apr. 10	Mar. 10-Apr. 10	Mar. 20-May 1	Apr. 1-May 10	Apr. 15-May 20	May 10-June 1	May 20-June 15.
Parsnip	Mar. 10-Apr. 10	Mar. 10-Apr. 10	Mar. 20-May 1	Apr. 1-May 15	Apr. 15-June 1	May 1-June 1	May 1-June 1.
Peas, garden	Feb. 20-Mar. 20	Mar. 1-Apr. 1	Mar. 10-Apr. 10	Apr. 1-May 1	Apr. 15-June 1	May 1-June 15	May 10-June 15.
Peas, black-eye	May 1-July 1	May 1-July 1	May 15-June 15	May 15-June 1	---	---	---
Pepper[1]	May 1-June 1	May 10-June 1	May 15-June 10	May 20-June 10	May 25-June 15	June 1-June 15	June 15.
Potato	Mar. 1-Apr. 1	Mar. 10-Apr. 1	Mar. 20-May 10	Apr. 1-June 1	Apr. 15-June 15	May 1-June 15	May 15-June 15.
Radish	Mar. 1-May 1	Mar. 10-May 10	Mar. 20-May 10	Apr. 1-June 1	Apr. 15-June 15	May 1-June 15	May 1-June 15.
Rhubarb[1]	Mar. 1-Apr. 1	Mar. 10-Apr. 10	Mar. 20-Apr. 15	Apr. 1-May 1	Apr. 15-May 1	May 1-20	May 15-June 1.
Rutabaga	Mar. 1-June 1	June 1-July 1	Mar. 10-June 1	Mar. 20-June 1	May 15-Apr. 20	May 10-20	May 20-June 10.
Salsify	Mar. 1-Apr. 15	Mar. 10-Apr. 15	Apr. 1-June 1	Apr. 15-June 1	May 20-June 10	Apr. 20-June 15	May 1-June 15.
Shallot	Mar. 1-Apr. 15	Mar. 15-Apr. 15	Mar. 20-May 1	Apr. 1-May 1	Apr. 10-May 1	June 1-15	May 1-June 15.
Sorrel	Mar. 1-Apr. 15	Mar. 15-Apr. 15	Apr. 1-May 1	Apr. 15-June 1	May 1-June 15	June 1-20	May 1-June 1.
Soybean	May 15-June 15	May 25-June 10	June 1-June 15	June 10-June 15	---	---	June 1-June 10.
Spinach	Feb. 15-Apr. 1	Mar. 1-Apr. 15	Mar. 20-Apr. 20	Apr. 1-June 15	Apr. 20-June 15	May 10-June 10	May 10-June 10.
Spinach, New Zealand	Apr. 20-June 1	May 1-June 15	May 1-June 15	May 10-June 15	May 20-June 15	June 10-June 15	---
Squash, summer	Apr. 20-June 1	May 1-June 15	May 1-June 15	May 1-June 1	June 10-July 1	June 10-July 1	---
Sweetpotato	May 1-June 1	May 1-June 1	May 10-June 1	Mar. 20-May 10	---	---	---
Tomato	Apr. 20-June 1	May 5-June 10	May 10-June 15	May 15-June 10	May 25-June 15	Apr. 20-June 15	May 1-June 15.
Turnip	Mar. 1-Apr. 1	Mar. 1-Apr. 1	Mar. 20-May 1	Apr. 1-June 1	Apr. 15-June 1	June 1-20	June 15-30.
Watermelon	Apr. 20-June 1	May 1-June 15	May 15-June 15	June 1-July 1	June 15-July 1	May 1-June 15	May 15-June 15.

[1] Plants.

[2] Generally fall-planted

SOURCE: Wester (1972).

The Great Plains region warms up rapidly in the spring and is subject to dry weather. In these areas, very early planting is essential for the vegetables to escape the heat and drought. Most cool season crops grow poorly when planted in the spring in the southern part of the Great Plains and southern Texas (Wester 1972). These plants are generally fall grown.

To determine the dates for late summer and fall plantings Fig. 1.13 and Table 1.3 are used. They are used in a similar manner to the method used to determine the spring planting dates. A planting date about in the middle of those given in Table 1.3 is usually best but in most areas of the USA, fair success can be achieved over the entire range of dates given. The late planting dates given in Table 1.3 are less exact and less dependable than the early date; particularly for gardens in the south where overwintered crops are grown. Rainfall, insects and diseases are often more important than temperature for the successful growing of late summer and fall crops in the south, especially in the southeast. In the pacific northwest, warm weather vegetables should not be planted quite as late as frost data (Table 1.3 and Figure 1.13) indicate. Frost occurs late but cool temperatures occur for some time before the frost occurs. This reduces the growth rate of warm weather vegetables, such as lima beans, sweet corn and tomatoes.

VARIETIES

Choosing the best varieties to grow in the garden is important. Gardeners should obtain a list of varieties recommended for their specific area from the state agricultural experiment station (See appendix for address). Gardeners too often purchase vegetable seeds without knowing if the variety is adapted to local climatic conditions.

Some varieties grow best in spring plantings, others grow best in late summer or fall plantings. In the southwest for example, some tomato varieties set fruit in spring and fall but do not set fruit during the summer. At high altitudes, a short growing season is encountered and the tomato variety grown must mature and set fruit rapidly.

All-America Selections.—This is a nonprofit organization of seed producers who develop and promote new varieties of vegetables and flowers. The vegetables are grown in various locations throughout the USA under various soil and climatic conditions. The vegetable variety must perform well under all of these conditions to be designated an All-American Selection or Award. Not all new varieties are tested under this program, however. In addition, a variety which performs best in one location may be unsuitable in another location and not be designated an All-American Selection.

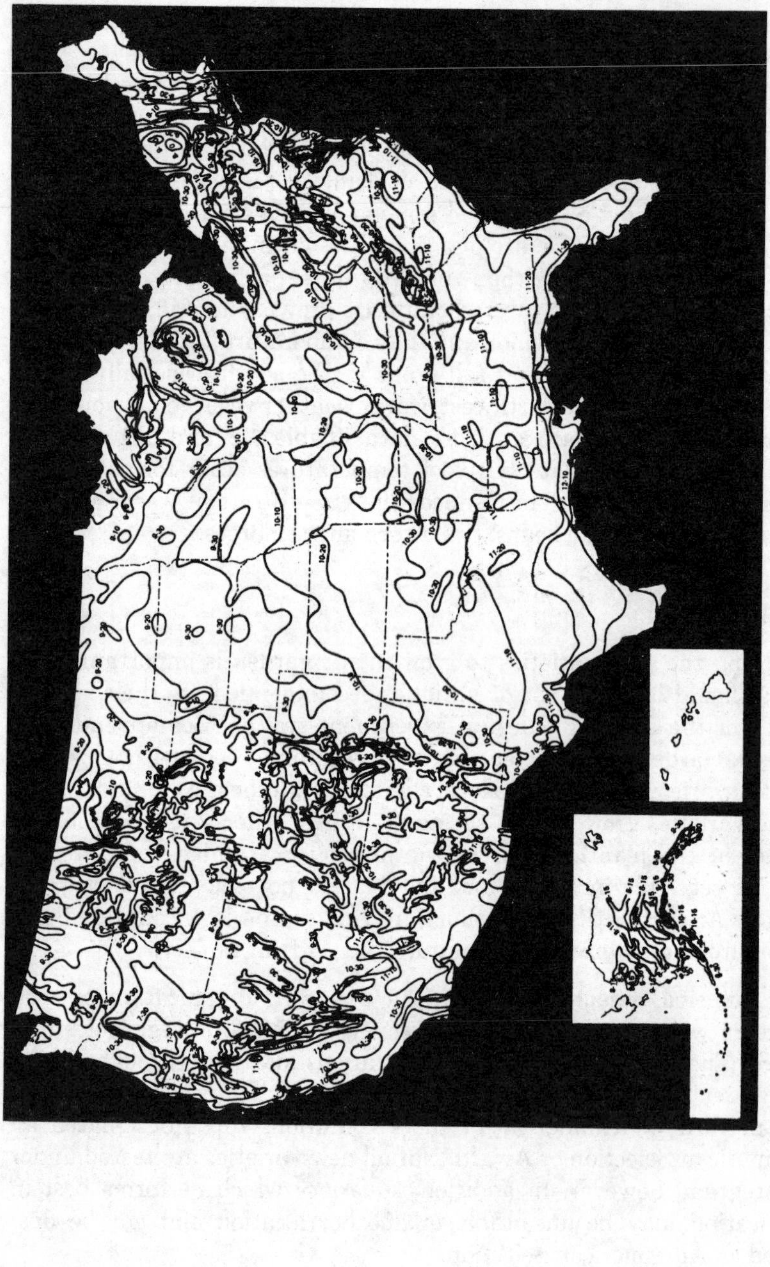

From Wester 1972

FIG. 1.13.   THE AVERAGE DATES OF THE FIRST KILLING FROST IN THE FALL

TABLE 1.3. THE LATEST DATES, AND A RANGE OF DATES, FOR SAFE PLANTING OF VEGETABLES IN THE FALL (SEE TEXT)

Crop	Planting dates for localities in which average dates of first freeze is—					
	Aug. 30	Sept. 10	Sept. 20	Sept. 30	Oct. 10	Oct. 20
Asparagus [1]					Oct. 20–Nov. 15	Nov. 1–Dec. 15.
Beans, lima				June 1–15	June 1–15	June 15–30.
Beans, snap		May 15–June 15	June 1–July 1	June 1–July 10	June 15–July 20	July 1–Aug. 1.
Beet	May 15–June 15	May 15–June 15	June 1–July 1	June 1–July 10	June 15–July 25	July 1–Aug. 5.
Broccoli, sprouting	May 1–June 1	May 1–June 1	May 1–June 15	June 1–30	June 15–July 15	July 1–Aug. 1.
Brussels sprouts	May 1–June 1	May 1–June 1	May 1–June 15	June 1–30	June 15–July 15	July 1–Aug. 1.
Cabbage [1]	May 1–June 1	May 1–June 1	May 1–June 15	June 1–July 10	June 1–July 15	July 1–20.
Cabbage, Chinese	May 15–June 15	May 15–June 15	June 1–July 1	June 1–July 15	June 15–Aug. 1	July 15–Aug. 15.
Carrot	May 15–June 15	May 15–June 15	June 1–July 1	June 1–July 10	June 1–July 20	June 15–Aug. 1.
Cauliflower [1]	May 1–June 1	May 1–July 1	May 1–July 1	May 10–July 15	June 1–July 25	July 1–Aug. 5.
Celery [1] and celeriac	May 15–June 15	May 15–June 15	May 15–July 1	June 1–July 5	June 1–July 15	June 1–Aug. 1.
Chard	May 15–June 15	May 15–July 1	June 1–July 1	June 1–July 5	June 1–July 20	June 1–Aug. 1.
Chervil and chives	May 10–June 10	May 1–June 15	May 15–June 15	(2)	(2)	(2)
Chicory, witloof	May 15–June 15	May 15–June 15	May 15–June 15	June 1–July 1	June 1–July 1	June 15–July 15.
Collards [1]	May 15–June 15	May 15–June 15	May 15–June 15	June 15–July 15	July 1–Aug. 1	July 15–Aug. 15.
Cornsalad	May 15–June 15	May 15–July 1	June 15–Aug. 1	July 15–Sept. 1	Aug. 15–Sept. 15	Sept. 1–Oct. 15.
Corn, sweet			June 1–July 1	June 1–July 1	June 1–July 10	June 1–July 20.
Cress, upland	May 15–June 15	May 15–July 1	June 15–Aug. 1	July 15–Sept. 1	Aug. 15–Sept. 15	Sept. 1–Oct. 15.
Cucumber			June 1–15	June 1–July 1	June 1–July 1	June 1–July 15.
Eggplant [1]				May 20–June 10	May 15–June 15	June 1–July 1.
Endive	June 1–July 1	June 1–July 1	June 1–July 15	June 15–Aug. 1	July 1–Aug. 15	July 15–Sept. 1.
Fennel, Florence	May 15–June 15	May 15–July 15	June 1–July 1	June 1–July 1	June 15–July 15	June 15–Aug. 1.
Garlic	(2)	(2)	(2)	(2)	(2)	(2)
Horseradish [1]	(2)	(2)	(2)	(2)	(2)	(2)
Kale	May 15–June 15	May 15–June 15	June 1–July 1	June 15–July 15	July 1–Aug. 1	July 15–Aug. 15.
Kohlrabi	May 15–June 15	June 1–July 1	June 1–July 15	June 15–July 15	July 1–Aug. 1	July 15–Aug. 15.
Leek	May 1–June 1	May 1–June 1	(2)	(2)	(2)	(2)
Lettuce, head [1]	May 15–July 1	May 15–July 1	June 1–July 15	June 15–Aug. 1	July 15–Aug. 15	Aug. 1–30.
Lettuce, leaf	May 15–July 15	May 15–July 15	June 1–Aug. 1	June 1–Aug. 1	July 15–Sept. 1	July 15–Sept. 1.
Muskmelon			May 1–June 15	May 15–June 1	June 1–June 15	June 15–July 20.
Mustard	May 15–July 15	May 15–July 15	June 1–Aug. 1	June 1–Aug. 1	July 15–Aug. 15	Aug. 1–Sept. 1.
Okra			June 1–20	June 1–July 1	June 1–July 15	June 1–Aug. 1.
Onion [1]	May 1–June 10	May 1–June 10	(2)	(2)	(2)	(2)
Onion, seed	May 1–June 1	May 1–June 1	(2)	(2)	(2)	(2)
Onion, sets	May 1–June 1	May 1–June 10	(2)	(2)	(2)	(2)
Parsley	May 15–June 15	May 1–June 15	June 1–July 1	June 1–July 15	June 15–Aug. 1	July 15–Aug. 15.
Parsnip	May 15–June 15	May 1–June 15	May 15–June 15	June 1–July 1	June 1–July 10	(2)
Peas, garden	May 10–June 15	May 1–July 1	June 1–July 15	June 1–Aug. 1	(2)	(2)
Peas, black-eye				June 1–July 1	June 1–July 1	June 1–July 1.
Pepper [1]			June 1–June 20	June 1–July 1	June 1–July 1	June 1–July 10.
Potato	May 15–June 1	May 1–June 15	May 1–June 15	May 1–June 15	May 15–June 15	June 15–July 15.
Radish	May 1–July 15	May 1–Aug. 1	June 1–Aug. 15	July 1–Sept. 1	July 15–Sept. 15	Aug. 1–Oct. 1.
Rhubarb [1]	Sept. 1–Oct. 1	Sept. 15–Oct. 15	Sept. 15–Nov. 1	Oct. 1–Nov. 1	Oct. 15–Nov. 15	Oct. 15–Dec. 1.
Rutabaga	May 15–June 15	May 1–June 15	June 1–July 1	June 1–July 1	June 15–July 15	July 10–20.
Salsify	May 15–June 1	May 10–June 10	May 20–June 20	June 1–20	June 1–July 1	June 1–July 1.
Shallot	(2)	(2)	(2)	(2)	(2)	(2)
Sorrel	May 15–June 15	May 1–June 15	June 1–July 1	June 1–July 15	July 1–Aug. 1	July 15–Aug. 15.
Soybean				May 25–June 10	June 1–25	June 1–July 5.
Spinach	May 15–July 1	June 1–July 15	June 1–Aug. 1	July 1–Aug. 15	Aug. 1–Sept. 1	Aug. 20–Sept. 10.
Spinach, New Zealand				May 15–July 1	June 1–July 15	June 1–Aug. 1.
Squash, summer	June 10–20	June 1–20	May 15–July 1	June 1–July 1	June 1–July 15	June 1–July 20.
Squash, winter			May 20–June 10	June 1–15	June 1–July 1	June 1–July 1.
Sweetpotato					May 20–June 10	June 1–15.
Tomato	June 20–30	June 10–20	June 1–20	June 1–20	June 1–20	June 1–July 1.
Turnip	May 15–June 15	June 1–July 1	June 1–July 15	June 1–Aug. 1	July 1–Aug. 1	July 15–Aug. 15.
Watermelon			May 1–June 15	May 15–June 1	June 1–June 15	June 15–July 20.

[1] Plants.
[2] Generally spring-planted

TABLE 1.3. (*Continued*)

Crop	Planting dates for localities in which average date of first freeze is—					
	Oct. 30	Nov. 10	Nov. 20	Nov. 30	Dec. 10	Dec. 20
Asparagus [1]	Nov. 15–Jan. 1	Dec. 1–Jan. 1				
Beans, lima	July 1–Aug. 1	July 1–Aug. 15	July 15–Sept. 1	Aug. 1–Sept. 15	Sept. 1–30	Sept. 1–Oct. 1.
Beans, snap	July 1–Aug. 15	July 1–Sept. 1	July 1–Sept. 10	Aug. 15–Sept. 20	Sept. 1–30	Sept. 1–Nov. 1.
Beet	Aug. 1–Sept. 1	Aug. 1–Oct. 1	Sept. 1–Dec. 1	Sept. 1–Dec. 15	Sept. 1–Dec. 31	Sept. 1–Dec. 31.
Broccoli, sprouting	July 1–Aug. 15	Aug. 1–Sept. 1	Aug. 1–Sept. 15	Aug. 1–Oct. 1	Aug. 1–Nov. 1	Sept. 1–Dec. 31.
Brussels sprouts	July 1–Aug. 15	Aug. 1–Sept. 1	Aug. 1–Sept. 15	Aug. 1–Oct. 1	Aug. 1–Nov. 1	Sept. 1–Dec. 31.
Cabbage [1]	Aug. 1–Sept. 1	Sept. 1–15	Sept. 1–Dec. 1	Sept. 1–Dec. 31	Sept. 1–Dec. 31	Sept. 1–Dec. 31.
Cabbage, Chinese	Aug. 1–Sept. 15	Aug. 15–Oct. 1	Sept. 1–Oct. 15	Sept. 1–Nov. 1	Sept. 1–Nov. 15	Sept. 1–Dec. 1.
Carrot	July 1–Aug. 15	Aug. 1–Sept. 1	Sept. 1–Nov. 1	Sept. 15–Dec. 1	Sept. 15–Dec. 1	Sept. 15–Dec. 1.
Cauliflower [1]	July 15–Aug. 15	Aug. 1–Sept. 1	Aug. 1–Sept. 15	Aug. 15–Oct. 10	Sept. 1–Oct. 20	Sept. 15–Nov. 1.
Celery [1] and celeriac	June 15–Aug. 15	July 1–Aug. 15	July 15–Sept. 1	Aug. 1–Dec. 1	Sept. 1–Dec. 31	Oct. 1–Dec. 31.
Chard	June 1–Sept. 10	June 1–Sept. 15	June 1–Oct. 1	June 1–Nov. 1	June 1–Dec. 1	June 1–Dec. 31.
Chervil and chives	(2)	(2)	Nov. 1–Dec. 31	Nov. 1–Dec. 31	Nov. 1–Dec. 31	Nov. 1–Dec. 31.
Chicory, witloof	July 1–Aug. 10	July 10–Aug. 20	July 20–Sept. 1	Aug. 15–Sept. 30	Aug. 15–Oct. 15	Aug. 15–Oct. 15.
Collards [1]	Aug. 1–Sept. 15	Aug. 15–Oct. 1	Aug. 25–Nov. 1	Sept. 1–Dec. 1	Sept. 1–Dec. 31	Sept. 1–Dec. 31.
Cornsalad	Sept. 15–Nov. 1	Oct. 1–Dec. 1	Oct. 1–Dec. 1	Oct. 1–Dec. 31	Oct. 1–Dec. 31	Oct. 1–Dec. 31.
Corn, sweet	June 1–Aug. 1	June 1–Aug. 15	June 1–Sept. 1			
Cress, upland	Sept. 15–Nov. 1	Oct. 1–Dec. 1	Oct. 1–Dec. 1	Oct. 1–Dec. 31	Oct. 1–Dec. 31	Oct. 1–Dec. 31.
Cucumber	June 1–Aug. 1	June 1–Aug. 15	June 1–Aug. 15	July 15–Sept. 15	Aug. 15–Oct. 1	Aug. 15–Oct. 1.
Eggplant [1]	June 1–July 1	June 1–July 15	June 1–Aug. 1	July 1–Sept. 1	Aug. 1–Sept. 30	Aug. 1–Sept. 30.
Endive	July 15–Aug. 15	Aug. 1–Sept. 1	Sept. 1–Oct. 1	Sept. 1–Nov. 15	Sept. 1–Dec. 31	Sept. 1–Dec. 31.
Fennel, Florence	July 1–Aug. 1	July 15–Aug. 15	Aug. 15–Sept. 15	Sept. 1–Nov. 15	Sept. 1–Dec. 1	Sept. 15–Nov. 1.
Garlic	(2)	Aug. 1–Oct. 1	Aug. 15–Oct. 1	Sept. 1–Nov. 15	Sept. 15–Nov. 15	Sept. 15–Nov. 15.
Horseradish [1]	(2)	(2)	(2)	(2)	(2)	(2)
Kale	July 15–Sept. 1	Aug. 1–Sept. 15	Aug. 15–Oct. 15	Sept. 1–Dec. 1	Sept. 1–Dec. 31	Sept. 1–Dec. 31.
Kohlrabi	Aug. 1–Sept. 1	Aug. 15–Sept. 15	Sept. 1–Oct. 15	Sept. 1–Nov. 1	Sept. 15–Dec. 31	Sept. 15–Dec. 31.
Leek	(2)	(2)	Sept. 1–Nov. 1	Sept. 1–Nov. 1	Sept. 1–Nov. 1	Sept. 15–Nov. 1
Lettuce, head [1]	Aug. 1–Sept. 15	Aug. 15–Oct. 15	Sept. 1–Nov. 1	Sept. 1–Dec. 1	Sept. 15–Dec. 31	Sept. 15–Dec. 31.
Lettuce, leaf	Aug. 15–Oct. 1	Aug. 25–Oct. 1	Sept. 1–Nov. 1	Sept. 1–Dec. 1	Sept. 15–Dec. 31	Sept. 15–Dec. 31.
Muskmelon	July 1–July 15	July 15–July 30				
Mustard	Aug. 15–Oct. 15	Aug. 15–Nov. 1	Sept. 1–Dec. 1	Sept. 1–Dec. 1	Sept. 1–Dec. 1	Sept. 15–Dec. 1.
Okra	June 1–Aug. 10	June 1–Aug. 20	June 1–Sept. 10	June 1–Sept. 20	June 1–Sept. 20	Aug. 1–Oct. 1.
Onion [1]		Sept. 1–Oct. 15	Oct. 1–Dec. 31	Oct. 1–Dec. 31	Oct. 1–Dec. 31	Oct. 1–Dec. 31.
Onion, seed			Sept. 1–Nov. 1	Sept. 1–Nov. 1	Sept. 1–Nov. 1	Sept. 15–Nov. 1.
Onion, sets		Oct. 1–Dec. 1	Nov. 1–Dec. 31	Nov. 1–Dec. 31	Nov. 1–Dec. 31	Nov. 1–Dec. 31.
Parsley	Aug. 1–Sept. 15	Sept. 1–Nov. 15	Sept. 1–Dec. 31	Sept. 1–Dec. 31	Sept. 1–Dec. 31	Sept. 1–Dec. 31.
Parsnip	(2)	(2)	Aug. 1–Sept. 1	Sept. 1–Nov. 15	Sept. 1–Dec. 1	Sept. 1–Dec. 1.
Peas, garden	Aug. 1–Sept. 15	Sept. 1–Nov. 1	Oct. 1–Dec. 1	Oct. 1–Dec. 31	Oct. 1–Dec. 31	Oct. 1–Dec. 31.
Peas, black-eye	June 1–Aug. 1	June 15–Aug. 15	July 1–Sept. 1	July 1–Sept. 10	July 1–Sept. 20	July 1–Sept. 20.
Pepper [1]	June 1–July 20	June 1–Aug. 1	June 1–Aug. 15	June 15–Sept. 1	Aug. 15–Oct. 1	Aug. 15–Oct. 1.
Potato	July 20–Aug. 10	July 25–Aug. 20	Aug. 10–Sept. 15	Aug. 1–Sept. 15	Aug. 1–Sept. 15	Aug. 1–Sept. 15.
Radish	Aug. 15–Oct. 15	Sept. 1–Nov. 15	Sept. 1–Dec. 1	Sept. 1–Dec. 31	Aug. 1–Sept. 15	Oct. 1–Dec. 31.
Rhubarb [1]	Nov. 1–Dec. 1					
Rutabaga	July 15–Aug. 1	July 15–Aug. 15	July 15–Aug. 15	Sept. 1–Nov. 15	Oct. 1–Nov. 15	Oct. 15–Nov. 15.
Salsify	June 1–July 10	June 15–July 20	July 15–Aug. 15	Aug. 15–Sept. 30	Aug. 15–Oct. 15	Sept. 1–Oct. 31.
Shallot	(2)	Aug. 1–Oct. 1	Aug. 15–Oct. 15	Sept. 15–Oct. 15	Sept. 15–Nov. 1	Sept. 15–Nov. 1.
Sorrel	Aug. 1–Sept. 15	Aug. 15–Oct. 1	Aug. 15–Oct. 15	Sept. 1–Nov. 15	Sept. 1–Dec. 15	Sept. 1–Dec. 31.
Soybean	June 1–July 15	June 1–July 25	June 1–July 30	June 1–July 30	June 1–July 30	June 1–July 30.
Spinach	Sept. 1–Oct. 1	Sept. 15–Nov. 1	Oct. 1–Dec. 1	Oct. 1–Dec. 31	Oct. 1–Dec. 31	Oct. 1–Dec. 31.
Spinach, New Zealand	June 1–Aug. 1	June 1–Aug. 15	June 1–Aug. 15			
Squash, summer	June 1–Aug. 1	June 1–Aug. 10	June 1–Aug. 20	June 1–Sept. 1	June 1–Sept. 15	June 1–Oct. 1.
Squash, winter	June 10–July 10	June 20–July 20	July 1–Aug. 1	July 15–Aug. 15	Aug. 1–Sept. 1	Aug. 1–Sept. 1.
Sweetpotato	June 1–15	June 1–July 1	June 1–July 1	June 1–July 1	June 1–July 1	June 1–July 1.
Tomato	June 1–July 1	June 1–July 15	June 1–Aug. 1	Aug. 1–Sept. 1	Aug. 15–Oct. 1	Sept. 1–Nov. 1.
Turnip	Aug. 1–Sept. 15	Sept. 1–Oct. 15	Sept. 1–Nov. 15	Sept. 1–Nov. 15	Oct. 1–Dec. 1	Oct. 1–Dec. 31.
Watermelon	July 1–July 15	July 15–July 30				

[1] Plants.

[2] Generally spring-planted

SOURCE: Wester (1972).

Hybrids.—Many new varieties of vegetables are hybrids and are usually superior to the older varieties. Hybrid varieties usually have resistance to one or more diseases, grow rapidly and produce more uniform plants. Hybrids usually cost more but the disease resistance alone is worth the extra cost. This is particularly true for gardeners who do not use pesticides.

Hybrids do not reproduce true to type in the second generation and it is usually not advisable to harvest and save your own seed. It is usually advisable to grow a limited number of new varieties beside your present variety for comparison.

Amount to Plant

The amount of a specific vegetable that a gardener should plant depends upon the preference of the gardener, the ultimate use of the vegetable, and the number of people consuming the vegetable. Table 1.4 gives the yield of some vegetables produced in a home garden. The amount individual gardens will produce depends upon the location of the garden within the USA and how much attention the vegetables receive. Good gardens may yield more; poor gardens will produce less.

TABLE 1.4. YIELD OF VEGETABLES PRODUCED IN A HOME GARDEN.

Vegetables	Average crop expected per 100 feet	Approximate planting per person	
		Fresh	Storage, canning or freezing
Asparagus	30 lb.	10–15 plants	10–15 plants
Beans, snap bush	120 lb.	15–16 feet	15–20 feet
Beans, snap pole	150 lb.	5–6 feet	8–10 feet
Beans, Lima bush	25 lb. shelled	10–15 feet	15–20 feet
Beans, Lima pole	50 lb. shelled	5–6 feet	8–10 feet
Beets	150 lb.	5–10 feet	10–20 feet
Broccoli	100 lb.	3–5 plants	5–6 plants
Brussels sprouts	75 lb.	2–5 plants	5–8 plants
Cabbage	150 lb.	3–4 plants	5–10 plants
Cabbage, Chinese	80 heads	3–10 feet	——
Carrots	100 lb.	5–10 feet	10–15 feet
Cauliflower	100 lb.	3–5 plants	8–12 plants
Celeriac	60 lb.	5 feet	5 feet
Celery	180 stalks	10 stalks	——
Chard, Swiss	75 lb.	3–5 plants	8–12 plants
Collards and kale	100 lb.	5–10 feet	5–10 feet
Corn, sweet	10 dozen	10–15 feet	30–50 feet
Cucumbers	120 lb.	1–2 hills	3–5 hills
Eggplant	100 lb.	2–3 plants	2–3 plants
Garlic	40 lb.	——	1–5 feet
Kohlrabi	75 lb.	3–5 feet	5–10 feet
Lettuce, head	100 heads	10 feet	——
Lettuce, leaf	50 lb.	10 feet	——
Muskmelon (cantaloupe)	100 fruits	3–5 hills	——
Mustard	100 lb.	5–10 feet	10–15 feet
Okra	100 lb.	4–6 feet	6–10 feet

TABLE 1.4. (*Continued*)

Onions (plants or sets)	100 lb.	3–5 feet	30–50 feet
Onions (seed)	100 lb.	3–5 feet	30–50 feet
Parsley	30 lb.	1–3 feet	1–3 feet
Parsnips	100 lb.	10 feet	10 feet
Peas, English	20 lb.	15–20 feet	40–60 feet
Peas, southern	40 lb.	10–15 feet	20–50 feet
Peppers	60 lb.	3–5 plants	3–5 plants
Potatoes, Irish	100 lb.	50–100 feet	——
Potatoes, sweet	100 lb.	5–10 plants	10–20 plants
Pumpkins	100 lb.	1–2 hills	1–2 hills
Radishes	100 bunches	3–5 feet	——
Salsify	100 lb.	5 feet	5 feet
Soybeans	20 lb.	50 feet	50 feet
Spinach	40–50 lb.	5–10 feet	10–15 feet
Squash, summer	150 lb.	2–3 hills	2–3 hills
Squash, winter	100 lb.	1–3 hills	1–3 hills
Tomatoes	100 lb.	3–5 plants	5–10 plants
Turnip greens	50–100 lb.	5–10 feet	——
Turnip, roots	50–100 lb.	5–10 feet	5–10 feet
Watermelon	40 fruits	2–4 hills	——

SOURCE: Abraham and Abraham (1977).

SELECTED REFERENCES

ANON. 1978. Asian Vegetable Research and Development Center Progress Report for 1977, Taiwan.

ABRAHAM, G, and ABRAHAM, K. 1977. Planning your vegetable garden—pots, pyramids and planters. *In* Growing your own vegetables. USDA Bulletin *409.*

ARTHURS, K.L. 1977. Vegetables in containers require enough sun, space, drainage. *In* Growing your own vegetables. USDA Bulletin *409.*

BLACKWELL, C. 1977. Why folks garden and what they face. *In* Gardening for food and fun. J. Hayes (Editor). USDA Yearbook of Agriculture.

CARBONNEAU, M.C. 1969. Gardening in containers. Il. Agri. Exp. Stn. Circular *997.*

GOMEZ, R. 1974. Home vegetable gardening. N.M. Ag. Exp. Stn. Circular *457.*

MANSOUR, N.S. and BAGGET, J.R. 1977. Root crops more or less trouble-free, produce lots of food in a small space. *In* Growing your own vegetables. USDA Bulletin *409.*

MARR, C.W. 1977. End of one season is start of another. *In* Gardening for food and fun. J. Hayes (Editor). USDA Yearbook of Agriculture.

SIMS, W.L. *et. al.* 1977. Home vegetable gardening. Calif. Agri. Exp. Stn. Leaflet *2989.*

UTZINGER, J. D. and CONNOLLY, H.E. 1978. Economic value of a home vegetable garden. HortScience *13*:148-149.

VANDEMARK, J.S., HOPEN, H.J., and COURTER, J.W. 1975. Eat well and save money by growing your own vegetables. Ill. Res. *17(2)*:8-9.

VANDEMARK, J.S., JACOBSEN, B.J. and RANDELL, R. 1977. Illinois vegetable garden guide. Ill. Agri. Exp. Stn. Circular *1091*.

VANDEMARK, J.S., and SPLITTSTOESSER, W.E. 1978. Size and composition of pots affect vegetable transplants' growth. Ill. Res *20(1)*:5.

WESTER, R.E. 1972. Growing vegetables in the home garden. USDA Home and Garden Bulletin *202*.

WILSON, J.W. 1977. Where to garden-setting your sites. *In* Gardening for food and fun. J. Hayes (Editor). USDA Yearbook of Agriculture.

2

Plant Growth

SEEDS

A seed is a dormant undeveloped plant. It usually contains its own food supply and is protected by a seed coat. The seed carries the genetic material from its two parents and controls the maximum quality and performance of the developed plant. The cost of most vegetable seed is a small part of the cost of producing the edible vegetable product and considerable care should be taken in purchasing the seed. Good vegetable seeds are clean, disease-free, viable and produce plants typical of the variety listed on the seed packet.

Diseases.—Vegetable seed should be disease-free. Some diseases are carried on the seed coat, such as black rot of cabbage, and can be controlled by seed treatment. Other diseases such as blackleg are carried within the seed of cabbage and cauliflower and can be fairly well controlled with a hot-water treatment. Such treatment must be precise in temperature and time or the seed will be injured and the gardener should not attempt this procedure. Instead the gardener should purchase seed which has been commercially treated and the seed packet will state "Hot Water Treated." Some diseases, such as anthracnose of beans are not controlled successfully by seed treatment. These types of diseases are particularly a problem if the gardeners save their own seed and they live in a humid climate. Commercial seed is produced under hot, dry conditions where anthracnose is not a problem.

Some seed will also be treated with a fungicide to control fungi which attacks the seedling during germination. This is particularly true with corn, cucumbers and melons. These seed packages will carry the warning "Do Not Use For Food, Feed or Oil."

Vitality.—Vegetable seed should have enough vitality to germinate, emerge from the soil and produce the plant. A good stand is important as a partial stand results in wasted space. Overseeding results in a costly

34

thinning operation, or frequently, reduced yields due to overcrowding. Much vegetable seed a year or two old is still usable but one should know its vitality to insure a good stand. National seed companies test their seeds and sell only seed with a high germination percentage. Minimum germination requirements for most vegetables are controlled by the Federal Government and some seed packets carry the germination percentage of the seed and the date the seed was tested. If the seed is below the minimum germination, the package will be labeled "Below Federal Standard" and the percent germination must be stated. Some seeds such as carrot are usually low in germination percentages while others such as cabbage frequently give 99 to 100% germination. Table 2.1 gives the federal standard for germination of the principal kinds of seed and the expected longevity of the seed. The longevity figures are for seeds stored under favorable conditions from the time of harvest (not time of purchase). Under proper conditions many seeds are viable longer than indicated but the author found that some kinds of lettuce, when stored under hot, humid conditons, were only viable for 18 months.

Variety.—Good vegetable seeds produce plants typical of the variety listed on the seed packet. A horticultural classification recognizes the gradations into kind, variety and strain and these will be listed on the seed package.

A "kind" of vegetable seed includes all plants which are recognized as a single vegetable such as cucumber, tomato or pumpkin. This is not the same as genus or species of botanical classification. The species *Brassica oleracea* includes many kinds of vegetables (cabbage, collards, kale, cauliflower and others).

A "variety" of vegetable includes all those plants of a given kind which are practically alike in their important characteristics. Each variety should be different from all others in one or more prominent and significant features. On the seed package the kind is listed, such as Hybrid Cucumber and then the variety, such as Burpless Hybrid or Saticoy.

A strain includes those plants of a given variety which have the general characteristics of the variety but are different from the variety in one important aspect or two or three minor respects. These differences are not great enough to justify a new variety name. Thus, Dickinson Field Pumpkin is the pumpkin used in over half of the commercial pumpkin pie mixes and the strain "Libby Select" is one strain selected by a commercial company for proper color and thickness of the edible flesh.

Gardeners who save their own seed may not have a pure variety. Some vegetables are entirely or readily cross-pollinated. These include beet, Brussels sprouts, broccoli, cabbage, cauliflower, collards, cress, cucumber, kale, kohlrabi, melon, mustard, onion, pumpkin, radish, spinach, squash, sweet corn and turnip. Sweet corn will cross with a nearby field of field

TABLE 2.1 VEGETABLE SEED: FEDERAL MINIMUM GERMINATION; AVERAGE NUMBER OF SEEDS PER OUNCE AND RELATIVE LONGEVITY.

Vegetable	Minimum Germination (Per cent)	Average Number of Seeds per Ounce	Relative Longevity (Years)
Asparagus	60	1,400	3
Bean, Lima	70	20 to 70	3
Bean, Snap	75	100	3
Beet	65	2,000	4
Broccoli	75	8,100	3
Brussels Sprouts	70	8,500	4
Cabbage	75	7,700	4
Carrot	55	22,000	3
Cauliflower	75	8,600	4
Celeriac	55	50,000	3
Celery	55	76,000	3
Chard, Swiss	65	1,500	4
Chicory	65	20,000	4
Chinese Cabbage	75	7,000	3
Cucumber	80	1,100	5
Eggplant	60	7,200	4
Endive	70	17,000	5
Kale	75	10,000	4
Kohlrabi	75	9,200	3
Leek	60	9,900	2
Lettuce	80	26,000	5
Muskmelon	75	1,100	5
New Zealand Spinach	40	430	3
Okra	50	500	2
Onion	70	8,500	1
Parsley	60	18,000	1
Parsnip	60	6,800	1
Pea	80	50 to 230	3
Pepper	55	4,500	2
Pumpkin	75	200	4
Radish	75	3,100	4
Rutabaga	75	11,000	4
Salsify	75	2,000	1
Spinach	60	2,900	3
Squash	75	180 to 380	4
Sweet Corn	75	140	2
Tomato	75	10,000	3
Turnip	80	14,000	4
Watermelon	70	320	4

SOURCE: Harrington and Minges (1954)

corn and it is unwise to save this seed. Broccoli, cabbage, cauliflower, collards, kale and kohlrabi all intercross readily and plants must be well isolated from each other if the seed is to be saved. Seed may be saved from watermelon if isolated from other watermelons and citrons. Muskmelon seed may be saved if isolated from other melons, even if it was grown near cucumbers as these two plants do not cross. Most beans are self-pollinated and their seed may be saved if the plants were not grown under hot, humid conditions which favor seed-borne diseases.

GERMINATION REQUIREMENTS

When a seed receives the proper amount of air, water and heat, it will begin to grow. With a few vegetable seeds, notably celery, light may also be required. Some germination will usually occur over a wide range of each of these factors. However, as the extremes are approached, above or below the optimum range for each factor, the total germination is reduced, the rate is slower and abnormal seedlings are more frequent. Beyond the minimum and maximum, no germination occurs.

Temperature.—The effect of temperature on seed germination has received much attention. Some vegetable seeds such as onion, will germinate at freezing temperatures but the rate of growth is extremely slow. At 32°F, it takes 135 days for the appearance of an onion seedling when planted one-half inch deep. This emphasizes that some seeds can withstand cold temperatures and the seed will be alive when the soil temperature increases. Some seeds, such as sweet corn and beans will rot if planted at low temperatures for long periods of time. Table 2.2 gives the minimum temperature for germination of some vegetable seeds. This minimum temperature can be used as an indication of when to plant the crops in the spring. When the temperatures have reached the minimum, the vegetable may be planted. It is assumed that the soil temperatures will continue to increase, however. Planting vegetables befre the minimum temperature required for germination is reached does not produce an earlier crop. Instead, the seed will not germinate and it gives more time for soil organisms to destroy the seed, resulting in reduced stands.

Some seed companies sell seeds by the number of degree days required to reach maturity instead of the number of days from planting to harvest. If we know the number of degree days for a variety to reach maturity, we can use this to determine when the crop should be harvested. There is a minimum temperature below which the vegetable will not grow (See Table 2.2). This minimum is 50°F for sweet corn. (Hortik and Arnold 1965). Above 50°F, the higher the temperature, the more rapidly the corn plant grows and approaches maturity. If the temperature becomes too high, the corn growth will slow down, but within reasonable limits, this error is not too important. The number of degree days required for Golden Cross Bantam sweet corn to reach maturity is 1,875. This number signifies the number of degrees that the mean temperature was above 50° (the minimum temperature for corn germination). Thus, if the mean (average of the highest and lowest temperature for that day) temperature was 74°F, the corn crop was exposed to 24 degree days, (74 minus 50). Any temperature below 50° represents 0° of effective temperature. These degree days are added together beginning with the date of germination. This number of degree days does not indicate how many calendar days are involved. If your sweet corn crop was exposed to a 56° mean temperature for four days, this would result in 24 degree days, (56 minus 50 equals 6 degree days for each of 4 days). This is the

TABLE 2.2   SOIL TEMPERATURES FOR VEGETABLE SEED GERMINATION

MINIMUM

32°F	40°F		50°F
Endive	Beet	Parsley	Asparagus
Lettuce	Broccoli	Pea	Sweet Corn
Onion	Cabbage	Radish	Tomato
Parsnip	Carrot	Swiss Chard	Turnip
Spinach	Cauliflower	Celery	

60°F	65°F
Bean, Lima	Eggplant
Bean, Snap	Muskmelon
Cucumber	Pumpkin
Okra	Squash
Pepper	Watermelon

OPTIMUM

70°F	75°F	80°F
Celery	Asparagus	Bean, Lima
Parsnip	Endive	Carrot
Spinach	Lettuce	Cauliflower
	Pea	Onion
		Radish
		Tomato
		Turnip

85°F		95°F
Bean, Snap	Parsley	Cucumber
Beet	Pepper	Muskmelon
Broccoli	Sweet Corn	Okra
Cabbage	Swiss Chard	Pumpkin
Eggplant		Squash
		Watermelon

MAXIMUM

75°F	85°F	95°F		105°F
Celery	Beans, Lima	Asparagus	Eggplant	Cucumber
Endive	Parsnip	Bean, Snap	Onion	Muskmelon
Lettuce	Pea	Beet	Parsley	Okra
Spinach		Broccoli	Pepper	Pumpkin
		Cabbage	Radish	Squash
		Carrot	Swiss Chard	Sweet Corn
		Cauliflower	Tomato	Turnip
				Watermelon

same number of degree days calculated when the mean temperature was 74°F for one day. It is important to recognize that the sweet corn plant will be just as far along toward maturity in one day at 74°F as it will be in four days at 56°F. Thus, if a gardener wants successive crops of sweet corn during the summer, the time between planting the first and second crop will be far apart in the spring when temperatures are cool and there are few degree days accumulating. As the temperature becomes hotter, the harvest dates become closer and closer together.

There is a maximum temperature at which vegetable seeds will germinate (Table 2.2) and high temperatures may kill many vegetable seeds outright. High soil temperatures are also damaging at the time of seedling emergence, and the seedling may die due to heat injury at the soil surface. Lettuce and endive, however, will not germinate at high temperatures and if the soil temperature has not reached the maximum and killed the seed, the seeds will germinate when the soil temperature has cooled. This is particularly important in summer plantings for a fall crop.

TABLE 2.3. SOIL MOISTURE REQUIRED FOR VEGETABLE SEED GERMINATION

Group 1. Seeds that give nearly as good germination at the permanent wilting percentage as at higher soil-moisture contents.

Cabbage	Pumpkins
Broccoli	Radish
Brussels sprouts	Sweet corn
Cauliflower	Squash
Kohlrabi	Turnip
Muskmelon	Watermelon
Mustard	

Group 2. Vegetable seeds that require a soil moisture content at least 25% above the permanent wilting percentage.

Bean, snap	Peanut
Carrot	Pepper
Cucumber	Spinach
Leeks	Tomato
Onion	

Group 3. Vegetable seeds needing a soil moisture content at least 35% above the permanent wilting percentage.

Lima bean	Pea

Group 4. Vegetable seeds needing a soil moisture content above 50% of the permanent wilting percentage.

Beet	Endive
Chinese cabbage	Lettuce

Group 5. Vegetable seeds needing a soil-moisture content close to field capacity.

Celery

Water.—Vegetable seeds require water to germinate. They can be divided into five groups, depending on how much water their seeds need in order to germinate (Table 2.3). It is important to recognize that this is the amount of water required for the seeds to germinate, not the amount of water required to produce the crop. The rate of germination is faster at higher moisture levels than at the minimum. The amount of water in soils ranges from field capacity to the permanent wilting percentage. Field capacity is the maximum amount of water your particular soil will hold. Any additional water will drain out of the soil. Permanent wilting percentage is that small amount of water remaining in the soil when the plant can no longer remove any more water and the plant wilts. This permanently wilted plant will not recover unless water is supplied to the soil.

Some bean varieties are susceptible to having the cotyledons crack when the seeds are very dry and the seeds absorb water rapidly (Jones 1971). The bean cotyledon is the food storage organ for the new bean plant and comprises over 95% of the dry seed. If the seed is very dry, planted, and immediately irrigated, the outer layers of the bean cotyledon absorb water rapidly and begin to expand. However, the inner layers of the cotyledon are still dry and when the outer layer expands, the dry inner layers crack. This disrupts the food transport system so the newly developing plant cannot receive any of the food which is beyond where the crack occurred and the plant frequently does not emerge from the soil. The gardener can overcome this problem by storing the beans for several days at 50-60% humidity to raise the bean seed moisture content to above 14%, or by planting the seeds at a low soil moisture (See Table 2.3) and not irrigating the garden for several days.

Planting depth and rate.—Vegetable seeds should be planted at a depth equal to about four times the diameter of the seed. This rule or the specific depth chart (Table 2.4) must be used with care. In wet weather or heavy soils, seeds should generally be planted shallow. In dry weather or light and sandy soils, seeds should be planted deeper. Some small seeds, like tomato, pepper and eggplant germinate slowly and are often planted in the garden as transplants. If they are planted directly in the garden, care must be taken to prevent the soil from drying out and forming a crust on the soil surface. This crust is often so hard that the germinating seed does not have the strength to break through the crust, resulting in poor stands. The gardener can overcome this problem by making a small trench, about one inch deep, planting the seed at the bottom of this trench and covering the seed with vermiculite or sawdust. This will prevent crusting and the gardener can reduce the frequency of irrigation.

Oxygen.—Oxygen is required for germination of a vegetable seed but is usually limiting only when the soil around the seed is saturated with water. This is particularly a problem where the garden is located at the low end of the homeowners lot and rainwater from their neighbor's house floods the garden. This condition removes all the oxygen from the soil and if the area remains flooded for any period of time the seed will be killed. It is not too much water that has killed the seed but a lack of oxygen. Some seeds such as the cucurbits (muskmelon, cucumber, watermelon, pumpkin) are particularly sensitive to low levels of oxygen. These

TABLE 2.4.   VEGETABLE PLANTING DEPTH AND RATE

Vegetables	Depth to plant seeds (inches)	Plants or seed per 100 feet	Spacing (inches) Rows	Plants	Number days ready to use
Asparagus	½	60 plants or 1 oz	36-48	18	(2 years)
Beans, snap bush	1-1½	½ lb.	24-36	3-4	45-60
Beans, snap pole	1-1½	½ lb.	36-48	4-6	60-70
Beans, Lima bush	1-1½	½ lb.	30-36	3-4	65-80
Beans, Lima pole	1-1½	¼ lb.	36-48	12-18	75-85
Beans, Fava, Broad Bean	2½	½ lb.	18-24	3-4	80-90
Beans, Garbanzo-Chickpea	1½-2	½ lb.	24-30	3-4	105
Beans, Yardlong or Asparagus	½-1	½ lb.	24-36	12-24	65-80
Beets	½	1 oz.	15-24	2	50-60
Broccoli	¼	¹40-50 pl. or ¼ oz.	24-36	14-24	60-80
Brussels sprouts	¼	¹50-60 pl. or ¼ oz.	24-36	14-24	90-100
Cabbage	¼	¹50-60 pl. or ¼ oz.	24-36	14-24	60-90
Cabbage, Chinese	¼	¹60-70 pl. or ¼ oz.	18-30	8-12	65-70
Carrots	¼	½ oz.	15-24	2	70-80
Cauliflower	¼	¹50-60 pl. or ¼ oz.	24-36	14-24	70-90
Celeriac	⅛	200 pl.	18-24	4-8	120
Celery	⅛	200 pl.	30-36	6	125
Chard Swiss	1	2 oz.	18-30	6	45-55
Chicory, witloof or French Endive	¼	½ oz.	18-24	8-12	90-120
Collards	¼	¼ oz.	18-36	8-16	50-80
Corn, sweet	2	3-4 oz.	24-36	12-18	70-90
Cress	¼	¼ oz.	12-16	2-3	25-45
Cucumber	1	½ oz.	48-72	24-48	50-70
Dandelion	½	½ oz.	12-16	8-10	70-90
Endive	½-1	¼ oz.	12-24	9-12	60-90
Eggplant	¼-½	⅛ oz.	24-36	18-24	80-90
Fennel	½	¼ oz.	18-24	6	˙ 120
Garlic (cloves)	1	1 lb.	15-24	2-4	140-150
Ground Cherry or Physalis	½	¼ oz.	36	24	90-100
Horseradish	4-6	100 roots	24	10-18	(6-8 months)
Jerusalem Artichoke	4	50-70 tubers	30-60	15-24	100-105
Kale	¼	¼ oz.	18-36	8-16	50-80
Kohlrabi	½	½ oz	15-24	4-6	55-75
Leeks	½-1	½ oz.	12-18	2-4	130-150
Lettuce, head	¼-½	¼ oz.	18-24	6-10	70-75
Lettuce, leaf	¼-½	¼ oz.	15-18	2-3	40-50
Muskmelon (cantaloupe)	1	¹50 pl. or ½ oz.	60-96	24-36	85-100
Mustard	½	¼ oz.	15-24	6-12	30-40
Okra	1	2 oz.	36-42	12-24	55-65
Onions	1-3	400-600 plants or sets	15-24	3-4	80-120
Onions (seed)	½	1 oz.	15-24	3-4	90-120
Parsley	¼-½	¼ oz.	15-24	6-8	70-90

TABLE 2.4 (*Continued*)

Parsnips	½	½ oz.	18-30	3-4	120-170
Peas, English	2	1 lb.	18-36	1	55-90
Peas, southern	½-1	½ lb.	24-36	4-6	60-70
Peppers	¼	⅛ oz.	24-36	18-24	60-90
Potatoes, Irish	4	6-10 lb. of seed tubers	30-36	10-15	75-100
Pumpkins	1-2	½ oz.	60-96	36-48	75-100
Radishes	½	1 oz.	14-24	1	25-40
Rhubarb	4	20 pl.	36-48	48	(2 years)
Salsify	½	½ oz.	15-18	3-4	150
Soybeans	1-2	1 lb.	24-30	2	120
Shallot	1-2	700 bulbs	12-18	2-4	60-75
Spinach	¾	1 oz.	14-24	3-4	40-60
Spinach, New Zealand	1½	½ oz.	24	18	70-80
Squash, summer	1	1 oz.	36-60	18-36	50-60
Squash, winter	1	½ oz.	60-96	24-48	85-100
Sunflower	1	4 oz.	36-48	16-24	80-90
Sweet potato	4	75-100 pl.	36-48	12-16	100-130
Tomatoes	½	¹50 pl. or ⅛ oz.	24-48	18-36	70-90
Turnip greens	½	½ oz.	14-24	2-3	30
Turnip, roots or Rutabaga	½	½ oz.	14-24	2-3	30-60
Watermelon	1	1 oz.	72-96	36-72	80-100

¹As Transplants

plants are frequently grown on sandy soils, not because they require less water, but because they require more oxygen. Sandy soils contain more air spaces than heavy soils.

TRANSPLANTS

The term "transplanting" means shifting of a plant from one soil or culture medium to another. Some vegetables grow best when they are planted indoors and then transplanted into a garden. There are a number of advantages for producing your own transplants including a) permitting the plant to grow before the danger of frost is over and the soil is dry enough to prepare; b) maximum numbers of plants can be obtained from costly seed; c) the problem of soil crusting can be avoided; d) depth for planting is more easily controlled; e) growing conditions can be controlled to produce suitable plants when needed, such as peppers which germinate slowly or pumpkins which require high germination temperatures; f) the gardener can grow special varieties of vegetable plants which may not be available locally, such as cherry or paste-type tomatoes, and g) the hazard of importing diseases with purchased transplants is eliminated.

Success in growing good transplants depends on four growing requirements: 1) an insect, weed and disease free growing media is needed; 2) adequate heat and moisture for growing the plants; 3) enough light to insure a stocky growth of the plant; 4) an adjustment or "hardening" period to prepare the plant grown indoors to grow successfully in the outdoor environment.

Containers.—Many types of containers can be used to grow vegetable plants for transplanting. Almost anything is satisfactory as a container as long as there is a hole in the bottom to allow adequate drainage. Some gardeners use large containers made from wood called flats. They may be made of metal or other material but are usually constructed from cedar, cypress or redwood. If the flats are made from other woods they should be treated with a wood preservative such as copper naphthenate. Pentachlorophenol or creosote should not be used as these materials will retard plant growth.

Clay or plastic pots can be used but are expensive and must be sterilized before re-use. However, cut off milk cartons, plastic jugs, tin cans, freezer boxes, cottage cheese or margarine tubs can also be used. There are a number of commercially prepared organic-composition pots, such as peat-pots, which can be used also. These pots minimize root disturbance when the plants are placed in the field as the entire pot is planted. However, the pots must be completely covered with soil and watered thoroughly so the plant roots can grow through them. If the pots are not covered completely, they act as a wick and draw the water from around the plants. All of the above containers require that some type of growing media be placed in them.

Seeds for transplanting may be sown into small blocks or pressed peat blocks. Kys-Kubes and BR8 Blocks are small cubes or blocks containing fertilizer. These are thoroughly watered and the seeds placed in them. Jiffy-7 pellets are compressed peat enclosed in a plastic container. These pellets are soaked in water and expand 3-4 times in size. The seed is then planted into the expanded pellet. These cubes, blocks and pellets containing the vegetable transplant, are placed directly into the soil and little root disturbance occurs (Figure 2.1).

The size of the container is more important than the kind of container. The size should be equivalent to the minimum size suggested for transplants in Table 2.5. Avoid close spacings which cause plants to compete with each other for light, nutrients, and moisture. Crowded seedlings tend to become weak and spindly and are more susceptible to disease. Wider spacings or larger containers generally give superior results. If you want to produce the highest quality plants, space them so the leaves of one plant do not touch those of another plant. However, it may not be economical to provide the space required for growing a volume of plants in this manner.

Plants are frequently overcrowded when seeded directly into hotbeds

Courtesy of Jiffy Products

FIG. 2.1. JIFFY-7 USED FOR TRANSPLANTING AS AN
INDIVIDUAL CONTAINER.

Left to right, dry, soaked in water and planted with a seed, and
plant ready for transplanting

where they remain undisturbed until ready for transplanting into the
field or garden. Such vegetable plants (cabbage, onion, pepper, and tomato) seeded at the recommended rates should be thinned to stand one-
half inch or more apart in the row.

Growing media.—The soil media for growing transplants should not
be soil from the garden or field. This type of soil usually lacks proper
structure (too much clay), contains insect pests, disease organisms, weed
seeds and may contain some residual herbicides. A good growing medium
should be sterile, uniformly fine, well aerated and well drained.

Composted soil and soil mixes are commonly used as medium for growing transplants. Frequently artificial media are also added to the soil mix
and include vermiculite, perlite, peat, and sand. Vermiculite is a light
weight expanded mica which absorbs large amounts of water (3-4 gal/
cubic foot) and contains a considerable amount of available magnesiun
and potassium. Perlite is a light weight expanded volcanic material
mined from lava flows which has no fertility value but has an excellent
water holding capacity.

Soil mixes for growing transplants should contain adequate nutrients,
be well drained and well aerated. Mixtures of: a) equal parts of soil, sand
and peat; b) equal parts of soil, peat, perlite; or c) two parts soil, one part

TABLE 2.5. SEED AND PLANT SPACING CHART FOR TRANSPLANTS

Crop	Planting depth (inches)	Seeds per inch of row (number)	Row width (inches)	Minimum space for transplants (inches)
Broccoli	¼-½	10	2-3	3 x 3
Brussels sprouts	¼-½	10	2-3	3 x 3
Cabbage				
For re-transplanting	½	10	2	3 x 3
For planting	½	3-6	4-6	—
Cauliflower	¼-½	10	2-3	3 x 3
Cucumber[1]	¾-1	—	—	3 x 3
Eggplant	¼-½	10	2-3	4 x 4
Lettuce (leaf, Bibb, head)	¼-½	10-15	2-3	2 x 2
Muskmelon[1]	¾-1	—	—	3 x 3
Onion (for planting)	½	10	3-4	—
Pepper				
For re-transplanting	¼-½	10	2-3	3 x 3[2]
For planting	½	3-6	4-6	—
Tomato				
For re-transplanting	¼-½	10	2-3	3 x 3[2]
For planting	¼-½	3-6	4-8	—
Watermelon[1]				
Regular	¾-1	—	—	3 x 3
Seedless	½-1	—	—	3 x 3

[1] These crops should be seeded directly in individual containers. Refer to following section on Techniques for Specific Vegetable Crops for seeding rates.
[2] For growing in flats, plants may be spaced 2 x 2 inches.

SOURCE: Courter et al. (1972)

sand and one part peat are good media. The soil provides the nutrients; the sand, perlite or vermiculite provide the aeration; and peat, vermiculite or perlite provide the water holding capacity. Sand alone is not recommended because it has low water holding capacity.

The growing media should be sterile. Small amounts of compost or garden soil may be sterilized by baking the soil in the oven. All of the soil should be heated to 180°F for 30 minutes. In a shallow pan, soil may reach this temperature in 45 minutes with the oven at 350°F. Over cooking releases toxic materials and kills various helpful microorganisms in the soil. These helpful microorganisms will degrade some of the organic matter in the soil and release nutrients, particularly nitrogen, for the plants growth. Without these microorganisms, the soil will usually be deficient in nitrogen.

There are a number of commercially prepared media suitable for starting and growing vegetable plants, such as Pro-mix, Jiffy Mix, Redi-Earth, and others.

Sowing.—The date to sow vegetables seeds for transplanting depends upon the date the transplants are to be planted into the field and the desired age of the transplant. How early you may plant the transplant depends upon the hardiness of the vegetable and the climate in your area. Some plants can withstand frost while others cannot. Table

2.6 gives the recommended growing periods and frost tolerance of the plants. Plants grown under less than optimum conditions will require longer growing times than those listed.

TABLE 2.6. TRANSPLANTING TOLERANCE AND TIME REQUIRED FROM SEEDING TO TRANSPLANTING

Vegetable	Transplanting Tolerance	Time to grow (weeks)	Frost Susceptibility
Broccoli	Survive well	5-7	Tolerant
Brussels sprouts	Survive well	5-7	Tolerant
Cabbage	Survive well	5-7	Tolerant
Cauliflower	Survive well	5-7	Tolerant
Celeriac	Survive well	8-10	Tolerant
Celery	Require care	8-10	Very susceptible
Cucumber[1]	Seed in container	3-4	Very susceptible
Eggplant	Require care	6-8	Very susceptible
Endive	Survive well	3-4	Tolerant
Kale	Survive well	5-7	Tolerant
Lettuce	Survive well	5-7	Moderately tolerant
Muskmelon[1]	Seed in container	3-4	Very susceptible
Onions, Dry	Survive well	8-10	Very tolerant
Parsley	Survive well	5-7	Tolerant
Pepper	Require care	6-8	Susceptible
Pumpkin[1]	Seed in container	4-6	Very susceptible
Squash[1]	Seed in container	4-6	Susceptible
Tomato	Survive well	4-7	Susceptible
Watermelon[1]			
Regular	Seed in container	4-6	Susceptible
Seedless	Seed in container	6-8	Susceptible

[1] Crops not generally successfully transplanted unless planted in individual containers, cubes, blocks or pellets. Any root disturbance hinders growth.

SOURCE: Courter *et al.* (1972)

A common practice is to sow the seed rather thickly in flats or large containers and then, when the first true leaves are fairly well developed, to transplant the seedlings spaced further apart into new flats. Suggested seed and plant spacings are given in Table 2.5. After seeds are sown in flats they are generally covered with a fine layer of sand, soil or vermiculite. Sprinkle the flat with water and then cover with a clear plastic film. This plastic film seals in moisture and air around the seeds and increases the temperature. The flat will require no further attention until the seedlings have begun to emerge.

When the seedlings have developed their first true leaves, they are ready to transplant into other containers. When transplanting, the seedling should be held by a leaf, not the stem. The slightest injury to the stem may cause permanent damage. Do not transplant weak, damaged or malformed seedlings. After transplanting, the seedlings will become established faster if they are kept shaded and moist for one or two days. Transplanting is not beneficial, and may be harmful, to the plants. The degree to which transplanting checks growth depends on the amount of injury to the root system, the age and size of the seedling, environmental conditions following transplanting, and the kind of vegetable seedling involved.

The seedlings of some vegetables, such as the cucurbits, are difficult to transplant successfully and should be seeded directly in individual containers. Thus, many gardeners initially sow seeds directly into individual containers (Peat pots, Jiffy-7 and the like) so that additional transplanting is not required.

Light, temperature and water for transplants.—It is seldom possible to keep transplanted plants in house windows without the plants becoming spindly and weak. They should be grown in a hotbed, cold frame or other place where they will receive enough sunlight, ventilation and suitable temperature.

There is no economical method of providing adequate artificial lighting to grow a volume of good plants. However, strong, vigorous seedlings can be started under 40 watt, 48 inch long fluorescent tubes, 6-8 inches above the seedlings. Best results are obtained if the fluorescent fixture is next to a window to increase the amount of light reaching the young plants, and that the plant receive 12 hours of total light (natural sunlight and artificial light). It is best to add one or two incandescent light bulbs with each four-tube fluorescent bank of lights to provide light which is more nearly like natural sunlight. "Plant-growth" type of lamps designed for growing plants indoors may also be used. These type of lamps emit a light which simulates sunlight but the color they emit may not be pleasing in a household environment. A timer to turn the lights on and off is very helpful.

Optimum day and night temperature ranges for growing plants are given in Table 2.7. During times of low light intensity, the lower temperatures should be used.

High temperatures (above the recommended range) at any time, and especially during conditions of low light, will cause plants to become spindly and weak. Temperatures lower than recommended will reduce growth and delay plant development, and they may also cause rough fruit in tomatoes and premature seeding of cabbage and cauliflower.

Use accurate thermometers to frequently check temperatures if the plants are being grown in a hotbed or cold frame. The thermometers should be located at the level of the plants being grown. Uniform temperatures are essential for adequate control of plant development and production of uniformly sized transplants.

Day time temperatures and humidity are primarily controlled by ventilation. This air exchange supplies carbon dioxide, which is used in photosynthesis, and helps to minimize disease problems. Ventilation at

TABLE 2.7. RECOMMENDED SEED–GERMINATION AND PLANT GROWING
TEMPERATURES

Crop	Optimum soil temperature range for germination (°F)	Days to emerge[1]	Plant-growing temperature[2] Day (°F)	Night
Broccoli	70-80	5	60-70	50-60
Brussels sprouts	70-80	5	60-70	50-60
Cabbage	70-80	4-5	60-70	50-60
Cauliflower	70-80	5-6	60-70	55-60
Cucumber	70-95	2-5	70-80	60-70
Eggplant	75-85	6-8	70-80	65-70
Lettuce	60-75	2-3	55-75	45-55
Muskmelon	75-95	3-4	70-80	60-70
Onion	65-80	4-5	60-70	45-55
Pepper	75-85	8-10	65-80	60-70
Tomato	75-80	6	60-75	60-65
Watermelon				
Regular	70-95	4-5	70-80	60-70
Seedless	85-95	5-6	70-80	60-70

[1] At optimum soil temperature range.
[2] The lower temperatures are recommended during cloudy weather.

SOURCE: Courter *et al.* (1972)

night, except during excessively windy or cold periods, insures adequate air circulation and reduced humidity. Avoid direct cold drafts, which may be harmful to the plants.

Plant growth can be regulated by careful watering. Water the plants only when moisture is needed and then wet the soil thoroughly. Too frequent watering is a common error in plant growing and results in soft, succulent plants with restricted root growth. It may also promote damping-off diseases. The less light, and the cooler the temperature, the less water is required by the plant. Plants should be watered in the morning to allow the foliage and soil surface to dry before night when the temperatures near the window or in the cold frame are cooler. Wet, cool conditions encourage damping off diseases.

Fertilizer.—Fertilizers can be easily supplied as the plants are watered. This allows a practical means of adjusting nutrient levels according to the stages of plant development and existing environmental conditions. You can control plant growth by the amount of and the strength of the fertilizer solution used, and the frequency of application.

Many soluble fertilizers are available for supplemental feeding. Starter fertilizers of various analyses, such as 10-52-17, 10-50-10, 20-20-20, 5-25-15, or 16-32-16 have been used with good results. These are high analysis, watersoluble fertilizers which are primarily mixtures of di-ammonium phosphate and mono-potassium phosphate. Potassium nitrate (14-0-46 analysis) and ammonium nitrate (33-0-0 analysis) have also been used successfully.

Many gardeners prefer to fertilize once each week. A rate of one tablespoonful of the above soluble fertilizers per gallon of water is suggested. After the plants are three weeks of age, the strength can be increased to two tablespoons of the fertilizer per gallon of water. To remove any fertilizer that might burn the foliage, give the plants a light watering with clear water.

Soluble salts can be a problem in plant-growing beds as a result of using too much fertilizer or improper fertilizer. Because it is easy to over-fertilize a small area, be careful not to use rates higher than those suggested. Also, avoid the use of muriate fertilizers which contain large amounts of chlorides. Symptoms of soluble salt injuries are poor seed germination, stunted plant growth, small dark leaves, and wilting. Wilting may occur even when the soil is sufficiently moist. Thus, it is a good practice to use plain water between fertilizer applications to prevent the accumulation of salts which could injure the transplants.

Cold frames And hot beds.—In determining the type of equipment for growing plants for later transplanting, the gardener must consider the climate of the area and the type of plants being grown. Frost tolerant plants (see Table 2.6) such as cabbage need only inexpensive, simple facilities while tender seedlings such as tomatoes or peppers require more elaborate facilities.

Cold frames are structures which depend on the sun for heat. In warmer parts of the USA and in protected locations, a coldframe or plastic covered pit on the sunny side of a building usually is sufficient. In cooler sections or in exposed areas, some additional heat is needed as a protection against cold damage and these heated coldframes are called hotbeds. The heat is provided by hot air, steam or hot water pipes, electric soil cables, infrared lights or fermenting manure.

The growing structure should be on well-drained land, free from danger of flooding in the spring. Covers for hotbeds and coldframes may be glass, fiberglass, plastic, canvas or muslin. The amount of covering is determined by the outside weather, the heat generated inside the structure and the type of plants being grown. In cold climates a tight, well-glazed structure is necessary.

Large plant hoods which resemble a small greenhouse may be made from tubular aluminum or steel pipe and plastic. Upright semi-circles of pipe are placed in the ground and a double layer of plastic film is placed over the pipes. This insulates against 5-10°frost temperatures. Clear plastic film transmits about as much visible light as glass and more ultraviolet and infrared (heating rays) than glass.

Electrically heated hotbeds are convenient for gardeners. A complete unit may be purchased, complete with frame, heating cables, switches and thermostats (Figure 2.2). Their cost is relatively low, depending on electric rates and the soil temperatures are easily controlled.

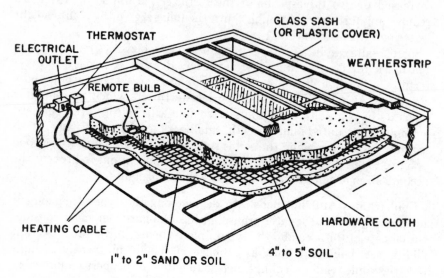

GLASS SASH
(OR PLASTIC COVER)

THERMOSTAT

ELECTRICAL
OUTLET

WEATHERSTRIP

REMOTE BULB

HEATING CABLE

HARDWARE CLOTH

1" to 2" SAND OR SOIL

4" to 5" SOIL

From Wester 1972

FIG. 2.2. AN ELECTRICALLY HEATED HOTBED FOR THE HOME GARDENER

Gardeners may construct a hot bed by building a cold frame on the south side of their house in front of a heated basement window. The heated basement will heat the hot bed and the temperature of the hotbed can then be controlled by opening and closing the basement window.

Hardening.—Hardening is a physiological process whereby plants accumulate carbohydrate reserves and produce additional cuticle on the leaves. This allows the plants to withstand such conditions as chilling, drying winds, shortage of water or high temperatures. Plants can be hardened by any method that stops growth, such as lowered temperature, withholding water or limiting fertility. During the marketing of vegetable transplants, a combination of these factors occurs, hardening the plants. Gardeners often place the plants outside in a protected area and expose them to lower temperatures for two weeks before planting. The plants should be brought inside or covered in a cold frame if frost is likely. The plants should be exposed to more sunlight which causes the plant to produce more cuticle thereby reducing water loss. Cabbage, lettuce, onion and some other plants can be hardened to withstand frost; tomatoes, peppers and eggplant cannot.

Hardening is not necessarily helpful to the plant and it may be detrimental. It is not recommended for most kinds of vegetable transplants. With the exception of tomatoes, plants which are susceptible to frost should not be hardened (see Table 2.6). Overly hardened plants may survive rigorous garden conditions but they begin growth slowly and they may never fully recover, reducing yields and delaying maturity. Some biennial crops such as cauliflower and cabbage can receive enough cold temperature below 50°F that, if they are large enough plants, they will be induced to produce a seed stalk instead of the edible part.

When hardening plants it is better to reduce growth of the plants than stop it completely. Hardening reduces the growth rate, thickens the cuticle, increases the wax on leaves of some plants, increases the carbohydrate reserve and induces a pink color, especially in the stems, petioles and veins of the leaves. Usually hardened plants contain leaves which are smaller and darker green than non-hardened plants. Hardened plants produce new roots faster than non-hardened plants and this is important for plants which are not grown in individual transplanting containers. The hardened plants have accumulated a food reserve which is used in the formation of new roots.

TRANSPLANTING TECHNIQUES FOR SPECIFIC CROPS.

Although all vegetables can be grown as transplants, they are not all grown in an identical manner. Some can only be transplanted if they are planted in an individual container so their roots are not disturbed. The best plants to transplant are those which do not contain fruit and still have the cotyledons (initial leaves) remaining on the plant.

Cabbage and broccoli.—These plants germinate and grow best at soil temperatures of 70°-80°F. If the seeds are sown in a hotbed it may be necessary to transplant the seedlings to a coldframe, because it is sometimes impractical to lower the hotbed temperature enough to grow good, stocky cabbage or broccoli plants. Although cabbage and broccoli thrive on relatively low temperatures, repeated chilling or exposure of the plants to low temperature (50°F) for a period of two weeks or more may cause them to prematurely form seedstalks after they are set in the field. In warm climates, cold frames can be used for growing cabbage and broccoli plants.

Cauliflower and brussels sprouts.—These vegetables are similar to cabbage, except that cauliflower requires slightly higher night temperatures. Cauliflower plants are delicate and require careful handling. The seedlings should not be crowded, exposed to low temperatures or inadequately watered, as this will slow or stunt growth of the plants. If the stems become woody or tough due to poor growing conditions, they will form small inferior cauliflower heads in the garden. Cauliflower plants should be grown in individual containers or when removing the plants from the flat for transplanting, the plants should be lifted out with as much soil on the roots as possible.

Eggplant.—Eggplant seeds require about a week to germinate in a flat and should be ready to transplant to other containers in an additional 10-15 days. Seedlings should be grown uniformly from germination onwards. If growth stops, the stems become hard and woody and plants do not produce satisfactory fruits. Eggplant is susceptible to low temperatures and should not be hardened. Plants should be planted in the garden when they have 4-5 true leaves and the soil is warm and there is no danger of frost.

Lettuce.—Lettuce seeds germinate in two or three days and can be transplanted into other containers after an additional week. Bibb lettuce has a higher optimum growing temperature than head or leaf lettuce and should be grown at temperatures higher than those listed in Table 2.3. Lettuce seedlings are spaced two inches apart and should be grown in individual containers. If they are grown in flats, as much soil as possible should be left on the roots when planted in the garden.

Onions.—Onions are grown from sets or seeds. The Spanish type is usually grown as a transplant. Seeds should be planted 90 days before they are to be planted in the garden. Onions do better if moderately hardened by watering less frequently and exposing the plants to night temperatures of 40-45°F for 7-10 days before transplanting. The tops of the plants are often clipped to a six inch height to reduce water loss and for ease of transplanting. Excessive clipping will delay onion growth and decrease yields.

Pepper.—The seed germinates slowly and requires about eight days. Seedlings should be ready for planting into other containers in an additional 10-15 days when the first true leaf has appeared. Peppers are grown similar to tomatoes.

Tomato.—Tomato seeds germinate in about six days but the time is influenced by the viability of the seed and the germination temperature. Lowered growing temperatures (see Table 2.7) and adequate light and water will produce short stocky plants. The seedlings should be transplanted into individual containers or flats 10-15 days after sowing. In general, container-grown seedlings produce earlier yields than plants grown in flats and pulled out bare-root prior to transplanting. When grown under good conditions, tomatoes should have stocky, thick, stems, well-developed root systems and visible flower buds on the first cluster. Flowers should not be in bloom and fruit should not be set. If fruit is set before the plant becomes established in the field, the plant will not develop properly and the fruit should be removed. Plants should not be pruned or trimmed to slow down growth. By removing the leaves, less food will be available for the plants' growth. Pruning will increase branching of the plants but this has not been found to be beneficial. Hardening of the plants often results in delayed establishment of the plants in the field, delaying harvest. Hardening frequently results in rough tomato fruit on the first two clusters. The plants can be held a week in good conditions if weather prevents transplanting into the garden.

Vine crops.—Watermelons, muskmelons, cucumbers, summer squash, pumpkins and gourds are generally planted directly into the garden. These crops do not transplant easily if grown in flats and they must be grown in individual containers about three inches or larger in size. This allows transplanting of the plant with minimum disturbance to the root system. Usually three to five seeds are sown and then thinned to the two strongest seedlings after emergence. Plants should be thinned by pinching off or cutting the stems with a knife. Pulling the excess plants out can result in injury to the roots of the remaining plants. The cost of some seedless and hybrid seed is such that many gardeners plant only one or two seeds per container.

Vegetative Propagation

Vegetative propagation of plants is asexual propagation and does not involve seeds. Asexual propagation involves the regeneration of the missing plant parts. A root cutting develops a new shoot, and a stem develops new roots. There are several advantages to vegetative propagation. Seeds do not always produce identical plants but vegetatively propagated plants are always identical with the mother plant. Any problems with seed dormancy are eliminated by this method. Some vegetables produce few viable seeds or they are not commercially available and vegetative propagation allows the production of these crops such as garlic, horseradish, potato and sweet potato. The following list summarizes various vegetables and the plant part that are vegetatively propagated.

Asparagus (crowns)	Sweet potato (slips or shoots)
Rhubarb (crowns)	Horseradish (root)
Potato (stem tuber)	Garlic (bulbs)
Jerusalem artichoke (tuber)	Shallots (bulbs)

The crown of a plant is that part just above or below ground level and may be thought of as a very short stem. Crowns produce buds which produce new plants, as occurs with rhubarb and asparagus. In these vegetables the crown also serves as a food storage organ.

Vegetables such as garlic and shallots are propagated by bulbs, which consist of many fleshy leaves and a very short stem. Bulbs produce new bulbs at the base of these leaves which may be used to produce new plants.

Potatoes and Jerusalem artichokes are propagated from tubers which are enlarged stems grown underground. This tuber contains a number of "eyes" or buds, each of which is capable of producing a new plant. Commonly three ounces of tuber containing at least two eyes are used as the seed piece. If the entire tuber is planted, the terminal "eye" or bud inhibits the other buds from growing.

Sweet potatoes are propagated from the edible part, the fleshy, swollen root (tuberous root). These roots are grown usually in sand and produce a number of new rooted plants. These plants (slips) are removed from the tuberous root and planted in the garden. Horseradish is commonly propagated vegetatively from a small root about three to five inches long. This root will produce a new plant.

GERMINATION

Germination of a seed involves four phases: 1) the absorption of water; 2) the formation of enzyme systems and the breakdown of the food reserves; 3) the growth of the new root and shoot, and 4) the growth of the seedling up to the time it has emerged from the soil.

When seeds absorb water, active metabolism begins and respiration (the breakdown of sugars into carbon dioxide and water with the release of energy) and protein synthesis begin. The growth of the small root and shoot (embryo) require large amounts of energy for new cell material. At the beginning of germination the embryo has enough carbohydrate, fat, and protein food reserve but this is soon depleted. The bulk of the seed is composed of food reserves and these must be broken down by various enzymes which are made of protein. The food reserves start to dissolve shortly after the embryo begins to grow. The cell walls are degraded; reserve protein is hydrolyzed to soluble amino acids; starch is hydrolyzed to sugar and fats are converted to sugar or energy. These events are controlled by various enzymes which have been synthesized and in about four days the food reserves have been liquified. Much of the food reserve has been transported to and used by the growing embryo.

The radical or root emerges first from the seed. The young root can now absorb water and nutrients from the soil. Shoot development begins after the root has emerged. The seedling now grows in the absence of light in the soil and is dependent upon the stored food reserves until the shoot emerges. If small seeds are planted deep in the soil, the seedling will run out of food reserve before it emerges from the soil. When plants are grown in the dark or in the soil, the shoot continues to elongate until it has emerged into the light. Plants have various ways in which they protect the shoot from damage as it moves through the soil toward the surface. In grasses such as sweet corn, the tip of the shoot is enclosed in a leaf cylinder called the coleoptile. The area between the seed and the coleoptile grows until light hits the coleoptile, and then secondary roots are formed. As the secondary roots form only when the light hits the coleoptile, these roots are always at the same depth in the soil, regardless of how deep the seed was planted.

In dicotyledonous plants, the stem forms a hook and as the shoot moves through the soil, it pulls the top of the shoot behind it. This prevents damage to the cotyledons and/or leaves which are pulled rather than pushed upward. Once the seedling is exposed to light, the shoot becomes unhooked and the leaves begin to expand. The cotyledons of some vegetables such as tomatoes, peppers, beans and squash emerge from the soil and function, as leaves. The cotyledons of peas remain undergound, however. The cucurbits (cucumber, squash, pumpkins) develop a "foot" on the shoot as it develops and this foot pries off the large seed coat from the cotyledons as they emerge or shortly thereafter.

VEGETATIVE GROWTH

Once the seedling has emerged from the soil, it is capable of continuous and uninterrupted growth until flowering. During this period of growth when the plant cannot readily be induced to flower, it is considered to be juvenile. Specific environmental conditions are also required (such as day length or low temperature) for some plants to flower.

There are a number of advantages to the plant for having a period of rapid vegetative growth. The plant can better compete with weeds and other plants if it is large. It maintains its competitive position and is able to receive more sunlight by growing rapidly. As a result, the plant will have more food produced from photosynthesis, and a large plant with more food reserve will produce a higher yield of the edible part. By maintaining a vegetative condition, the food reserve of beets, carrots, onions and radish is used to produce the edible part. When these plants flower, however, the food reserve is used to produce flowers and seeds. These plants are not capable of developing the edible part and also producing flowers and seeds. In those vegetables in which fruit is desired, a larger plant can withstand the stresses of flowering much easier than a small plant. A small plant often produces seed and then dies. A build-up of food materials occurs in the leaves during vegetative growth and these materials are used in the flowering process. In many plants, once flowering begins, vegetative growth stops and no more food accumulates. After flowering and fruit set, the plant often stops growing, but if the fruit is removed, the plant continues to grow and produce new flowers and fruit, as occurs in pepper and beans. In some plants, such as sweet corn, the vegetative part of the plant becomes the flowering part (the tassel on sweet corn) and the plant cannot continue to grow or produce new flower parts even if the flower or fruit (sweet corn ear) is removed.

Often vegetative and reproductive growth proceed together. In peanuts, flower parts often develop in the seed while it is still in the soil. In sweet corn, the plant has formed the ear and tassel before the plant has reached the sixth leaf stage.

Vegetative growth is influenced by the environment. Pungency of onions and radish develop rapidly at high temperatures and most gardeners do not want "hot" radishes. If radishes are grown in the greenhouse, high temperatures frequently occur resulting in radishes with a high pungency content. The amount of solids and starch of potato tubers is also affected by temperature.

FLOWERING

Once the plant has reached a certain developmental stage and the plant has overcome juvenility, and certain environmental conditions have been met, the plant will flower. Many environmental factors affect flowering; and water, nutrition, light, and temperature play a vital role. The actual environmental conditions which promote flowering do not have to be present during the flowering process. The gardener is interested in producing two types of vegetables; those in which the edible part is the flower bud, fruit or seed, and those in which the edible part is the leaf, root, stem or petiole. The plants in the latter group may, however, produce flowers instead of a satisfactory edible part.

Temperature.—Temperature is one critical environmental factor which affects flowering. Many vegetables are induced to flower by low temperatures, particularly biennial and perennial plants. Some, such as spinach, are induced to flower at high temperatures. Tomatoes will produce more flowers if grown at 80°F during the day and 65°F at night than at higher or lower night temperatures.

The induction of flowering due to low temperature is called vernalization. Biennial plants normally grow one year, are induced to flower during the winter, and flower the next year. They may, however, be induced to flower the first year and if this happens, the plant does not produce a satisfactory edible plant part. As the plants become older, they respond more easily to low temperature flower induction. However, the gardener can manipulate the plants so as to prevent flowering. The vernalization process requires water, oxygen, a growing point or bud, cold temperature, and a food reserve. If any of these requirements are lacking, the plant will not flower.

Horseradish is commonly grown from a small root cutting obtained one year and planted the next year. This root cutting is a section of a side root. When this root is planted early in the spring, it receives a cold treatment but does not flower that year. The root appears to have enough food reserve but lacks an active growing point, a requirement for vernalization. Thus, the root cutting produces a new fleshy root instead of flowers. If the plant is left in the ground over winter, it will flower the next year as the plant now has an active growing point and is vernalized.

Broccoli and cauliflower require very little chilling for vernalization. The gardener can transplant these plants when they are small and do not have enough food reserve for vernalization to occur, or can transplant them as larger plants after the soil temperatures have warmed up. If the plants receive a cold treatment, and they have enough food reserve, they will flower and produce a head so early that it will be very small.

Carrot varieties are highly variable in their vernalization response. The large root of carrot is easily vernalized at 60°F to induce it to flower.

Onions are vernalized if they receive two weeks at 40-50°F. Onions sets are normally stored during the winter at temperatures just above freezing to prevent spoilage. During this storage the sets are vernalized and if they were planted immediately they would flower and would not form a bulb. However, the sets can be converted back to their original non-flowering condition by high temperatures. Exposing the sets to 80°F for two or three weeks will de-vernalize the sets and they will form bulbs instead of flowers. If the sets are not exposed to high temperatures, the gardener should select medium sized sets about one-half inch in diameter for use as dry onions or bulbs. These sets are small enough so that even if they have been exposed to low temperatures when planted in the spring, the sets do not have enough food reserve to allow them to become vernalized. The larger sets should be used to produce green onions.

Beets, cabbage and celery may also be vernalized by cold temperature. To prevent this, it is best to plant beets when the temperature is warming up rapidly in the spring and the seedling does not have enough food reserve to be vernalized and the cold temperatures do not remain long enough. Small cabbage transplants with low food reserves or larger plants planted late will produce satisfactory heads instead of flowers.

Nutrition.—When some vegetables are given a large amount of nitrogen fertilizer, the plants produce large amounts of vegetative growth but few flowers and fruit. This is particularly a problem when large amounts of manure are applied to a garden and tomatoes are produced.

Light.—A large number of vegetables respond to the variations in the length of the light and dark periods, or daylengths. Some vegetables initiate flowers during long days (12 hours or more of light) such as radish, lettuce, spinach, potato and beets. Other vegetables initiate flowers during short days, such as some gourds and beans. Still other vegetables such as tomatoes and peppers, produce flowers under either long or short days. As a result, different varieties of vegetables are grown in the south than are grown in the north. Some types of sweet corn are adapted to short days and, if grown under long day conditions, the plants will grow vegetatively but will not flower and produce an ear. Some gourds and beans are short day plants and will not flower under long days. In northern climates, they grow vegetatively under the long days of summer and flower in the fall. Frequently a frost occurs before the fruit has reached an acceptable size.

Flower types.—Most vegetables, of which the edible part is the fruit or seed, produce complete flowers. Complete flowers are those containing both male and female parts. The cucurbits (cucumber, squash, pumpkins), however, have separate male and female flowers (Figure 2.3). These plants produce a number of male flowers and as the vine grows, they begin to produce both male and female flowers. The fruit is produced only by the female flowers and the gardener should not be concerned with a lack of fruit on the first part of the vine. The production of male flowers insures a larger amount of vegetative growth before fruit set, thereby providing more food material to produce more and larger fruit.

FRUIT SET

Pollination.—The changes which mark the transition of the flower into a young fruit are called fruit set. The first event a gardener notices is pollination. In peas, beans, and some other legumes, they are already pollinated when the flowers emerge. In others like tomato, the flower must be shaken (wind pollinated) or visited by bees or insects to transfer the pollen from the male to female parts of the flower. Pollination allows seed production and also prevents the flower or young fruit from falling off the plant.

In gourds and squash (Figure 2.3), there are separate male and female flowers and bees or some other insect must transfer the pollen from the male to the female. Commercial seeds of these plants are produced in

From MacGillivray et al. 1968

FIG. 2.3. SUMMER SQUASH SHOWING MALE FLOWER (LEFT) AND FEMALE
FLOWER (RIGHT) WITH IMMATURE SQUASH FRUIT

isolated areas where no other variety is grown. The gourds, pumpkins and squash are all members of the family *Cucurbitaceae* and of the genus *Cucurbita*. Varieties within a species will cross-pollinate with each other, even though they may be called a gourd or a pumpkin or a squash. This cross-pollination does not affect the shape, color or taste of the fruit presently produced. However if the seed from these fruits is saved and planted the next year, a vast array of colors, shapes, sizes, textures and tastes of fruit will be produced. Within the *Cucurbita* genus, some species will also sometimes cross-pollinate with another species, although only a few seeds are usually produced. Thus, varieties in the species *pepo* and *maxima* will sometimes cross with *moschata*.

Parthenocarpy.—Some vegetables can have fruit set without the production of seeds, and this is called parthenocarpy. Fruit development by this means can occur 1) without any pollination; 2) with pollination but without fertilization; or 3) by pollination and fertilization but the embryo aborts.

Fruit development without pollination is often noted by gardeners who use auxin-like herbicides to kill weeds in their lawn. A small amount of this material will stimulate production of tomato fruit with no seeds inside the fruit. Frequently, the inside of the fruit will be hollow. Parthenocarpic fruit produced without pollination occasionally occurs naturally with tomato, pepper, pumpkins and cucumbers. There are several varie-

TABLE 2.8.   VARIETIES WITHIN THE *CUCURBITA* GENUS WHICH ARE FREQUENTLY CROSS-POLLINATED WITHIN A GIVEN SPECIES.

Genus and species	Gourds and Ornamentals[1]	Variety Squash Summer	Variety Squash Winter	Pumpkin
Cucurbita pepo	Apple Bicolor Bird nest Crown of Thorns Miniature Miniature Bottle Orange Pear Spoon Warted Other small hard shelled types	(*Yellow elongated types*) Butterbar Crook Neck Eldorado Goldbar Golden Girl Golden Zucchini Straight Neck (*Flat-shaped types*) Green Tint Pattie Pan Scallopini White Scallop (*Green elongated types*) Caserta Cocozelle Zucchini	(*Acorn types*) Acorn Ebony Table Ace Table King Table Queen (*Novelty types*) Vegetable Spaghetti Vegetable Gourd Edible Gourd	(*Naked seed types*) Eat-All Lady Godiva Triple Treat (*Standard types*) Big Tom Cinderella Connecticut Field Early Sweet Sugar Funny Face Halloween Howden's Field Jack-O'-Lantern Jackpot Luxury Small Sugar Spirit Sugar Pie Tricky Jack Young's Beauty
Cucurbita moschata			(*Butternut types*) Butternut Hercules Hybrid Butternut Patriot Ponca Waltham	(*Standard types*) Cheese Dickinson Field Golden Cushaw Kentucky Field
Cucurbita maxima	Aladdin Turk's Turban		Baby Blue Hubbard Banana Boston Marrow Buttercup Delicious Emerald Gold Nugget Golden Turban Hubbard Hybrid R Kindred Marblehead Sweet Meat	(*Standard types*) Big Max King of the Mammoths Mammoth Chili Mammoth Prize
Cucurbita mixta				Green-Striped Cushaw Japanese Pie Tennessee Sweet Potato White Cushaw

[1] Although listed as gourds and ornamentals, some of these are eaten, particularly Turks Turban.

SOURCE: Adapted from Doty (1973) and Vandemark and Courter (1978).

FIG. 2.4. PARTHENOCARPIC CUCUMBERS PRODUCED IN A GARDEN WHERE NO
OTHER CUCUMBERS WERE GROWN NEARBY

ties of cucumbers for greenhouse production which produce fruit without pollination. Most of these varieties will produce seed if grown outdoors and are pollinated.

Fruit development with pollination but without fertilization can occur in tomato. Below 59°F, pollination of the flower can occur but the pollen tube does not grow so that fertilization does not occur. In this case, various hormones (such as "Blossomset") can be applied by the home gardener to induce fruit set.

Production of parthenocarpic fruit by embryo abortion occurs in seedless watermelons. Although no seeds are produced, the fruit still contains small seed coats which are sometimes confused with true seeds.

FRUIT DEVELOPMENT AND GROWTH

The control of fruit development is extremely complex. There are many growth hormones involved and there is considerable competition between various growth substances. It is obvious that fruits which contain a large amount of food material must obtain this from the rest of the plant. The seeds in the developing fruit produce new growth substances which induce the production of a conducting system between the fruit and the plant. Usually this conducting system is between certain leaves nearest the developing fruit. In peas and cucumbers, about 80% of the sugar is provided by the leaves nearest the fruit. When the fruit is removed, very little sugar moves out to the rest of the plant. Thus, old leaves may fall off or be shaded by new growth without any yield reduction. These old leaves are not providing much food material to the new developing fruit anyway. When the food material is being rapidly transported to the fruit, a nutrient deficiency sometimes occurs in the leaves due to this rapid transport.

Without the production of growth hormones by the developing seed, the fruit usually falls off. In cucumber, however, if two flowers which are at the same node are pollinated at the same time, both fruits develop simultaneously. If there is one day difference in pollination, the one pollinated first develops first. The other fruit remains small and does not develop until the first fruit is developed or picked. Sometimes the food material may move from the second fruit into the first fruit, causing the later pollinated fruit to fall off the plant.

Fruit may stop growing without falling off the plant. If the young developing fruit is removed, other fruits continue to grow. In okra, if the old fruit is allowed to mature and remain on the plant, yield is drastically reduced. In tomato, it normally takes about 45 days to go from pollination to incipient color (just turning red). If fruit growth is stopped, it may take as long as 130 days to get color. The seeds in these fruit are still viable and these fruits begin to grow when other fruits are removed from the plant.

In sweet corn and peas, the young seeds are watery and high in sugar content. As they continue to develop, they make starch, which is not sweet tasting, and form woody-like material in the seed coat making the seeds tough. In peas, development and enlargement of the pod begins first. Development of the embryo is second and seed enlargement is the last development stage. We can make use of this knowledge and harvest edible-podded peas when pod enlargement is complete and before embryo and seed development begins.

Fruit size depends upon 1) the number of leaves, 2) the amount of sunlight received by these leaves, 3) an ample supply of water, 4) the right temperature and 5) the competition between fruit. The plant only has so much food material available for the developing fruit. If the plant is large and has ample food, it is capable of producing more and larger fruit than a small plant. If a tomato transplant is planted with a small fruit on the plant, the fruit will be small. This transplant cannot grow vegetatively and develop an adequate sized fruit at the same time. The plant will use the available energy to produce this fruit and will have limited energy for new growth and additional fruit. Fruit on a tomato transplant should be removed before planting in the garden. Gardeners prefer smaller fruit on cucumbers which are grown for pickles. The cucumber plant is capable of producing many medium-sized fruit or a few large fruit. However, total weight of the fruit produced by the plant is about the same. Gardeners frequently prefer one large pumpkin instead of several small ones. To produce the largest pumpkin fruit, the first and second female flowers that the plant produces should be removed and the next female flowers should be pollinated. Total numbers of fruit will be reduced but the weight of the fruit that is produced will be increased as all the plant's energy is being directed into this one fruit.

FRUIT RIPENING

When a fruit has reached its maximum size, it is mature. A tomato fruit which is beginning to turn red is mature and will not increase further in size and may be picked. Ripening of fruit refers to the processes which change in the mature fruit. The general changes which occur during ripening are: 1) softening of the fruit flesh, 2) hydrolysis of stored materials into soluble material, 3) changes in the pigment content (color) of the fruit, 4) changes in flavor and 5) changes in respiration.

During ripening, cell walls are broken down, making the fruit soft. Various insoluble starches are converted to sugar. Ripe bell peppers are sweeter than green ones due to this increased sugar. However, the hydrolysis of starch in pumpkin or winter squash makes the product watery and this is not desirable.

Most gardeners consider a fruit ripe when it has changed to a characteristic color. Tomato and bell peppers become red. Winter squash turns light yellow or orange, starting at the area which was in contact with the ground. Usually this color is due to new pigments being synthesized. In summer beets, there is a high sugar content and a small amount of red color. In the fall, under cooler temperatures, the red color increases greatly, and as there is less photosynthesis occurring, the sugar content declines. A summer grown red beet has about the same percentage of sugar as a typical sugar beet.

During ripening, various flavor components appear. In snap beans, over 40 volatile flavor components appear although only 6 or 7 of these are important. Sweetness and acidity are often important in flavor, and sugar usually accumulates during ripening and acid levels decline.

It is not desirable to have all the ripening changes occur at the same time. Color development and softening of tomato fruit for example, are greatly influenced by temperature. At high temperatures (85°F), the fruit becomes soft but color development is slow. The fruit becomes partially colored or becomes orangish instead of red in color and is soft. Tomato fruit should be exposed to temperatures in the 70's to produce a red, firm fruit. This can be achieved by picking the fruit when the first sign of color appears and allowing the fruit to ripen in the light in the air-conditioned house (or another cooler place).

BULB AND TUBER FORMATION

A tuber is an inflated stem produced by a swelling type of growth. This tuber has a number of buds called "eyes" in potatoes. In a bulb, the stem does not increase in size but the base of the leaves swell. Bulb formation results from an increase in cell size while tubers increase due to an increase in both cell size and cell number.

Both bulb and tuber formation are affected by day length. Tuber formation of potatoes is accelerated by short days but some varieties produce tubers over a wide range of daylengths. Potato tuber formation is greatest at 70°F. Where summer temperatures are greater than this, the crop must be planted as early as possible and mulched with about eight inches of straw to keep temperatures as low as possible.

Onions require cool temperatures during early growth, and high temperatures and long daylengths for bulb formation. Therefore, if onion seedlings are grown in the house under artificial light of 18 hours, the seedlings will not grow faster; instead these seedlings will form very small bulbs and the tops will die.

Tubers and bulbs do not ripen as fruits do. Tubers should be stored two weeks at warm temperatures after harvest to allow a thicker skin and suberin layers to form. This protects the tubers from a high rate of water loss and covers over bruises which may have occured.

SELECTED REFERENCES

COURTER, J.W., VANDEMARK, J.S., and SHURTLEFF, M.C. 1972. Growing vegetable transplants. U. Ill. Coll. Agri. Circular *884*.

DOTY, W.L. 1973. All about vegetables. Chevron Chemical Company, San Francisco, CA.

HARRINGTON, J.F., and MINGES, P.A. 1954. Vegetable seed germination. U. Calif. Coll. Agri. Leaflet.

HORTIK, H.J. and ARNOLD, C.Y. 1965. Temperature and the rate of development of sweet corn. Proc. Amer. Soc. Hort. Sci. *87*, 303-312.

JONES, T.L. 1971. Injury to beans (*Phaseoeus vulgaris L.*) in relation to imbibition. Ph.D. Thesis. University of Illinois.

MACGILLIVRAY, J.H., SIMS, W.L., and JOHNSON, H. JR. 1968. Home vegetable gardening. Calif. Agri. Exp. Stn. Circular *499*.

VANDEMARK, J.S. and COURTER, J.W. 1978. Vegetable gardening for Illinois. U. Ill. Agri. Circular *1150*.

WESTER, R.E. 1972. Growing vegetables in the home garden. USDA Home and Garden Bulletin *202*.

3

Soils and Plant Nutrition

SOIL

An ideal garden soil is fertile, deep, friable, well drained and high in organic matter. The exact type of soil is not as important if the soil is well drained, adequately supplied with organic matter and retains moisture. The kind of subsoil is also important. Hard shale, rock ledges, gravel beds, deep sand or a hardpan under the surface are particularly undesirable. They make the development of a good garden soil difficult or impossible. However, if the soil has good physical properties but is just unproductive, this soil can be made productive by adding organic matter, fertilizer and adjusting the pH.

Good water drainage is essential. The garden should not contain low places where water would stand after heavy rains. Good air drainage is also important. The garden may be on a slight slope that allows the air to move downward to lower levels on the hill. This allows the garden to escape early and late frosts.

Soil composition.—Soil is made up of inorganic substances, decaying organic material, air, water and various amounts of insects, earthworms, bacteria, fungi and microorganisms. The living organisms degrade the organic material into a residual material called humus. Humus is dark in color and can absorb large amounts of water and nutrients.

Soil type.—Soils which contain 20-65% organic matter are called muck soils. Soils containing over 65% organic matter are peat soils. These soils retain large amounts of moisture but are deficient in several plant nutrients.

Most soils contain less than 20% organic matter and are mineral soils. These soils contain various sized particles of decreasing size: sand, silt

66

and clay. These materials are bound together into soil particles and the coarseness or fineness of these particles is referred to as soil texture. Texture is important because the area between the particles is filled with organic matter, air and water. The total area is not as important as the size of the individual spaces. Clay soils have more total space than sandy soils and clays can hold more water than sands. However, the individual spaces between particles is so small in the clays that air and water movement is slow, and when filled with water, prevent air movement which is essential for root growth. Sands allow this water to drain out and the spaces become filled with air. This allows for good aeration but without this water, plant nutrients are not kept in solution to be absorbed by the plant. The best garden soils contain a mixture of sand (for aeration), silt and clay(holds water and nutrients).

Mineral soils may be separated into sandy soils, loam soils and clayey soils. Sandy soils contain less than 15% silt or clay. They are well aerated, dry out and warm up rapidly. They are low in fertility and cannot hold much added nutrients or water.

Loam soils contain a relatively even mixture of sand, silt and clay. They contain less than 20% clay, 30-50% silt and 30-50% sand. These soils are ideal for most vegetables.

Clay soils contain 20-30% clay. Clay soils retain water and dry out slowly making them difficult to cultivate and work properly. Root growth is poor due to the small spaces between particles. These soil surfaces crust easily, reducing stands of some vegetables.

Sand and clay soils may be modified in the garden by adding organic matter and various soil amendments. The relative composition of desirable soils is 45% mineral matter, 5% organic matter, 25% air and 25% water (Bartelli, Slusher and Anderson 1977).

Cation exchange.—Cation exchange is the ability of clay and humus, which are negatively charged, to attract and exchange positively charged ions called cations. These cations, such as calcium, magnesium, potassium and ammonia, are thus held in the soil and are not lost by leaching. These cations become dissolved in the soil solution and are absorbed by the plant. The cations are replenished by the application of fertilizer or released from the degradation of organic matter or decomposition of rocks. The amount of material able to exchange cations is important. The more cation exchange capacity available, the more nutrients the soil can hold and fewer are lost. Cation exchange capacity is equivalent to the milligrams of hydrogen ions that will combine with 100 grams of dry soil. The actual amount varies with the amount of humus and the amount and type of clay present. The cation exchange capacity range for typical garden soils is: sands 2-10; loams 2-40; clays 5-60.

Soil preparation.—Vegetables grow best on fairly deep soils. If the garden soil is shallow it should be deepened gradually by increasing the depth of plowing an inch or two a year until the desired depth is reached. Organic matter should be incorporated into these shallow soils to make the subsoils more productive (see section on Soil Amendments— page 90). The deeper the soil is prepared, the greater is its capacity for holding air and moisture. One of the purposes of turning over the soil is to separate soil particles and allow air to come into contact with as many particles as possible and thereby provide a good growing media for the growth of roots and soil microorganisms.

The garden can be plowed, tilled or spaded in the spring or fall. Fall preparation has several advantages over spring preparation: 1) organic matter decomposes more rapidly; 2) insect and disease problems are reduced by burying them in the soil or exposing them to the weather, 3) more water is absorbed; 4) the physical condition of clay soils is improved by exposing them to frost action, 5) the soil can be worked and planted earlier in the spring and 6) the trapped air acts as insulation for increasing the survival of earthworms. Fall preparation is particularly desirable when sod, manure or a large amount of organic material is to be turned under. These materials will decompose during the fall and early spring and be of value to the crops planted the next season.

Spring preparation of soils is desirable where soil erosion occurs, where shallow tilling is practiced or on sandy soils. In the south, where conditions are hot and dry, the gardener may wish to consider a type of mulch system (see section on Mulches—page 97), instead of spring soil preparation.

Garden soils should not be worked when they are wet. When a handful of soil is squeezed in the hand, it should readily crumble and not feel sticky when the pressure is released. If the soil forms a compact, muddy ball, it is too wet to be worked. When examining the soil to determine if it is dry enough to work, samples should be taken both at and a few inches below the surface. The soil may be dry at the surface, but the lower layers may be wet. Soil that sticks to a shovel or other tools is usually too wet. Shiny unbroken surfaces of spaded soil is another indication of a wet soil condition. Clay soils low in organic matter lose their crumbly texture if they are worked when wet and become hard, compact, and unproductive.

Fertilizer can be added before soil preparation, and organic fertilizers and natural deposits particularly should be added at this time. If fertilizer is added after the soil is prepared, the fertilizer should be worked into the soil to a depth of two or three inches.

Before planting, the seedbed can be smoothed with a harrow or rake. A freshly prepared seedbed will prevent weeds from emerging before the vegetable plants. Each soil has its own characteristics which determine the best physical condition or tilth suitable for planting. Soils should not be worked to such a fine consistency that crusting occurs after rains. Clay soils particularly crust easily and prevent emergence of seedlings. These soils should be left comparatively rough and cloddy to reduce crusting of the soil surface.

WATER

Adequate soil moisture is essential to the production of vegetables. Water dissolves plant nutrients in the soil, plays an important role in biological activities, keeps the plant cool, and transports food and nutrients in the plant. Many vegetables are about 80% water. Plants require hydrogen (H) and obtain this from water (H_2O). Plants cannot use hydrogen from the air. Water for plant growth comes from rain or snowfall, surface drainage water and underground water. There are usually dry periods during the growing season when additional water will be required to begin germination, keep vegetables growing rapidly, and insure continual fruit production. The critical periods to insure that vegetables have adequate water are given in Table 3.1. Rain showers which provide less than one-fourth inch of water barely wet the soil surface and most of this water is lost by evaporation. Whenever the rainfall is less than one inch during the week, the garden should be irrigated. About one inch of water a week, including rainfall, is desirable. It is better to thoroughly soak the soil to a depth of at least a foot (two feet in southern and western soils) than to lightly sprinkle the area frequently. Watering in the morning or before 2:00 p.m. will allow the plants to become completely dry and help reduce diseases from mildew, blight, damping off and others. An easy way to determine how much water has been received by the garden is to place four or five cans at various spots in the garden and measure the amount of irrigation water received in these cans.

Water is often required to establish a garden, particularly summer or fall gardens. If the soil is dry when it is time to plant, about one inch of water should be applied to the area. The surface should be allowed to dry out and the surface then raked or very lightly cultivated to prepare the seedbed. This entire procedure often takes one day. The vegetables should then be planted but no additional water applied for two days. If no rainfall occurs, the area should receive one-half inch of water every other day until the seedlings have emerged. This procedure is particularly important for green, wax and lima beans as heavy watering results in reduced stands and yields (see germination requirements-water—page 39).

TABLE 3.1.   CRITICAL PERIODS OF WATER NEEDS OF VEGETABLES

Critical period	Vegetables
Germination	All, particularly summer or fall crops
Pollination	Lima beans
Pod enlargement	Lima and snap beans
	Edible podded peas
Head development	Broccoli, cabbage, cauliflower
Root, bulb and tuber enlargement	Carrot, onion, parsnip, potato, radish, turnip
Flowering and ear, fruit and seed development	Sweet corn, cucumber, pea, squash
Fruit set and early development	Melons
Uniform supply from flowering to harvest	Eggplant, pepper, tomato

Sprinkle and furrow irrigation.—Most gardeners will apply water with overhead sprinklers. Sprinkler irrigation can be applied at a slow rate to allow the water to be absorbed in compacted soils and to reduce run-off on sloping gardens. Winds may disturb the sprinkler pattern and it is best to water when the air is still. Sprinklers should be placed so the spray pattern overlaps with each nearby sprinkler. Less water is received at the edges of the sprinkler spray than at the center (Figure 3.1).

In the west and southwest, many gardeners use furrow irrigation. The beds growing the vegetables should be about six inches high and three feet apart. The irrigation water is applied in furrows between the beds (Figure 3.1). Raised beds are also useful in rainy areas as they allow the excess rain water to drain off the beds.

Trickle irrigation.—Trickle irrigation or drip irrigation is a method of applying small amounts of water directly to the growing plant (Figure 3.2). The system consists of a network of water-conducting plastic tubes which allow water to move through the walls of the tube at a slow rate. The tubes are placed at one side of the row and frequently buried one or two inches deep in the soil. Trickle irrigation uses less water than sprinkler irrigation and gives a more uniform supply of water to the plant. It is especially useful in dry regions where evaporation causes salts to accumulate near the surface. Trickle irrigation will leach the high concentrations of salt from around the plant roots reducing the salt problem. The major disadvantage of trickle irrigation is its high cost.

AIR

All plants require air to provide oxygen (O_2) and carbon dioxide (CO_2). Oxygen is required by the above ground parts at night for respiration and

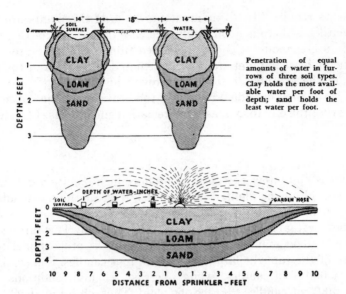

Penetration of equal amounts of water in furrows of three soil types. Clay holds the most available water per foot of depth; sand holds the least water per foot.

From MacGillivray et al. 1968

FIG. 3.1. WATER PENETRATION PATTERNS FROM SPRINKLER AND FURROW IRRIGATION ON DIFFERENT SOIL TYPES

From Kenworthy 1975

FIG. 3.2. A TRICKLE IRRIGATION SYSTEM INSTALLED

is required all the time for the roots. When too much water is applied and the drainage is poor the plant roots die, not from too much water, but from a lack of oxygen.

All plants require CO_2 to manufacture food. If the plants are being grown outdoors there is little way to increase the amount of CO_2 to the plant. In a greenhouse, CO_2 can be added from a CO_2 generator and a dramatic increase in plant growth can be noted. In the winter time, CO_2 is used in the greenhouse for plant growth and CO_2 levels inside are usually lower than outside. Frequently the vents are opened during the warm part of the day to increase air circulation and increase CO_2 levels.

LIGHT

Sunlight is absolutely necessary to produce high-quality vegetables. A garden should not be planted near shrubs, trees or the north side of a building where shading occurs. Leafy vegetables can be grown in partial shade but vegetables producing fruit need full sun. The rate of photosynthesis (food manufacture) of green plants is proportional to the intensity of the sunlight up to about 1200 foot-candles. Full sunlight is about 10,000 foot-candles, while overcast, cloudy conditions allow about 1,000 foot-candles to reach the plant. Thus, on sunny days a little over 10% of the available sunlight is used in photosynthesis while on cloudy days, all the light is utilized.

The amount of light received indoors near a window is about 100 foot-candles or about 10% of the light needed to grow quality vegetables. It is not economical to grow vegetables under artificial light.

ESSENTIAL PLANT ELEMENTS

Many different chemical elements are found in plants but only 16 have been shown to be essential. Most of the plant is composed of carbon, hydrogen and oxygen and these are obtained from air and water. The remaining 13 elements are phosphorus, potassium, nitrogen, sulfur, calcium, iron, magnesium, molybdenum, boron, copper, manganese, zinc and chlorine. These are absorbed from the soil as inorganic salts. Any of these elements in a high enough concentration will be toxic to the plant and reduce yields. A deficiency of any element results in typical plant symptoms as shown in Table 3.2.

Carbon, hydrogen and oxygen.—These three elements make up the bulk of the plant tissue. Much of the live plant is made up of water (hydrogen and oxygen) which is used to keep the plant cool, keep materials in solution, transport minerals from the soil through the plant, and transport food from the leaves. About 90% of the dry weight of the plant is cellulose and various sugars, much of this being in the cell walls. These materials are composed of carbon, hydrogen and oxygen.

TABLE 3.2. A KEY TO NUTRIENT DEFICIENCY SYMPTOMS OF VEGETABLES.

A. Symptoms on leaves, stems or petioles. . . . . B
Flowering or fruiting affected . . . . M
Storage organs affected. . . . . N
Variable plant growth throughout the field. Some plants appear normal, some show severe marginal leaf
necrosis, while others are stunted. Determine soil pH . . . . ACID or
ALKALINE
SOIL COMPl

B. Youngest leaves affected first. C
Entire plant affected or oldest leaves affected first. I

C. Chlorosis appears on youngest leaves. . . . . D
Chlorosis is not a dominant symptom. Growing points eventually die and storage organs are affected . . . . H

D. Leaves uniformly light green, followed by yellowing. . . . and poor, spindly growth . . . Most common in
areas with acidic, highly leached, sandy soils low in organic matter . . . . SULFUR
Uniform chlorosis does not occur. . . . . E

E. Leaves wilt, become chlorotic, then necrotic. Onion bulbs are undersize and outer scales are thin and
lightly colored. May occur on acidic soils, on soils high in organic matter, or on alkaline soils . . . . COPPER
Wilting and necrosis are not dominant symptoms. . . . . F

F. Distinct yellow or white areas appear between veins, and veins eventually become chlorotic. Symptoms
rare on mature leaves   Necrosis usually absent . . . . Most common on calcareous soils . . . ("lime
induced chlorosis") . . . . IRON
Yellow/white areas are not so distinct, and veins remain green . . . . G

G. Chlorosis is less marked near veins. Some mottling occurs in interveinal areas. . . . . . .Chlorotic areas eventually become brown, transparent, or necrotic. Symptoms may appear later on older leaves . . . . In
peas and beans, the radical and central tissue of cotyledons of ungerminated seeds become brown
("marsh spot") . . . Most common on soils with pH over 6.8 . . . . MANGANES
Leaves may be abnormally small and necrotic . . . . Internodes are shortened . . . . . . Beans, sweet
corn ("white bud" of maize)· · · ·and lima beans most affected; potatoes, tomatoes and onions somewhat affected; uncommon with peas, asparagus and carrots. Reduced availability in acidic, highly
leached, sandy soils, in alkaline soils, and in organic soils. . . . . ZINC

H. Brittle tissues . . . . . Young, expanding leaves may be necrotic or distorted followed by death of growing
points . . . . Internodes may be short, especially at shoot terminals . . . . Stems may be rough,
cracked . . . . . . or split along the vascular bundles (hollow stem of crucifers · · · · cracked stem of
celery . . . .) . Most likely on highly leached, acidic soils and on organic soils with free lime. . . . . BORON
**Brittle tissues not a dominant symptom. Growing points usually damaged or dead ("dieback") . . .
Margins of leaves developing from the growing point are first to turn brown or necrotic, expanding
corn leaf margins are gelatinous and necrotic· · · · expanding cruciferous seedling leaves are cupped
and have necrotic margins; old leaves remain green. Common on acidic, highly leached, sandy soils.
May result from excess Na, K, or Mg from irrigation waters, fertilizers or dolomitic limestone. (Celery
blackheart, brown heart of escarole, lettuce tipburn, internal tipburn of cabbage, internal browning of
Brussels sprouts, hypocotyl necrosis of snapbeans. . .)** . . . . CALCIUM

I. **Plant exhibits chlorosis.** . . . . J
Chlorosis is not a dominant symptom L

J. Interveinal or marginal chlorosis. . . . . : . . . . K
General chlorosis. Chlorosis progresses from light green to yellow. Entire plant becomes yellow under
prolonged stress . . . . Growth is immediately restricted and plants soon become spindly . . . . . and
drop older leaves . . . . Most common on highly leached soils or with high organic matter soils at low
temperatures. Soil applications of N show dramatic improvements · NITROGEN

K. **Marginal** chlorosis or chlorotic blotches which later merge . . . Leaves show yellow chlorotic interveinal
tissue on some species, reddish purple progressing to necrosis on others . . . Younger leaves affected
with continued stress . . . . Chlorotic areas may become necrotic, brittle, and curl upward . . . .
Symptoms usually occur late in growing season. . . . Most common on acidic, highly leached, sandy
soils . . . or on soils with high K . . . or high Ca . . . . MAGNESIUM
Interveinal chlorosis, with early symptoms resembling N deficiency (Mo is required for nitrate reduction);
older leaves chlorotic or blotched with veins remaining pale green. Leaf margins become necrotic and
may roll or curl . . . Symptoms appear on younger leaves as deficiency progresses. In brassicas, leaf
margins become necrotic and disintegrate, leaving behind a thin strip of leaf ("whiptail", especially of
cauliflower . . . . Common on acidic soils or highly leached alkaline soils · · · · · · · · · · · · · MOLYBDENUM

L. Leaf margins tanned, scorched, or have necrotic spots . . . . . (may be small black dots which later coalesce
. .) . Margins become brown and cup downward . . . . Growth is restricted and dieback may occur · · ·
Mild symptoms appear first on recently matured leaves, then become pronounced on older leaves, and
finally on young leaves . . . . Symptoms may be more common late in the growing season due to
translocation of K to developing storage organs. Most common on highly leached, acidic soils and on
organic soils due to fixation . . . . POTASSIUM

TABLE 3.2 (*Continued*)

Leaves appear dull, dark green, blue-green or red-purple, especially on the underside, and especially at the midrib and veins . . . . Petioles may also exhibit purpling . . . Restriction in growth may be noticed . . . . Availability reduced in acidic and alkaline soils, and in cold, dry, or organic soils	PHOSPHORUS
Terminal leaflets wilt with slight water stress. Wilted areas later become bronzed, and finally necrotic . . . . . . Very infrequently observed	CHLORINE
M. Fruit appears rough, cracked or spotted . . . . . . Flowering is greatly reduced. Tomato fruits show open locule, internal browning, blotchy ripening or stem-end russeting. Occurs on acidic soils, on organic soils with free lime, and on highly leached soils	BORON
Cracking and roughness are not dominant symptoms. Fruits exhibit water-soaked lesions at blossom end, later becoming sunken, dark or leathery (blossom-end rot of tomato, pepper, and watermelon) . . . . . . Common on acidic, highly leached soils	CALCIUM
N. Internal or external necrotic or water soaked areas of irregular shape (hollow stem of crucifers, internal browning of turnip and rutabaga, canker or blackheart of beet, water core of turnip) . . . . May occur on acidic soils on alkaline soils with free lime, or on highly leached soils	BORON
Cavities develop in the root phloem, followed by collapse of the epidermis, causing pitted lesions. (Cavity spot of carrots or parsnips.) Common on acidic, highly leached soils	CALCIUM

SOURCE: English and Maynard (1978).

Plants receive carbon and oxygen from the air and hydrogen from water. All other nutrients are obtained from the soil solution.

Nitrogen.—Nitrogen is usually more responsible for increasing plant growth than any other element. It is used in the formation of various proteins needed by the plant to do useful work. Although nitrogen is about 80% of the earth's atmosphere, it cannot be used in this form. It must be converted by various microorganisms or industrial processes into a form the plant can use. The two main forms are ammonium (NH_4+) and nitrate (NO_3-) ions. If various organic nitrogen forms are added as a fertilizer, this material must be broken down into these ions by soil microbes before the plant can use the nitrogen. Plants cannot use the nitrogen in the organic form. The organic material (whether added as a fertilizer or plowed under plant debris) is converted to the ammonium ion by various soil bacteria and this ion moves little in the soil. However, the ammonium ion is converted by other soil bacteria into the nitrate ion, which is soluble and easily leached from the soil. These conversion processes are dependent upon air, temperature and moisture. When air is lacking in the soil, various bacteria convert nitrates to atmospheric nitrogen and the nitrogen is lost. Under cool temperatures, little ammonium is converted to nitrate but warm temperatures cause some of the ammonia to be lost to the atmosphere by volatilization and also hasten its conversion to nitrate. Large amounts of moisture will result in leaching of these nitrates.

Four fates await any nitrogen applied to the soil (Luckhardt 1976), whether the nitrogen is found in a commercial fertilizer, an organic fertilizer, or crop residue; 1) it escapes into the air as a gas; 2) it is leached by water; 3) it is incorporated into new organic matter and; 4) the crop can use the remainder. Some 15-20% of the applied nitrogen is lost by volatility and about 50% of the nitrogen in manure is frequently

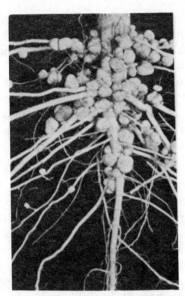

From Shanmugam and Valentine
1976 (U. Calif. Div. Ag. Sci.).

FIG. 3.3. BEAN PLANT WITH NODULES CONTAINING BACTERIA WHICH FIX
ATMOSPHERIC NITROGEN

lost by volatility. Leaching of the nitrates amounts to a lot on sandy soils and less on heavy clay soils. However, on clay soils saturated with water, the nitrates are converted to atmospheric nitrogen and are lost. Thus, heavy clay soils may lose as much nitrogen as sandy soils. The added nitrogen may be used by microorganisms involved in the breakdown of plant debris. These microbes use whatever amounts of nitrogen they require and the crop gets what is left. Thus, 30-60% of the applied nitrogen is tied up in organic matter. The nitrogen available to the vegetable crop is 15-75% of that applied and averages about 50%.

Snap beans and peas are legumes and these crops require a comparatively small amount of nitrogen compared to other vegetable crops (Janssen 1976). These legumes are associated with symbiotic bacteria (Figure 3.3) which convert atmospheric nitrogen into forms the plant can use. These bacteria depend directly upon the plant for their energy supply and cannot convert atmospheric nitrogen into a usable form unless they are associated with a specific plant. The amount of nitrogen converted into a useable form depends upon the vegetable involved, and the estimated pounds of nitrogen fixed per acre for some vegetables are as follows: peas 72 lbs; peanuts 42 lbs.; beans 40 lbs.; soybeans 58 lbs. (Delwiche 1970).

Usable nitrogen is also added to the soil by non-symbiotic types of bacteria and by lightning and rainfall. The amount of nitrogen added by these methods is unreliable for the typical gardener and can be ignored in fertilizer recommendations. The amount of nitrogen released from decaying organic matter for plant use depends upon the amount of organic matter in the soil.

Large amounts of nitrogen are used by plants when they are growing vegetatively and developing their roots, stems and leaves. Nitrogen stimulates the production of these parts at the expense of the fruiting and food storage parts. Leafy vegetables such as cabbage, kale, lettuce and spinach require more nitrogen than other garden crops. They may be stimulated to produce more leaves by side-dressings of nitrogen.

Phosphorus.—Phosphorus promotes root growth, flower, fruit and seed development, and stimulates stiffer stems. Many soils contain large amounts of phosphorus in a form not available to the plant. The availability of phosphorus is related to soil pH and is most readily available at pH 5-7. Phosphorus is not very soluble and little is removed by leaching. However, movement of phosphorus in the soil is low and added phosphorus fertilizer remains where it is placed. Thus, phosphorus should be worked into the soil to make it available to be absorbed by plant roots. When transplants are planted in the spring, a starter fertilizer is frequently applied around the plants. This fertilizer contains a large amount of water-soluble phosphorus to stimulate root growth and provide available phosphorus directly to the roots that are there.

Potassium.—Potassium is soluble in the soil and its loss by leaching is controlled by the amount of organic matter and the type of clay in the soil. Potassium is attracted to these types of materials and is held in reserve by them for later plant use. In soils high in organic matter such as peat and muck soils, potassium is usually limiting.

Potassium contributes heavily to the growth of root crops and has a stimulating effect on plant vigor and health. Root and tuber crops, such as carrots, beets, parsnips, potatoes, sweet potatoes and turnips require larger amounts of potassium than other vegetables.

Calcium.—Calcium is seldom lacking in the soil as a plant nutrient. It is frequently added as limestone to adjust the pH of the soil. In many mixed fertilizers calcium is combined with phosphorus and added incidentally to the soil. Calcium is used by the plant for the formation of new cell walls.

Magnesium.—Magnesium is frequently deficient in sandy, well drained soils. It is soluble in the soil solution but held to the clays and organic matter. Magnesium is important in chlorophyll formation and is involved in photosynthesis.

Sulfur.—Sulfur is not present in large amounts in soil and is easily removed from the soil by leaching. Sulfur makes the soil acidic and has been used to control soil pH. It is added to the soil in various organic material and in association with superphosphate types of fertilizer. Sulfur is seldom limiting in a garden soil.

Other essential elements.—Manganese, iron, zinc, boron, molybdenum, copper and chlorine are usually not limiting in garden soils. Manganese and iron, however, may be unavailable if the soil pH is alkaline. These two elements must then be applied in a water soluble form or the soil pH made slightly acid.

Soil Test and pH

In order to determine what elements are deficient in your soil, a soil test should be taken. This test will indicate the amount and availability of nitrogen, potassium and phosphorus and the soil pH. A small amount of soil from six to eight representative areas in the garden should be collected, dried and taken to the nearest county soil testing laboratory or contact the local county agent or farm adviser.

The acidity or alkalinity of the soil is expressed as pH, with pH 7 being neutral. The pH of the soil is regulated by the amount of hydrogen ions and mineral cations found attached to the soil colloids. A large number of hydrogen ions makes the soil acid (below pH 7) while a large number of mineral cations makes the soil alkaline (above pH 7). A change of one pH unit is a 10-fold increase in acidity or alkalinity from pH 7. Orange juice is acid (about pH 4), pure water is neutral (pH 7) and most soap solutions are alkaline (about pH 9). A pH above 9 or below 4 is toxic to plant roots. Plants grow best at a slightly acid pH of 6.5. Soil pH determines the availability (not total amount) of many nutrients. Calcium, phosphorus and magnesium may be unavailable at an acid pH below 6, and at this low pH, manganese, boron, zinc, iron and aluminum may become so available to the plant that they are toxic. An alkaline pH frequently renders iron unavailable for plant growth. The optimum pH for vegetable crops is given in Table 3.3. When a number of crops are grown in the same area, a common pH must be chosen, preferably about 6.5. Potatoes are often grown at pH 4.5 or 5 to prevent damage from potato scab disease, as this disease increases with increasing pH. The club root disease thrives in acid soils and cabbage is sometimes grown about pH 7 to reduce damage from this organism.

Soil pH is adjusted with limestone (calcium) to increase alkalinity or sulfur to increase acidity. The material can be applied the same time fertilizer is added in the fall and the soil then plowed or spaded. Spring applications are of little value that growing season. The amount of limestone or sulfur needed to adjust soil pH is given in Table 3.4.

TABLE 3.3.   OPTIMUM pH FOR VEGETABLES

pH	Crops
6-8	Asparagus
6-7.5	Beet; cabbage; muskmelon; peas; spinach; summer squash
6-7.0	Celery, chives, endive, horseradish, lettuce, onion, radish, cauliflower
5.5-7.5	Sweet corn, pumpkin, tomato
5.5-7	Snap beans, lima beans, carrots, cucumbers, parsnips, peppers, rutabaga, hubbard squash
5.5-6.5	Eggplant, watermelon
4.5-6.5	Potato

SOURCE: ANON. (1968)

TABLE 3.4.   AMOUNTS OF LIMESTONE OR SULFUR NEEDED TO ADJUST SOIL pH

	Raising pH to pH 6.5 Pounds of limestone per 1,000 sq. feet[1]		
Change in pH desired	Sandy Soil	Loamy Soil	Clayey Soil
From 6.2 to 6.4	40	80	80
From 5.8 to 6.4	120	200	200
From 5.4 to 6.4	320	360	400
From 4.8 to 5.3	160	240	280
From 4.2 to 4.7	200	320	—

	Lowering pH Pounds of sulfur per 1,000 sq. feet		
Change in pH desired	Sandy Soil	Loamy Soil	Clayey Soil
From 8.5 to 6.5	40	50	60
From 7.5 to 6.5	10	15	20
From 6.5 to 5.5	10	15	20
From 7.5 to 5.5	20	30	40
From 8.5 to 5.5	50	65	80

SOURCE: Adapted from Vandemark (1973)
[1]A similar amount of wood ashes or oyster shells may be used in place of limestone.

Dolomitic limestone contains about 5% magnesium oxide and should be used to adjust soil pH if the soil is deficient in magnesium. Wood ashes contain about as much calcium as dolomitic limestone and may be used to adjust soil pH in place of limestone (Fletcher and Ferretti undated).

FERTILIZER

A fertilizer improves plant growth directly by providing one or more necessary plant nutrients. Organic fertilizers are directly derived from plant and animal sources. Inorganic fertilizers are not derived from plant and animal sources although many such materials come from naturally occurring deposits. If these materials are not refined they are often referred to as "organic." Refined or inorganic fertilizers are referred to as chemical fertilizers. Both forms can be equally good. Organic materials are degraded by soil microorganisms into inorganic, water-soluble forms. Chemical fertilizers are supplied in this form. Plants can only use the inorganic, water-soluble form and cannot determine if the nutrient came from organic matter, a chemical fertilizer, a natural deposit or natural weathering of rocks (Gowans and Rauschkolb 1971, Utzinger et al. 1973).

Analysis.—By law, a commercial fertilizer must show the analysis of the material. Usually this is shown as first, the percent of nitrogen; second, the percent of phosphorus expressed as phosphorus pentoxide (P_2O_5); and third, the percent of potassium expressed as potassium oxide (K_2O). Only nitrogen is expressed in the elemental form. There is 43.7% phosphorus in phosphorus pentoxide and 83% potassium in potassium oxide. A fertilizer showing an analysis of 12-5-10 would contain 12% nitrogen, 5% phosphorus pentoxide and 10% potassium oxide. When the total amount of nutrients is below 30% the fertilizer is considered a low analysis fertilizer and above 30%, a high analysis fertilizer. Transportation costs per amount of nutrient are higher with low analysis fertilizer. However, with low analysis fertilizers, gardeners have less problem with applying the fertilizer evenly, have less problem with the fertilizer burning the plant, and frequently the mineral impurities in low analysis fertilizers are of value.

Natural deposits as fertilizers.—Natural deposits of material are usable as fertilizers. Limestone and sulfur are used to correct soil pH and often not thought of as fertilizers. However, dolomite limestone contains about 9% magnesium and about 25% calcium. Other natural deposits are used as fertilizer but the rock must be pulverized. Grinding of the material is the only change that is made and the smaller the particle size, the more readily available are the nutrients. The value of these natural materials depends upon the availability of the nutrients to the plant, not the total amount of nutrients present. This can be demonstrated with rock phosphate. Raw rock phosphate has been ineffective on soils with a pH higher than 6.0, even though it was finely ground (Fletcher and Ferretti undated). Above pH 6.0 the phosphorous in rock phosphate is only slightly soluble and is released from the rock very slowly. Rock phosphate needs acid to release the phosphate for plant use, and is therefore more effective on acid soils. Rock phosphate contains from 20 to 32% phosphorous pentoxide but the amount which is available for plant use is less than 5%. However, in acid soils, the phosphorus may be slowly released for plant use in subsequent years after application.

TABLE 3.5.   AVERAGE NUTRIENT VALUE OF SOME NATURAL DEPOSITS[1]

Material	N	P_2O_5	K_2O	Relative Availability
		Percent		
Granite meal	0	0	3	Very slow
Greensand	0	1	7	Medium
Rock phosphate	0	30	0	Very slow
Sodium nitrate	16	0	0	Rapid

[1]The amount of plant nutrients is highly variable, depending upon the material's origin. Their availability depends upon soil conditions and the fineness to which the material was ground.

Rock phosphate.—Rock phosphate is best used for reinforcing manure and compost piles. If used as a garden fertilizer, large amounts of rock phosphate must be applied to provide enough phosphorus for plant growth. The best rock phosphate comes from North Africa, followed by North and South Carolina, Florida and Tennessee.

Granite meal and greensand.—Granite meal and greensand are used as a source of potassium. Granite meal is ground up granite rock, often a by-product of the granite building stone industry and often contains some phosphorus. Greensand is obtained from sandy deposits. The potassium in greensand dissolves rapidly into the soil solution but the total amount of potassium in greensand is quite small. Because of this low concentration of nutrients, substantially more greensand is required than chemical fertilizer. The potassium in granite meal is not readily available and granite meal is better used as a soil amendment than a fertilizer. Granite dissolves slowly and this is one of the reasons it is used as grave headstones in cemeteries.

Sodium nitrate.—Sodium nitrate is a source of nitrogen which is rapidly available for plant growth. The availability of this nitrogen is similar to a chemical fertilizer.

Natural deposits vary widely in their composition of plant nutrients. They also vary widely in the nutrient availability. Table 3.5 lists the average amount of nutrients in some natural deposits.

Organic fertilizers.—Organic fertilizers are usually low in nitrogen, the one nutrient that must be added in large amounts. When organic matter is added to the soil and is low in nitrogen, the microorganisms which degrade this organic matter use the available soil nitrogen. The plants receive what is left and deficiencies often develop. The cost per unit of nutrient in organic fertilizers is almost always higher than chemical fertilizers. Organic fertilizers do have a number of advantages. Their nutrients are released slowly making them available to the plant over the entire growing season; the nutrients are less likely to be lost from the soil; many organic fertilizers also act as soil amendments,

TABLE 3.6. NUTRIENT VALUE OF SOME ORGANIC FERTILIZERS

Material	Percent		
	N	P_2O_5	K_2O
Animal tankage	9	10	1
Bonemeal, steamed	2	22	0
Blood, dried	13	1	0
Compost	2	1	1
Cotton seed meal	6	3	1
Fish meal	10	5	0
Guano	10	4	2
Mushroom compost	1	1	1
Wood ashes[1]	0	1	5
Sawdust	0.2	0.1	0.2
Seaweed	1	1	11
Sewage sludge	2	2	1
Soybean meal	6	1	2
Manure	See section on Manures		

[1]Burning removes all nitrogen. The K_2O content depends upon the tree species burned. Wood ashes contain about 23% calcium and are alkaline.

improving the physical condition of the soil and indirectly improving plant growth. The nutrient content of some common organic fertilizers is given in Table 3.6. These values are averages as the percent of plant nutrients is highly variable. From an ecology and conservation viewpoint, bonemeal, dried blood, cotton seed and soybean meal are more useful and valuable as a livestock feed than as a fertilizer. These products should first be used as an animal feed and the manure recycled and used as an organic fertilizer. Manure will be discussed in a separate section later.

Bonemeal and blood.—Steamed bonemeal is a by-product of the meat industry and is an excellent source of phosphorus, calcium and trace elements. Dried blood is also a by-product of the meat industry and is sold for its nitrogen content. The supply is governed by the number of cattle being slaughtered. It is used mainly as a feed making it expensive for gardeners to use. Fish meal is also sold for its nitrogen and phosphorus content, which becomes slowly available to the plant.

Cotton seed and soybean meal.—Cotton seed and soybean meal are good sources of nitrogen which is moderately available to the plant. They are also used in cattle feed, making them expensive to use as a fertilizer.

Compost.—Compost is composed of decayed organic material and the nutritive value depends upon the material added to the compost pile. The major value of compost is as a soil amendment as discussed later, and not as a fertilizer.

Mushroom compost is often available in areas where commercial mushrooms are produced. It is inexpensive and an excellent source of organic matter. For soils low in organic matter, about four inches may be spaded into the soil. Sawdust is a common material but a nitrogen deficiency is almost inevitable unless other fertilizers are applied. Sawdust contains too much carbon for the soil microorganisms to decompose without additional nitrogen. For each bushel of sawdust added, about one-half pound of a 33-0-0 fertilizer is needed. Wood ashes contain no nitrogen as this is lost during burning. The amount of potassium in wood ashes depends upon the tree species burned. Wood ashes contain about 23% calcium, are alkaline and can be used to increase soil pH.

Seaweed.—Seaweed (kelp) is a good source of trace elements. During World War I kelp were harvested to produce explosives and for fertilizer. Because kelp grows in the oceans, it contains large amounts of soluble salts including common table salt. Heavy applications of seaweed should be avoided as these salts may reduce plant growth.

Sewage sludge.—Sewage sludge varies greatly in composition. Raw sewage, untreated or improperly treated sewage sludge should not be applied to the garden soil as these sludges often carry human diseases which are absorbed by the plant and found in the edible part. Heat treated sludges are normally safe from a sanitary viewpoint. Another potential hazard is the toxicity from non-essential elements such as cadmium and possibly selenium. Other toxic elements like nickel, lead, chromium and arsenic are less hazardous than cadmium, selenium and mercury as they are less readily absorbed by plants and transferred to man. Most municipal sludges from industrial areas contain some, or all of the toxic elements and it is not possible to use sludge as a fertilizer without adding toxic elements to the soil. Leafy vegetables like lettuce, cabbage, spinach, asparagus and swiss chard are effective in transporting a toxic element like cadmium between the soil and man. The cadmium hazard is difficult to evaluate and becomes a personal judgment assessment. Present state-of-knowledge does not permit establishment of *safe critical leaf composition levels* for cadmium in vegetable crops. Neither do we know the *critical soil levels* that are acceptable without serious potential food quality damage to leafy vegetables. Small additions, 50-100 lbs. per 1,000 square feet of dry sludge that is high, 100 to 300 ppm, in cadmium can cause a significant increase in the cadmium content of leafy vegetables and moderate increase in certain root crops. How harmful such increases are to man will depend on the background cadmium level in the total diet and the amount and composition of the leafy vegetable consumed.

Not all sludges will contain dangerous levels of cadmium or the other hazardous elements. Some may contain one or two, others will contain none. Sludges from urban and non-industrial cities are usually very low in cadmium, and other hazardous elements, and are a good source of plant nutrients for the garden. Sludges from industrial cities are more likely to contain cadmium levels that are *unacceptable* for garden fertilization. Because such sludges vary greatly in composition, no one fixed rate of application can be considered ideal to supply needed nitrogen and phosphorus and at the same time be completely safe from health hazards. The gardener needs to be *aware of the chemical composition* of the sludge before purchase and use. Properly sterilized sludges from non-industrial cities are acceptable as fertilizer for all garden purposes. Sludges that exceed 50 ppm cadmium should probably not be used where leafy vegetables, carrots, radishes and turnips are to be grown, and used only with caution on other garden crops. Most sludges may be used on lawns, flowers, shrubs, and trees. Theoretically all sludges can pose small health hazard risks, but when used with utmost discretion as described above can be used successfully as fertilizer (Melsted 1976).

Chemical fertilizers.—Many chemical fertilizers, are derived from natural deposits. The nutrients are concentrated and converted into a form that is readily available in the soil for the plant to absorb. This is particularly true of phosphorus and potassium. Much of the nitrogen fertilizer is synthesized from the nitrogen in the air. The three major forms are ammonia, nitrate and urea. Urea is an organic compound so technically it is an organic fertilizer. Because it is manufactured commercially it is referred to here as a chemical fertilizer.

Chemical fertilizers are usually concentrated and so only a small amount is added to the soil to provide the needed nutrients. Since chemical fertilizers do not contain a lot of non-nutrient material, they are usually more economical than organic fertilizers or natural deposits. Chemical fertilizers are immediately available for plant use. The use of a concentrated, readily available fertilizer can also become a disadvantage instead of an advantage. Many gardeners apply too much chemical fertilizer since only small amounts are needed. Because they are soluble and readily available, there may be large amounts of nutrients in the root zone, which results in salt injury to the plant. Some nutrients in chemical fertilizers are very water soluble and can be leached from the root zone and lost. Table 3.7 gives some common chemical fertilizers and their nutrient value.

Unmixed fertilizers contain only one element. The nitrogen carriers are the most important. Urea is a common chemical fertilizer and it is rapidly broken down by soil microorganisms into ammonia. Ureaform types of chemical fertilizers are broken down slowly to release nitrogen for plant use. The nitrogen is made available to the plant for a longer period of time during the growing season. In addition, these ureaform fertilizers do not burn the plant if applied to the foliage and there is less problem of salt injury. These slow-release types of chemical fertilizers are similar in many respects to organic fertilizers but lack the soil amendment properties of the organic fertilizers.

TABLE 3.7. APPROXIMATE COMPOSITION OF CHEMICAL FERTILIZERS

Material	Percent		
	N	P_2O_5	K_2O
Urea	42-46	0	0
Ureaform	30-40	0	0
Ammonium nitrate	33.5	0	0
Ammonium sulfate	20.5	0	0
Superphosphate	0	16-20	0
Triple superphosphate	0	46	0
Muriate of potash	0	0	48-62

Mixed fertilizers contain nitrogen, phosphorus and potassium in various amounts. Various analysis suitable for general garden use are: 5-10-5; 3-12-12; 5-10-10; 8-16-8; 10-10-10; 12-12-12. Several highly water soluble, high phosphate fertilizers are available for use when transplanting to promote faster initial growth of the plants, such as 10-55-10 or 11-52-17.

Fertilizer recommendations.—The natural fertility of a soil is dependent upon the factors which built the initial soil: the initial rock formation, climate, time, topography and the native vegetation. Soil which has not been disturbed reaches an equilibrium. The amount of nutrients released into the soil by the breakdown of organic matter, weathering of the rocks, etc., equals the amount of nutrients removed from the soil by leaching, formation of new plant material, etc. However, when the soil is used to grow vegetables, some of the nutrients are tied up in the formation of new plants and some are removed in the edible parts. The amount which is removed varies with the vegetable and the yield. The approximate amount of the major nutrients removed by vegetables is shown in Table 3.8. The major nutrients which need replenishment are nitrogen, phosphorus and potassium. These three nutrients are the major ingredients of most fertilizers.

The amount of fertilizer to add to the soil depends upon many factors. These include: 1) the amount removed in the edible part shown in Table 3.8; 2) the disposition of the plant debris. About one-third the nitrogen and half of the phosphorus and potassium absorbed by a sweet corn plant remains in the non-edible part of the plant. If this material is returned to the soil, these nutrients are not lost; 3) the type of plant. Bacteria on legumes (peas, beans) have the capacity to convert atmospheric nitrogen (see Figure 3.3) into a form the plant can use and these plants do not need as much nitrogen fertilizer; 4) the type of soil. Soils differ in the amount and availability of nutrients and some Midwest soils contain adequate amounts of phosphorus; and 5) the organic matter content of the soil. If corn stalks, sawdust, unfinished compost, manure or straw is added to the soil, soil microorganisms will use the available nitrogen to

TABLE 3.8. NUTRIENTS REMOVED BY THE EDIBLE PLANT PART OF VEGETABLES

Crop	Yield (lbs./ 1,000 sq. ft.)	lb. removed/1,000 sq. ft.		
		N	P_2O_5	K_2O
Asparagus	90	0.5	0.1	0.2
Beans, snap	90	0.3	0.1	0.3
Beans, dry	54	1.8	0.1	0.7
Beets (without tops)	450	1.1	0.5	1.9
Cabbage	450	1.4	0.3	1.3
Carrots	580	1.4	0.6	3.4
Cauliflower	420	1.4	0.5	1.1
Corn, sweet	135	0.6	0.1	0.2
Cucumbers	430	0.5	0.2	1.1
Eggplant	260	0.5	0.2	1.1
Horseradish	90	0.9	0.4	0.7
Lettuce	270	0.9	0.1	0.5
Muskmelon	150	0.3	0.1	0.6
Onions, bulbs	450	1.0	0.05	0.5
Parsnips	570	1.4	1.0	5.0
Peppers	240	0.6	0.1	0.5
Potatoes	410	1.4	0.6	2.0
Pumpkin	580	1.4	0.6	3.9
Spinach	135	0.7	0.1	1.3
Squash, summer	455	0.5	0.1	0.9
Squash, winter	580	1.4	0.6	3.9
Sweet potato	320	0.9	0.3	2.0
Tomato	570	1.1	0.3	1.7
Turnip	510	1.1	0.5	1.4
Watermelon	225	0.2	0.07	0.3

break down these materials, and additional nitrogen is required. Dark-colored soils contain organic matter which is continuously being broken down and the nitrogen is released for plant use. Light-colored soils contain little organic matter and will release little nitrogen. Dark-colored soils release about a half pound of nitrogen per 1,000 square feet and would require less nitrogen fertilizer than a light-colored soil.

If this is your first year in your present location, have your soil tested and follow those fertilizer recommendations. If you do not have your soil tested, follow the general recommendations in Table 3.9 or 3.10. Most nutrients in organic fertilizers and natural deposits are slowly available to the plant and much more of these must be applied than chemical fertilizers. Soil nutrients can be present in unbalanced amounts by using organic fertilizers just as well as by using chemical fertilizers. A specific balance among elements is necessary for each vegetable to achieve maximum yield and quality. Few organic fertilizers contain a balanced amount of nitrogen, phosphorus and potassium, as chemical fertilizers do. Three different organic fertilizers (see Table 3.10) are needed to provide the proper amount of nitrogen, phosphorus and potassium. Fertilizers which are high in nitrogen only promote vegetative growth, rather than fruits, seeds or root and tuber crops. High nitrogen fertilizers should be used on lawns instead of on gardens.

TABLE 3.9.   CHEMICAL FERTILIZER RECOMMENDATIONS FOR VEGETABLES

Previous fertilizer treatment	Fertilizer analysis	Fertilizer to apply (lb./ 1,000 sq. ft)	amount applied (lb/1,000 sq. ft.)		
			N	P_2O_5	K_2O
None or little	3-12-12	40	1.2	4.8	4.8
	or				
	5-20-20	30	1.5	6.0	6.0
Some	5-10-10	25	1.2	2.5	2.5
Heavy (previous gardens have produced well)	10-10-10	12	1.2	1.2	1.2
	or				
	15-15-15	10	1.5	1.5	1.5

SOURCE: Adapted from Vandemark *et al.* (1977).

TABLE 3.10.   ORGANIC FERTILIZER RECOMMENDATIONS FOR VEGETABLES

Organic material	Previous fertilizer treatment	Main nutrient applied	Amount to apply	Amount of available nutrient applied
			lb./1,000 sq. ft.	
Dried blood	All treatments	N	10	1.2
Fish meal	All treatments	N	15	1.2
Cotton seed or Soybean meal	All treatments	N	20	1.2
Steamed bonemeal	Little or none	P	25	4.8
	Some	P	15	2.4
	Heavy	P	5	1.1
Rock phosphate[1]	Little or none	P	300	5.0
	Some	P	150	2.5
	Heavy	P	75	1.2
Greensand	Little or none	K	300	5
	Some	K	150	2.5
	Heavy	K	75	1.2
Wood ashes	Little or none	K	100	5
	Some	K	50	2.5
	Heavy	K	25	1.2
Manure	See section on Manures			

[1]Nutrients in rock phosphate are not readily available the first year but become more available subsequent seasons, resulting in high initial application rates.

It is usually not harmful to add excess plant nutrients to a soil. However, large amounts may injure some plants. Large amounts of nitrogen induce vegetative growth rather than seed production and result in poor storage quality of vegetables. All plant nutrients will kill plants if added to the soil in large amounts.

When to apply.—Chemical fertilizer should generally be applied during the growing season of the plant. The fertilizer should be spread over the garden area in the fall or spring and the soil spaded or plowed. If organic fertilizers, slow-release chemical fertilizers, sulfur or limestone are used, they are best applied in the fall to allow them to partially decompose and make the nutrients available for plant growth. Chemical fertilizer can be applied just before planting the crop, if they are worked into the soil. Phosphate fertilizers particularly give best results when worked into the soils, so plant roots can contact the fertilizer.

When transplants are used, a starter fertilizer should be applied to give faster plant growth. About one tablespoon of 10-52-17 or 10-50-10 per gallon of water should be made up and one cup of this solution applied around the roots of each plant. A solution of one cup of 0-45-0 or similar fertilizer in 12 quarts of water may also be used and one cup of this solution used for each plant. As nutrients in organic fertilizers are not readily available, there are no good organic fertilizers that can be used as a transplant fertilizer.

Often the plants require more fertilizer during the growing season. Nitrogen particularly becomes limiting late in the growing season. Fertilizer can be applied in a band along one side of the row about four inches from the crop, a process called sidedressing. This fertilizer can be applied to leafy crops, sweet corn, greens, and root crops when they are half-grown; and to tomatoes, peppers, cucumbers and squash when they begin to produce fruit. About two and one-half pounds of ammonium nitrate (33-0-0) or two pounds of urea (42-0-0) per 1,000 square feet should be used, or about eight pounds of dried blood or fish meal. The chemical fertilizer should not come into contact with the plant leaves as it will burn them. All sidedressed fertilizers should be hoed or worked into the soil and in dry weather, water should be applied to make the fertilizer more quickly available.

Effect on soil microorganisms and earthworms.—Microorganisms and earthworms live on organic matter in the soil. When fertilizer is used, more crop is produced and more plant residues are returned to the soil, providing more food. Microorganisms require relatively large amounts of nitrogen to degrade organic matter, and fertilizer stimulates their growth. When organic matter and insulative cover during the winter is given, earthworms prosper, even if the soil is spaded or plowed each year. Earthworm populations are limited most by a lack of fertilizer, water and adequate insulation during cold temperatures.

Manure

Stable or barnyard manure was practically the only fertilizer available in the early days of vegetable production. The use of manure can greatly affect the amount of fertilizer needed as it contains many plant nutrients and supplies an important source of nitrogen. Manure does more than add nutrients, and sometimes produces better results than chemical fertilizers alone. Manure provides needed organic matter which improves the physical condition of the soil (see Soil Amendments—Organic, page 90) and in this manner also improves plant growth. If animal manure can be obtained cheaply, it is the best material for maintaining the organic matter content of the soil and supplying a source of nutrients. Manure is best used for vegetables which require a large amount of nitrogen. Manure is usually low in phosphorus and fresh manure should be reinforced with superphosphate at 50 pounds per ton of cattle or horse manure. This phosphate will absorb ammonia and reduce the loss of nitrogen and increase the phosphorus content of the manure.

TABLE 3.11.   APPROXIMATE PERCENT OF THE PRIMARY NUTRIENTS IN ANIMAL MANURES

Animal	Percent		
	N	P_2O_5	K_2O
Cattle, fresh	0.5	0.2	0.5
Cattle, dried	1.5	2.0	2.3
Goat, dried	1.4	1.0	3.0
Horse, fresh	0.7	0.3	0.5
Swine, fresh	0.7	0.6	0.7
Sheep, fresh	1.4	0.7	1.5
Sheep, dry	4.2	2.5	6.0
Chicken, fresh	1.5	1.0	0.5
Chicken, dry	4.5	3.5	2.0

Continued heavy applications to the garden can create soil fertility and excessive salt problems. Some manures contain excessive salts and these must be leached from the soil by adequate rainfall or irrigation. Manures not reinforced with phosphate can lead to soils where the level of nitrogen and potassium are excessive or out of balance with other nutrients. This can result in excessive vegetative growth without fruit production, delayed maturity and poor storage quality of vegetables. In addition, the large amounts of potassium found in some manures can "salt out" and reduce the amount of magnesium in the soil, creating a magnesium deficiency. If a soil test indicates that the soil contains an excessive amount of potassium, the application of manure should be avoided. If manure is used where carrots are grown, misshapen roots frequently result (Mansour and Baggett 1977). The approximate percent of the primary nutrients in some manures is given in Table 3.11. Manure contains numerous micronutrients which are required for plant growth in small amounts. Soils low in these nutrients would greatly benefit from the use of manure (see Table 3.12). Manures vary greatly in their nutrient content, depending upon the type of feed used, the amount of bedding or straw, the moisture content, losses in the liquid portion and degree of rotting. About half the nutrient content is in the liquid portion

TABLE 3.12.   MICRONUTRIENTS IN ANIMAL MANURE[1]

| | lbs. of nutrient / 1,000 lbs. of manure | | | | | | | |
Animal	B	Ca	Cu	Fe	Mg	Mn	Mo	S	Zn
Cattle	0.08	15.0	0.03	0.21	5.9	0.05	0.005	2.7	0.08
Horse	0.06	31.4	0.02	0.54	5.6	0.04	0.004	2.8	0.06
Sheep	0.04	25.4	0.02	0.69	8.0	0.04	0.004	3.9	0.11
Swine	0.20	28.5	0.03	1.40	4.0	0.10	0.005	6.8	0.30
Chicken	0.20	123.6	0.05	1.55	9.7	0.30	0.018	10.4	0.30

[1]Based upon dry (15% moisture) manure. B = boron; Ca = calcium; Cu = copper; Fe = iron; Mg = magnesium; Mn = manganese; Mo = molybdenum; S = sulfur; Zn = zinc.

and this is easily lost by leaching, run-off and volatility. Cat, dog, bird and other pet wastes should not be added as they may contain diseases which are readily transmitted to humans eating the plants. Fresh manure is best applied to the garden in the fall. The advantage of applying the material fresh is that 1) less loss of nutrients has occurred; 2) more microorganisms are added to the soil and 3) more organic material is supplied. This provides food for microorganisms resulting in some additional release of nutrients. Decomposed manure can be applied either in the fall or spring. It has the advantage of 1) containing a higher percentage of nutrients (but not total amount); 2) the nutrients are in a more readily available form; 3) it will not burn the crop if applied just before planting; 4) it contains more phosphorus in relation to nitrogen and potassium; 5) it is easier to plow or spade into the soil; and 6) many weed seeds in the manure have been destroyed.

The availability of the nutrients in fresh manure depend partly upon the amount of bedding or straw. Microorganisms will degrade this organic material and compete with the plants for use of the nitrogen. The amount of manure to apply to the garden is shown in Table 3.13. These amounts are based upon the nitrogen requirements only and take into account the fact that much of the nitrogen will be used by microorganisms to degrade the organic matter. If the garden has previously received heavy applications of fertilizer, about one or two pounds of P_2O_5 and K_2O are needed per 1,000 square feet. At the recommended rates to provide nitrogen, ample potassium is also supplied but many of the manures are short of phosphorus. The addition of superphosphate or rock phosphate would also be needed to provide an adequate balance of nutrients. The amount of manure applied should not exceed that recommended in Table 3.13. If excessive vine or foliage growth of vegetables occurs, chicken or sheep manure should not be used (Hinish and Jordan undated). The nutrients in sheep and chicken manure are available the year the material is applied and may cause this excessive growth.

Manure is best applied in the fall and plowed or spaded under as soon as possible after spreading. This will conserve the nutrients, minimize

TABLE 3.13.   ACCEPTABLE RATES OF MANURE FOR VEGETABLES

Type of Manure	Amount to apply[1] (lbs./1,000 sq. ft.)	Approximate amount of available nutrient applied (lbs./1,000 sq. ft.)		
		N	P$_2$O$_5$	K$_2$O
Cattle, fresh	500	1.5	0.5	1.3
Cattle, dry	180	1.2	1.6	1.8
Horse, fresh	500	1.2	0.5	0.9
Swine, fresh	500	1.2	1.1	1.2
Sheep, fresh	285	1.4	0.6	1.3
Sheep, dry	100	1.3	0.8	1.8
Chicken, fresh	280	1.4	0.8	0.4
Chicken, dry	100	1.4	1.1	1.6

[1]Rates are based upon the nitrogen requirement only. One bushel of manure weighs about 50 pounds.

odors and flies, and speed up the decomposition of the organic matter. Manure can often be obtained from local riding stables, race tracks and the county fairgrounds. Frequently it can be obtained for the hauling as manures are becoming a disposal problem for many livestock producers.

Soil Amendments

The tilth or physical condition of the soil is important in relation to plant growth. If the soil is in poor physical condition, it will be hard and crusty when dry, and sticky when wet. Vegetables will not grow and develop properly. The physical condition of a soil may be improved by the addition of a soil amendment. A soil amendment is a material that improves the chemical and/or physical condition of the soil and in this way indirectly improves plant growth. They may be organic or non-organic and do not have to supply nutrients.

Non-organic amendments.—The most common amendments are limestone and sulfur which are used to adjust the soil pH. By adjusting soil pH, many insoluble nutrients are made available for plant growth. Heavy clay soils can be improved by the addition of coarse sand, cinders, vermiculite or perlite. About two inches of these materials can be worked into the soil to improve drainage, aeration, and workability. These non-organic soil amendments are of limited value compared to organic soil amendments.

Organic amendments.—Organic matter affects soil structure and fertility. The rate organic matter is decomposed depends upon adequate water, nitrogen and temperature. This decomposed organic matter improves the soil (Fletcher and Dutt undated) in the following ways: 1) it serves as a source of food for microorganisms and earthworms which help condition the soil; 2) it increases the water holding capacity of sandy soils

TABLE 3.14.   THE C:N RATIO OF SOME COMMON ORGANIC MATERIALS

Material	C:N ratio
Liquid manure	10:1
Alfalfa or sweet clover hay	12:1
Lawn clippings	20:1
Composted manure	20:1
Kitchen garbage	30:1
Green rye or oats	36:1
Corn stalks	60:1
Leaves	70:1
Straw	75:1
Strawy manure	80:1
Sawdust, wood chips	400:1
Corn cobs	420:1

by filling in the excess spaces between particles; 3) it increases the amount of usable water in clay soils by keeping the tiny particles apart, allowing excess water to drain away; 4) it keeps the tiny particles in clay soils from cementing together, thereby reducing crusting and allowing easier root penetration; 5) it provides more pore space in clay soils which allows more aeration for better root growth; 6) it keeps more even soil temperatures; 7) it releases plant nutrients when the organic matter decays; 8) the acids produced in the decay process help dissolve mineral nutrients from the soil and applied natural deposits; and 9) when decayed, it increases the cation exchange capacity, thereby allowing the soil to retain more nutrients.

Types of organic amendments.—For the organic material to be of value in improving the soil, it must decompose. The microorganisms which decay the organic material need about one part of nitrogen for every 15-30 parts of carbon present in the material. This is called the carbon-nitrogen or C:N ratio. If this value is greater than 30:1, then nitrogen will be deficient. Whatever nitrogen is present in the soil will be used by the microorganisms to decay the organic matter and will not be available for use by the vegetables. Table 3.14 lists the C:N ratio of some common organic materials. The organic matter in a garden soil can be increased by the addition of manure, sawdust, leaves, lawn clippings, compost and similar materials. These materials vary greatly in nitrogen content. Nitrogen may have to be added to these materials when they are applied in the garden and again during the growing season, if a nitrogen deficiency develops. Walnut leaves contain toxic materials and should not be used. They may be burned and the ash used, however. Lawn clippings from lawns that have been treated with pesticide sprays (weed killers, insecticides, fungicides) should not be added to the garden. The amount of organic matter which can be added to the garden soil and the amount of available nitrogen required to be added to decompose the material without causing a nitrogen deficiency is given in Table 3.15.

TABLE 3.15. AMOUNT OF ORGANIC MATERIAL AND THE NITROGEN REQUIRED
TO BE ADDED TO A GARDEN SOIL

Organic material[1]	Amount to add per 1,000 square feet	Actual nitrogen available in fertilizer to be added with the organic material[2]
Lawn clippings	40 bushels	none
Compost	750 pounds (15 bushels)	none
Manure (cattle or horse)	750 pounds (15 bushels)	none
Manure (sheep, chicken)	300 pounds (6 bushels)	none
Hay	600 pounds (10 bales)	none
Straw	600 pounds (10 bales)	½ to 1 pound
Leaves	750 pounds (40 bushels)	½ to 1 pound
Sawdust, wood chips	500 pounds (20 bushels)	1 to 1½ pounds
Corn cobs	500 pounds (20 bushels)	1 to 1½ pounds

[1]See section on manures for nutrients added with the various manures.
[2]See section on fertilizers for nitrogen sources.

Either chemical or organic nitrogen sources may be used as the nitrogen source. As manure varies greatly in its nutrient composition, about 750 pounds per 1,000 square feet of cattle or horse may be used, and about 300 pounds of sheep or chicken manure. Organic matter is best added in the fall and spaded or plowed under with whatever additional nitrogen is required. This allows the material to partially decompose over winter. Probably, the easiest obtainable source of organic matter is leaves. These can frequently be obtained from homeowners for the asking. Many cities collect and grind used Christmas trees, and these wood chips are also a good source.

Organic matter can be added to the soil by growing a green manure or cover crop and plowing this crop under. About three pounds of annual rye, one pound of ryegrass or one and one-half pounds of oat seeds should be seeded per 1,000 square feet (Fletcher et. al 1972). The seed can be planted in the fall between rows of fall vegetables or broadcast over the entire area where no vegetables are growing. The seed should be worked into the soil with a rake or hand cultivator. The crops are plowed under in the spring before planting vegetables. Cover crops will produce little organic matter and not be of much value if they are planted in late fall and plowed under in very early spring. They should be planted about a month before the first killing frost. Cover crops will not only provide organic matter but also utilize nutrients in the soil which might otherwise be leached from the soil by fall rains. In addition, they will help prevent erosion on sloping sites and in windy, sandy areas.

In an undisturbed soil, the organic matter content reaches an equilibrium. The major losses of organic matter result from crop removal and oxidation as a result of cultivation. In large fields it is seldom possible to increase the percentage of organic matter to any degree. However, garden soils can be increased in organic matter content, particularly the sands and clays. The importance of organic matter should not be overlooked and gardeners should attempt to add organic matter yearly until their soil contains at least 5% organic matter (Bartelli *et al.* 1977). Most sands and clays contain 1% or less.

Compost

Compost is basically decomposed organic material. It is best described as a soil amendment since the amounts of nitrogen, phosphorus and potassium are low. It can be added to the garden soil, used with soil to grow transplants or used as a mulch. Through the use of compost, organic materials are not wasted and higher quality and yields of vegetables can be achieved.

Decomposition of organic materials requires adequate nitrogen, air and water. The microbes in the compost pile will decompose the carbon from the organic material into CO_2, and this CO_2 will escape into the air. This reduces the size of the compost pile and concentrates the remaining nutrients. However, some diseases and pesticides are not decomposed and they will also be concentrated in the compost and be a problem when added to the garden. Some weed seeds and non-viral and non-spore disease organisms are killed by the temperatures produced in the decomposition process. The outside layers of the compost pile must be turned into the center so that weed seeds and disease organisms in these outer layers are destroyed by the heat. In the decomposition process, heat is released and temperatures may become 120 to 175°F. The intensity depends upon the amount of nitrogen material included. When the pile starts to cool, it can be considered finished. Gardeners can use the "look and touch" method. If the organic material is broken up and not recognizable as the original material and has developed a dark, rich color, the material is composted.

Materials for compost.—Virtually any organic material can be composted: kitchen wastes, egg shells, coffee grounds, nut shells, leaves, lawn clippings, garden residues that are not eaten, straw, hay, weeds, manure, newspaper, etc. Material which should not be added to a compost pile include metal and glass as these will not decompose. In addition, there are a number of organic materials gardeners should not compost. Eggs, cheese, grease, fat and meat scraps should be avoided as they decompose slowly and may develop offensive odors and attract rodents and flies. Walnut wastes (leaves, nuts, limbs) contain material which inhibit plant growth and should not be included. Cooked bones which are meat free and ground in a shredder may be included as they are similar to steamed bonemeal. Avoid lawn clippings which have been treated with insecticides and herbicides and avoid obviously diseased plants and weed seeds (Erhardt and Littlefield 1973). Some diseases, weed seeds, and pesticides are not destroyed during composting and they are then added back to the garden with the compost. Pet wastes may contain diseases which can be transmitted to humans and should not be included.

Time required to produce compost.—The time required to produce compost depends upon two major factors: the amount of nitrogen in the compost pile and the particle size of the organic material added. Ordinarily 12 to 18 months are required to make coarse materials usable (Vandemark and Shurtleff 1970) but fertilizer and grinding of the organic material will greatly reduce this time. The microorganisms derive their energy from the organic material and require nitrogen to live and multiply rapidly. About 15—30 parts of carbon for every part of nitrogen is ideal. If the organic material has a C:N ratio of greater than 30:1 (see Table 3.14) fertilizer should be added. The decomposition process will make the compost slightly acid and limestone should be added unless the compost is for use with acid-loving plants. For each 40 pounds of green material (10 pounds dry material) about one pound of the chemical fertilizer or three pounds of the organic fertilizer mixture shown in Table 3.16 should be mixed with the compost. A one or three pound coffee can is easily used as an approximate measure.

TABLE 3.16.   CHEMICAL AND ORGANIC FERTILIZERS FOR USE IN MAKING COMPOST[1]

Chemical fertilizer

25 lbs. - 10-10-10 Fertilizer
10 lbs. - Finely ground limestone
Organic fertilizer

15 lbs. - Wood ashes
7 lbs. - Dried blood or fishmeal
4 lbs. - Steamed bonemeal

[1]The fertilizer is first mixed thoroughly together. Use 1 pound of the chemical or 3 pounds of the organic fertilizer per 10 pounds dry weight (40 pounds green). Other organic fertilizers which will supply 0.07 lbs. each of N, P_2O_5 and K_2O per 10 pounds dry weight of organic material to be composted may be substituted (see Table 3.6).

The size of the particles of organic matter also influence the speed of decomposition. The smaller the particle size, the greater is the surface area exposed to the microorganisms and fungi to decompose the material. Leaves and such may be chopped with a rotary grass mower. Limbs, cornstalks, and other coarse material should be ground to less than one-half inch in a chipper-shredder, if possible. If tree branches are ground they will decompose in less than a year, while whole tree limbs will take several years to decompose.

Crop residues naturally contain all the microbes that are needed for the decomposition process. Various types of compost activators do little to speed up this process (Fletcher *et. al* 1972). A small amount of soil, manure or old compost can be added to increase the number of microbes in the compost pile. The addition of fertilizer and grinding the organic material will speed up the composting process more than anything else.

Pit and trench composting.—Before a compost pile is built, local ordinances should be checked to be sure that composting is permitted in the community. The pile should be in an area screened from the public and care taken to prevent the pile from becoming a home for various rodents. Compost pits are often six feet square and two feet deep. A compost trench is rectangular in shape and varies in size, depending upon the available space. A compost pit and trench are similar in all other aspects.

From Anon 1971

FIG. 3.4. COMPOSTING LEAVES IN A WIRE BIN (TOP) AND A WOODEN BOX (BOTTOM) FOR NEXT YEAR'S GARDEN

A compost pile can be built on the open ground if drainage is not a problem or be made of a bin above ground. Above ground bins are often made with snow fence, boards or stakes and chicken wire (Figure 3.4). A layer of strong plastic on the inside of the fence helps speed decomposition, especially during long dry periods. The organic material is spread out to a depth of about six inches and the fertilizer mixture added. A few shovels full of soil, manure or old compost can be sprinkled over each layer to prevent the organic material from blowing away and to help hold water. The layer is moistened thoroughly but not to the extent that the fertilizer mixture is leached out. Additional six inch layers of organic material, fertilizer mixture, soil and water are added until all the organic material has been added. The top of the pile should be flat and slant slightly to the center to assure even penetration of rainfall. During dry periods, the compost pile may have to be watered to speed the decomposition process. The pile should be turned about 45 days after it was constructed. The center should be turned to the outer edges and the outer edges and top should be placed toward the center. This will speed the process and make a more uniform compost. Additional water should be added if needed.

Container composting.—Aerobic composting can take place in almost any container as long as air and water requirements are met. A standard garbage can can be used. About eight slots are made in the sides of the can to allow ventilation and five made in the bottom to allow drainage. Leaves, lawn cuttings, weeds, straw or other materials are run through a shredder-grinder or chopped with a rotary mower and collected with a grass catcher. This will increase the surface area for decomposition. These shredded materials are mixed with fertilizer (see Table 3.16) and placed in the garbage can. The can is placed on an elevated rack about one foot off the ground to allow drainage and ventilation. The material is watered until a slight dripping is observed through the bottom of the can. The lid is placed on the can and in about three days the temperature inside the can should have reached about 138°F. In 10-14 days the material is composted and ready to use.

Some gardeners prefer anerobic decomposition; composting without air. A 32-gallon plastic garbage or trash bag can be filled with chopped leaves, garden debris and fertilizer. When the bag is full about a quart of water is added (more if dry material is used) and the bag tied tightly and set outside. The anerobic method should be used outdoors and sufficient water added. The process involved is similar to the process involved in spontaneous combustion which has resulted in fires in moldy hay and accumulated used paint rags.

Sheet composting.—Sheet composting grew out of the needs of large-scale gardeners. Instead of composting in piles, the organic material can be spread on the soil and it will be composted at the soil surface. The basis for sheet composting is to provide the soil with the material to produce its own compost. The organic material can be spread between the vegetable rows three to six inches deep. Green material will decompose rapidly while dry material will act as a mulch and slowly decompose at the soil surface. Green material should not be placed next to the plants. The heat produced during decomposition and the microorganisms and insects may damage some of the vegetable plants. The undecomposed material can be spaded under at the end of the growing season. Sheet composting works best with shredded, dry material placed around trees, shrubs and with perennial vegetables such as rhubarb, asparagus and perennial herbs.

Mulches

In a broad sense, a mulch is any substance applied to the soil surface which protects the roots of plants from extremes in temperature, or drought, or keeps fruit clean. Mulching vegetables can increase yields, promote early harvest and reduce fruit defects when the plant is growing under less than ideal conditions (Courter et al. 1969). Mulches modify the soil and air microclimate in which a plant is growing and specific mulches are used to create this favorable environment. Mulches do not always increase crop yields and may, under some conditions, reduce yields.

Temperature.—Mulches may either increase or decrease soil temperature. Loose dry material such as straw or wood chips act as insulation and protect against high temperatures. Light reflective mulches such as white paper or aluminum foil, can reflect sunlight and also decrease the soil temperature. Soil mulched with these materials is about 5-10°F cooler than bare soil (Courter et al. 1969). During the spring growing season, this lower soil temperature may reduce plant growth and yields. If these mulches are applied when soil temperatures have increased, yields may increase; particularly with potatoes which require cooler temperatures for tuber formation, or late summer plantings of zucchini squash and cool season crops such as Brussels sprouts and lettuce.

Black paper or black and transparent plastic mulches increase soil temperatures 10-15°F compared to bare soil (Courter et al. 1969). This hastens early plant development, particularly for the production of warm-season crops under cool conditions or in northern climates. Melons, cucumbers, pumpkins, squash, watermelons and early crops of sweet corn and tomatoes respond well to soil-warming mulches (Figure 3.5).

Moisture.—Mulches reduce evaporation of water by 10-50% or more. Permeable organic mulches increase the rate at which the soil will absorb rainfall. These permeable mulches will also absorb irrigation water. Nonpermeable mulches such as plastic, aluminum and paper will not absorb water. Adequate moisture should be available before applying the material or a trickle irrigation system installed. In rainy seasons, mulching may keep the soil too wet for adequate aeration. Mulches also save water for crop use by reducing competition from weeds. Plastic mulches prevent water loss by evaporation and frequently increased growth of these

From Topoleski 1972

IG. 3.5. YIELD OF MUSKMELONS GROWN ON BARE SOIL (LEFT) AND SOIL
MULCHED WITH BLACK PLASTIC (RIGHT).

From Anon 1971

FIG. 3.6. MULCHING THE GARDEN TO CONSERVE
WATER AND HELP CONTROL WEEDS

plants is noted. This increased plant growth on mulched plots results in greater water use as the plants are larger and transpire more. Thus, on sandy, well-drained soils under dry conditions these crops may require more irrigation water than unmulched crops.

Weed control.—Mulches help control weeds (Figure 3.6) but do not reduce weed infestations if the weeds are already present and established. If the material is weed-free and applied properly, weed seeds do not have a chance to germinate or the mulch layer is so deep that the germinated seedlings cannot push through it. Perennial weeds and grasses will grow through most organic mulches. Black plastic or paper mulches prevent light penetration which is necessary for the weeds to grow. Weeds will grow under a clear plastic mulch. Shredded organic material is more effective and provides longer weed control than loose, porous materials.

Soil structure.—Mulches help maintain good soil structure by preventing soil crusting and compaction. Mulched soil remains loose, providing good aeration for root growth. Many plants develop an extensive root system in the upper two inches of mulched soil while in unmulched soil these roots are reduced due to drying, crusting and cultivation. The mulch provides a physical barrier that prevents root pruning and injury due to cultivation and hoeing. An extensive root system allows more efficient use of nutrients. Organic mulches which are spaded under after the growing season improve soil tilth as they decompose and provide some nutrients.

Disease control.—Mulches do not eliminate plant diseases but keep the fruit from coming into contact with the soil where the disease is located. Tomato fruit rots and fruit defects in cucumber and melons can be reduced by mulching. The fruits are also cleaner than when in contact with the soil. Tomatoes should either be grown in wire cages or mulched (Figure 3.7) to prevent fruit rots in areas where rainfall is plentiful during the summer.

Organic mulches.—Organic materials which have been used for mulching include 1) plant residues such as straw, hay, crushed corncobs, leaves, composts, dry lawn clippings, and peanut hulls; 2) peat; 3) wood products such as sawdust, wood chips, wood bark, old newspapers and shavings and 4) animal manure.

Many mulching materials require the addition of nitrogen fertilizer to reduce the chance of nitrogen deficiency in the plants that have been mulched (see Table 3.15). The fertilizer should be added with the mulch at a rate of about two pounds of 5-10-5 per 100 square feet. Additional fertilizer should be applied if the lower foliage of the plants become

From Vandemark et al. 1973
(University of Illinois)

FIG. 3.7. TOMATO MULCHED WITH STRAW TO PREVENT FRUIT ROTS

yellow or the plants appear stunted during the growing season.

Organic mulches should be placed on the soil after the plant is well established and preferably when the soil has warmed up sufficiently for active root growth. A mulch placed on cool soil will slow root development. A three to six inch layer of material can be spread between the rows and around the plants, making certain you do not cover the plants.

Plant residues.—Plant residues are commonly used as a mulch. Legume hay does not require additional nitrogen. Straw should be weed-free and should not be used where a cigarette could carelessly create a fire hazard. Leaves are the least expensive mulch available where trees are abundant. Large leaves such as from sycamore should be chopped with a rotary mower to prevent them from matting down and preventing water penetration. Lawn clippings are best used when dry. If applied fresh, they mat down, produce heat during decomposition which damages the plants and gives off an offensive odor. Do not use the lawn clippings for a mulch if they have been treated with a pesticide. Compost is probably the best mulch you can use.

Peat.—Peat is one of the most commonly used mulches. The fine grade of peat has a tendency to blow away. When very dry, peat sheds water rather than allowing it to soak in.

Wood products.—Wood products decompose slowly and may create a nitrogen deficiency if additional nitrogen is not added. Wood chips can frequently be obtained from park districts, cities and electric power companies which remove and grind limbs overhanging streets or electric lines, and dispose of used Christmas trees as wood chips. Shredded newspapers are used to a limited extent. Unshredded paper mats down and prevents water penetration.

Manure.—Well-rotted manures can be used but chicken manure should be excluded as a mulch since it burns plants too easily. Manure should not have been treated with odor-reducing chemicals as these substances sometimes injure the vegetable plants.

Synthetic mulches.—Synthetic mulches include paper, aluminum foil, plastic and various combinations of these. Aluminum foil and some types of plastic are not biodegradable and they must be removed at the end of the growing season. The plastic mulches are usually used to increase the soil temperature and obtain an early crop and are applied to the soil before the crop is planted. The edge of the plastic is covered with soil to prevent it from blowing away and holes then punched in the plastic. The seeds are planted in the soil beneath these holes.

Permanent mulch systems.—Some gardeners prefer to leave a mulch on the garden all year around and not plow or spade the soil. The decision to use a permanent mulch system depends upon the climate, the type of mulch and the vegetables the gardener wishes to grow. Perennial vegetables, such as asparagus and rhubarb can be organically mulched permanently and new mulch added each year. Organic mulches lower the soil temperature and conserve moisture. In northern climates or in rainy areas, a permanent mulch will prevent adequate drying and warming of the soil in the spring. The soil will remain cool and wet and planting dates for the vegetables will be delayed. The mulch will have to be moved aside for planting to occur and small-seeded crops such as lettuce, carrots, beets and radishes will have difficulty emerging through the mulch, particularly sawdust and wood chip mulches. Frequently, no small-seeded plants emerge through a three inch layer of mulch, and seeds of vine crops, such as pumpkins and squash, rot due to the cold, wet germination conditions.

A permanent mulch system can be used to an advantage in warm climates with low rainfall and sandy soils. A loose, porous organic mulch such as straw or hay, should be used and a three to six inch layer of mulch spread over the area. The hay or straw is easily moved to one side in the spring to allow the planting of small-seeded crops, and once they are established, the straw can be moved around the plants. The mulch can be placed around transplanted plants immediately. Sandy soils are well-drained and soil temperatures increase rapidly in southern areas, eliminating the cool, wet soil conditions. As the soil temperatures increase rapidly, a permanent mulch will decrease the soil temperature in the spring increasing the time various cool-season crops can be grown. The mulch will partially decompose during the year and less material will have to be moved aside to plant small-seeded crops. If legume (alfalfa, clover) hay is used, no additional nitrogen is needed but straw will require about two pounds of fertilizer (5-10-5; 6-10-4 or similar) per 100 square feet to prevent any nitrogen deficiency occurring in the vegetable crops growing through the straw.

A variation of the permanent mulch system has been used successfully in cooler, wetter climates. The hay or straw is moved to one side of the garden in early spring, allowing the soil to dry out and warm-up. The vegetables are seeded and once established, the mulch is replaced over the area.

SELECTED REFERENCES

ANON. 1968. Optimum pH range for vegetable crops. Ill. Agri. Exp. Stn. *H-420*.

ANON. 1971. Mulches for your garden. USDA Home and Garden bulletin *185*.

BARTELLI, L.J., SLUSHER, D.F. and ANDERSON, K.L. 1977. Know your soil and how to manage it. *In* Growing your own vegetables. USDA Bulletin *409*.

COURTER, J.W., HOPEN H.J., and VANDEMARK, J.S. 1969. Mulching vegetables. Ill. Agri. Exp. Stn. Circular 1009.

DELWICHE, C.C. 1970. The nitrogen cycle. Sci. Amer. *223*: 126-146.

ENGLISH, J.E. and MAYNARD, D.N. 1978. A key to nutrient disorders of vegetable plants. HortScience *13*: 28-29.

ERHARDT, W.H. and LITTLEFIELD, L.E. 1973. Natural gardening. Maine Agri. Exp. Stn. Bulletin *567*.

FLETCHER, R.F. and FERRETTI, P.A. undated. Soil testing for the organic gardner. Penn. State Agri. Exp. Stn. Hort. Series *1*.

FLETCHER, R.F. and DUTT, J.O. undated. Garden soil management. Penn. Agri. Exp. Stn. Circular *540*.

FLETCHER, R.F. *et al.* 1972. Extension agent's guide to organic gardening, culture, and soil management. Penn. Agri. Expt. Stn.

GOWANS, K.D. and RAUSCHKOLB, R.S. 1971. Organic and inorganic fertilizers and soil amendments. Calif. Agri. Exp. Stn. AXT-*357*.

HINISH, W.W. and JORDAN, H.C. undated. Profitable use of poultry manure. Penn. Agri. Exp. Stn. Spc. Circular *146*.

JANSSEN, K.A. 1976. Snap bean nitrogen needs. Virg. Truck Orn. Exp. Stn. *30(10)*.

KENWORTHY, A.L. 1975. Trickle Irrigation. *In* Science and the home garden. Mich. State U. Agri. Exp. Stn. Series no. *28*.

LUCKHARDT, R.L. 1976. What happens to applied nitrogen. Agrichemical Age (Sept-Oct): 27.

MACGILLIVRAY, J.H., SIMS, W.L. and JOHNSON, H. JR. 1968. Home vegetable gardening. Calif. Agri. Exp. Stn. Circular 499.

MANSOUR, N.S. and BAGGETT, J.R. 1977. Root crops more or less trouble free, produce lots of food in a small space. In Growing your own vegetables. USDA Bulletin 409.

MELSTED, S.W. 1976. Municipal sludges as vegetable garden fertilizers. Personal communication. Urbana, Ill.

SHANMUGAM, K.T. and VALENTINE, R.C. 1976. Solar protein. Calif. Ag. 30(11): 4-7.

TOPOLESKI, L.D. 1972. Growing vegetables organically. N.Y. Agri. Exp. Stn. Bulletin 39.

UTZINGER, J.D. et. al 1973. Organic gardening. Ohio Agri. Exp. Stn. Bulletin 555.

VANDEMARK, J.S. 1973. Home garden recommendations for soil test interpretations. Ill. Agri. Exp. Stn. Veg. Grow. 25.

VANDEMARK, J.S., JACOBSEN, B.J. and RANDELL, R. 1977. Illinois Vegetable garden guide. Ill. Agri. Exp. Stn. Circular 1091.

VANDEMARK, J.S. and SHURTLEFF, M.C. 1970. The garden compost pile. Ill. Agri. Exp. Stn. Vegetable growing no. 1.

VANDEMARK, J.S., SPLITTSTOESSER, W.E., and RANDELL, R. 1973. Organic gardening can be successful if you follow sound principles. Ill. Res. 15(2): 5.

4

Pest Control

Very few gardens will escape attack from various pests. Weeds and insect pests will usually be the major problem. Some vegetables, however, can·be grown with little or no danger from insect or disease pests. Other vegetables will require pest control measures to reduce the pest population to a tolerable level. Home gardeners use mechanical, cultural and biological methods of pest control. If a chemical or botanical pesticide is used they must be used with care. Pesticides are generally sold as dusts, emulsible concentrates, wettable powders and granulars. Dusts are used in the form they are purchased. Emulsible concentrates and wettable powders are diluted with water and sprayed on the area. Granulars are small clay pellets which are impregnated with pesticide and usually applied to the soil to reduce soil-borne pests.

The use of pesticides should be limited to those crops which would otherwise be seriously damaged by insects or diseases. Sprays and dusts can drift to other crops in the garden or garden area and damage these plants. Gardeners are limited in the number of pesticides that can be economically used and some vegetable crops do not have any pesticides which have been cleared for use by the U.S. Government. If pesticides are handled or applied improperly, or if unused pesticides are disposed of improperly, they may be injurious to humans, domestic animals, desirable plants, pollinating insects, and fish or other wildlife, and they may contaminate water supplies. Use pesticides only when needed and handle them with care. Follow the directions and heed all precautions on the container labels.

Store all pesticides in a cool, dry, locked storage area so that they are not accessible to children, irresponsible persons, and animals. Do not dispose of pesticides through sewage systems. Haul them or have them hauled to a sanitary land fill for burial. Various pressurized pesticide cans should not be placed on a stove or heater or near a source of heat that might exceed 120°F as they may explode. They should also be stored in a

104

cool place and empty cans should be disposed of in a sanitary landfill. Pesticide containers should never be used for anything except to contain the original pesticide and pesticides should not be stored in anything but the original container. By the time any publication on insect or disease control reaches the gardener, it is already outdated by more recent research. Thus, the chemical pesticides listed here are general control measures rather than specific ones. Reliable, current insect and disease control measures can be obtained from state agricultural experiment stations and county agricultural extension agents (see Appendix) or the U.S. Department of Agriculture. Insects or diseased plants which the gardener cannot identify can be taken to the local county agricultural extension agent or sent to agricultural specialists at the agricultural experiment stations (see Appendix). Insect pests should be carefully wrapped in facial tissue and placed in a strong container and sent by first class mail to the Extension Entomologist. Diseased plants should contain the roots wrapped in moist soil or peat, packed in a strong container and sent by first class mail to the Extension Plant Pathologist. Insects and diseased plants should be sent to arrive during a weekday and accompanied by a letter describing the crop, location in the state, pesticides used on the area and type of damage noted. The more information available, the easier it will be for the specialist to identify the problem and recommend a solution.

TOXICITY AND HAZARDS OF PESTICIDES

Pesticides are poisonous. They have to be poisonous to kill undesirable plants, insects, diseases or other pests. Safe and proper use of pesticides depends upon a knowledge of their use.

Toxicity is the inherent capacity of a material to produce injury or death (Bever *et al.* 1975). If you know the toxicity of a pesticide, you will know what precautions to take.

Tests are performed with each pesticide to determine the toxicity to rats, rabbits, guinea pigs, or other animals. These tests are helpful in determining how hazardous the pesticide probably would be to humans.

In oral tests, the animal is given quantities of the pesticide by mouth according to the animals' body weight. The dose is increased until the dose which will kill 50% of the test animals is found. This lethal dose is called "Oral LD_{50}". The dose is expressed in milligrams of pesticide per kilogram of body weight (mg/kg). (There are 1,000 mg in a gram and 454 grams in a pound. A kilogram [kg] is 2.2 pounds). If a pesticide has an Oral LD_{50} of 100, then 100 mg of the pesticide are required to kill 5 out of 10 test animals each weighing a kilogram. A compound with an Oral LD_{50} of 100 is dangerous because 1/90 of a pound (one or two tea-spoons) could kill a human (Bever *et al.* 1975). The lower the LD_{50} number, the more toxic the pesticide.

In dermal tests, the pesticide is placed on the skin of the test animal and covered with a bandage so that it will remain on the skin for 24 hours. If 500 mg of the pesticide are required to kill 5 out of 10 test animals weighing one kilogram, the Dermal LD_{50} is 500. Most materials are absorbed more rapidly by the body when taken by mouth than when placed on the skin. Thus the Oral LD_{50} is almost always lower than the Dermal LD_{50}.

In inhalation tests, the test animals are placed in an airtight container with specific quantities of the pesticide. The animals remain in the container for one hour. Inhalation values called LC_{50}'s are measured in micrograms per liter ($\mu g/1$). The LC_{50} is the lethal concentration that will kill 50% of the test animals. (NOTE: There are 1,000 micrograms [μg] in one milligram [mg]. One liter is equal to 1.06 quarts). An LC_{50} of 100 means that 100 micrograms per one quart of air are required to kill 5 out of 10 test animals when they are exposed for one hour. LC_{50} also refers to the toxicity of a material to fish in water, and then is expressed in parts per million (ppm). Table 4.1 gives the oral and dermal LD_{50} and the inhalation LC_{50} for pesticides with high, moderate, low and slight toxicity. Highly toxic materials contain a drawing of a skull and crossbones and the words "Danger-Poison" on the label. Moderately toxic pesticides contain the word "Warning" on the label; and pesticides with low and slight toxicity contain the word "Caution" on the label. All pesticide labels carry a "Keep Out of Reach of Children" warning.

Oral exposure can occur because of an accident but it is more likely a result of carelessness. Blowing out a plugged spray nozzle by mouth and smoking or eating without washing contaminated hands can result in oral exposure. Dermal exposure is skin contamination and can occur anytime a pesticide is handled, mixed or applied. Inhalation exposure results from breathing in pesticide vapors, dust or spray particles. This can occur from smoking, breathing smoke from burning pesticide containers or inhaling the pesticide immediately after applying it.

The lethal dose is dependent upon the body weight of the person. A person who weighs 150 pounds can tolerate 50% more of the material than a 100 pound person, while a 50 pound child can only tolerate one-third as much as the 150 pound person. This is another reason for keeping all toxic materials out of reach of children.

It should be emphasized that *all* materials are toxic at some concentration. Remember that toxicity is the inherent capacity of a material to produce injury or death; but that does not mean it will if handled

TABLE 4.1. ORAL, DERMAL, AND INHALATION TOXICITY RATINGS OF PESTICIDES.[1]

Toxicity rating	Label signal words	Oral LD$_{50}$ (mg.kg)	Dermal LD$_{50}$ (mg/kg)	Inhalation LD$_{50}$ (μg/1 or ppm)	Lethal oral dose, 150-pound person
high	Danger-Poison	0-50	0-200	0-2,000	few drops to 1 tsp.
moderate	Warning	50-500	200-2,000	2,000-20,000	1 tsp. to 1 oz.
low	Caution	500-5,000	2,000-20,000	20,000 +	1 oz. to 1 pt. + or 1 pound
slight	Caution	5,000 +	20,000 +	— —	1 pt. + or 1 lb. +

SOURCE: Bever et al. (1975)
[1]tsp.=teaspoon; oz=ounce; pt=pint; lb=pound.

properly. Some common household materials are as toxic or more so than some pesticides. In Illinois, there were 11 deaths due to aspirin in 1977 while 35 persons died in the past 18 years due to all agricultural chemicals (Gentry 1978). Table 4.2 lists the various insecticides and fungicides that are discussed in this section on pest control. It is obvious from Table 4.2 that the materials which are derived from plant sources are also toxic to humans, and some of them are more toxic than man-made chemical products. This point needs to be re-emphasized as many organic gardeners think that if the material is a botanical insecticide (or "organic") it is not poisonous.

The toxicity values alone are not a measure of the hazards of a material to humans. Hazard and toxicity are not the same. Hazard is a combination of toxicity and exposure. It is the potential threat that injury will result from the use of a material in a particular formulation or quantity. Some hazards do not involve toxicity to humans or other animals. For example, oils, and numerous other chemicals are considered safe or relatively safe to animals but may cause considerable injury to some plants.

A compound may be extremely toxic but present little hazard when used 1) in a very dilute formulation, such as 2% or 5% dusts; 2) in a formulation that is not inhaled or absorbed through the skin; or 3) only occasionally and under conditions in which people are protected. Conversely, a chemical may be relatively nontoxic but present a hazard because it is used in a concentrated form or carelessly applied. A concentrated material may be toxic if taken orally but may not be a hazard when diluted with water. Chemicals are sold in different forms so that highly toxic materials are less of a hazard. Rotenone, nicotine sulfate and sevin are sold as 2% or 5% dusts. Diazinon is impregnated on a granule and sold in this form. Dichlorvos (Vapona or DDVP) is a highly toxic material but is impregnated on a resin strip ("no-pest strip") and enclosed in a container to reduce the hazard to humans. Thus hazard and toxicity are *not* the same.

TABLE 4.2.   RELATIVE TOXICITY OF SOME PESTICIDES AND COMMON HOUSEHOLD ITEMS.

Material (Trade Name)	Oral LD_{50}[1] (mg/kg)	Chemical Class
High toxicity		
Nicotine (tobacco)	10	Botanical Insecticide
Kerosene	50	Mechanical Insecticide
Moderate toxicity		
Diazinon	80	Chemical Insecticide
Nicotine sulfate	83	Botanical Insecticide
Gasoline	150	(for comparison only)
Rotenone	80-400	Botanical Insecticide
PNCB (Terraclor, Sanasol)	200-12,000	Chemical Fungicide
Caffeine (Coffee, Tea, Cola)	200	(for comparison only)
Low toxicity		
Carbaryl (Sevin)	700	Chemical Insecticide
Pyrethrum	1,000-1,300	Botanical Insecticide
Malathion	1,100-1,300	Chemical Insecticide
Ryania	1,200	Botanical Insecticide
Aspirin (various brands)	1,300	(for comparison only)
Ziram (Zerlate, Karlate, Karbam White Z-C spray dust)	1,400	Chemical Fungicide
Table Salt (various brands)	3,300	(for comparison only)
Ethyl alcohol (various brands)	4,500	(for comparison only)
Slight toxicity		
Zineb (Dithane 78, Zineb 75)	5,200	Chemical Fungicide
Maneb (Manzate D, Dithane M22)	6,750-7,500	Chemical Fungicide
Captan (Captan, Orthocide 50)	9,000-15,000	Chemical Fungicide
Bacillus thuringiensis (Dipel, Biotrol, Thuricide)	— —	Biological Control Insecticide

[1](mg/kg) means milligrams of actual material taken by mouth (orally) per kilogram of body weight; 1 kilogram=2.2 pounds; 454 grams=1 pound; 1 milligram=1/1000 of a gram.

WEEDS AND THEIR CONTROL

Weeds have been defined by some ecologists as "a plant growing out of place." If this definition is used then the growing of a "weed" cannot be done intentionally; the growing of a weed is the only thing that could be done only by accident. A better definition of a weed is a plant which is unsightly (crabgrass in your lawn), causes disease (ragweed for hayfever or poison ivy), reduces yield (sunflower with sweet corn) or grows where it is not wanted (volunteer pumpkin seeds from the added compost among your cucumbers). Weeds compete with vegetables for water, nutrients and sunlight. Weeds also harbor insects and diseases that may attack plants around the house and garden.

Herbicides.—There has been a substantial amount of research conducted on the use of weed-killers (herbicides) to control weeds without harming the vegetable plant. These materials do an excellent job of controlling weeds on commercial farms. However they are not recommended for the homeowner (with the possible exception of a herbicide on a large planting of asparagus).

The problems associated with herbicides used by the homeowner in the garden are as follows:

1. Herbicides are manufactured for specific crops to control specific weeds and some vegetable crops do not have any herbicide which has been cleared for use by the U.S. Government. No one specific herbicide can be used on all the crops growing in the garden. The gardener would need to apply a herbicide to vegetables in one or two rows, then apply a different herbicide to the different vegetables in the next row and so on. In addition some herbicides are applied before the seeds are planted and many gardeners forget which area was treated and which was not. The gardener would need to purchase, safely use and store several different materials. This would be expensive and create a storage problem as some herbicides cannot be frozen.

From Linn et al. 1966

FIG. 4.1. DAMAGE TO A TOMATO PLANT CAUSED BY DRIFT
FROM AN AUXIN-TYPE HERBICIDE.

Wavy edges and elongated leaflet tips (left) and heartshaped fruit (top right) are typical. The cracks on the tomatoes (bottom right) were induced by spraying the plant directly.

2. Gardens will contain many different types of vegetables at different stages of growth and drift from sprays can damage the veg-

etable plants. Similarly, spray drift from herbicides used on the lawn or yard can damage vegetable plants in the garden. The damage created by herbicide drift (Figure 4.1) has frequently resulted in legal action against the herbicide user.

3. Herbicides must be applied at the proper time and at the proper rate. There is a tendency to apply high rates if the quantity measured out "looks" as if it is not enough. These excessive rates not only damage plants this season but also may damage plants the next growing season. These high rates prevent the gardener from growing two or more crops of different vegetables in the same area. If rates lower than recommended are used, weeds are not killed.

4. Some weeds cannot be controlled easily with herbicides, particularly perennials. Excessive rates would be required which would also damage the vegetable plants (Utzinger *et al.* 1973).

Mechanical methods.—Cultivation and mechanical removal are the most common methods for controlling weeds in a garden (Hopen 1972). The best time to remove weeds is just as they appear on the soil surface. If the weeds are allowed to grow too large, they will shade the vegetables, causing them to grow poorly. Only those weeds that are present can be controlled and repeated cultivations are necessary.

FIG. 4.2.   HOEING IS THE MOST COMMON METHOD OF
WEED CONTROL IN A GARDEN

Weeds should be cut off just below the surface with a sharp hoe. On some soils, cultivation early in the season may loosen the soil, break up the soil crust and aerate the roots better. Shallow hoeing is best as roots of many vegetables are near the soil surface and can be easily damaged. In large gardens, rototillers or garden-type tractors can be used but they should cultivate shallow. Deep tillage brings buried weed seed to the surface where it can germinate and require additional cultivations.

Mulching.—The easiest and best method of weed control in the garden is to mechanically remove the weeds and then apply an organic mulch. An organic mulch six inches deep or an opaque synthetic mulch will control weeds by preventing light from reaching the seedlings (Binning 1975). This will control annual weeds which germinate from seeds each year but not perennial or established annual weeds. These must be removed before the mulch is applied and perennial weeds mechanically removed if they come through the mulch. (see Section on Mulches for types of mulch to use, page 97).

INSECTS AND THEIR CONTROL

There are now 1,100 species of alien insects in the USA. Most of these were introduced by the immigrants who brought fruits and vegetables with them when they settled here. Such pests as Hessian fly on grains, codling moth on apples, San Jose scale, gyspy moth, European corn borer and oriental fruit moth are only a few of the imported pests (Sailer 1972). There are 615 species of imported insects which have some adverse effect on our plants, and 217 are pests of major importance. When the settlers came, they brought few beneficial insects and there are few native beneficial insects which attack the imported destructive ones. The insect ecosystem in North America is not as well developed as many European countries. Since 1888 (Sailer 1972), the USDA has been combing the world for beneficial insects and so far has introduced 128 species of beneficial insects. Gardeners recognize, however, that not all destructive insects are under control.

It is usually necessary to use a variety of methods to obtain satisfactory control of insects in the home garden. The first step is to learn to recognize both destructive and beneficial insects. This point must be re-emphasized as too many gardeners do not recognize the larval stage of the lady beetle for example. After the insect is recognized as a destructive one, make sure it is doing economic damage to your garden. If you see three or four cabbage moths you can be sure you will have cabbage worms; but a small infestation of aphids will probably be controlled biologically and not create much damage. Make sure a problem exists before applying either a chemical or botanical (organic) insecticide. Some years, destructive insects fail to appear in large enough numbers to cause damage (Utzinger *et al.* 1973). Other years, considerable damage or complete loss may occur. The rainfall, humidity, temperature and beneficial insects all influence the level of destructive insects.

If you decide to garden without the use of any insecticide, either chemical or botanical, the following recommendations (Utzinger *et al.* 1973) should be considered:

1. Grow few or no vegetables which are highly susceptible to insect damage. Vegetables which have little or no insect problems include beets, chard, Chinese cabbage, chives, leeks, lettuce, mustard, onions, parsnips, peas, salsify, spinach, an early crop of sweet corn in northern areas, sweet potatoes, tomatoes, turnips and most herbs (Vandemark *et al.* 1973).

2. Expect a certain amount of insect damage to occur.

3. Be prepared to spend considerably more time and effort using mechanical methods of control.

4. Plant and take care of a larger garden than what is required for your needs. This will allow you to obtain the necessary yields to offset losses due to insects.

5. Expect considerable damage from soil insects if they are a problem in your garden. Frequently these insects do little damage, but areas of lawn which are converted into a garden are often infested with various grubs.

Destructive Insects

Many destructive insects can be found in the garden, but not all of these are important. Figure 4.3 and Table 4.3 (page 128) show some vegetable insects which are important garden pests.

Cabbage Worms.—Cabbage looper and imported cabbage worms are serious pests of cabbage, cauliflower, broccoli and sometimes lettuce. They overwinter as pupa attached to the stems of last years plants. In the spring, white moths emerge and lay white to yellow eggs on the lower side of leaves. The eggs hatch and the larvae eat the leaves and stems. Frequently they can be found in the heads of cabbage and cauliflower causing them to rot.

Aphids.—There are several species which may damage vegetables. They overwinter as an egg. Nymphs hatch out in the spring, mature and give birth to young aphids. Many generations occur over a summer and large populations can be built up rapidly. Aphids suck the plant juices from leaves, pods, blossoms and stems, and dwarfed plants may result.

Cabbage looper (light green) and imported cabbageworm (dark green)

Cabbage aphid. Other species damage many crops.

Hornworm showing cocoons of parasite on back

Two-spotted spider mite (enlarged). Not an insect.

Bean leaf beetle

Mexican bean beetle adult, pupa, larvae, eggs, and damage

Thrips (enlarged)

Root maggot and damage

Striped cucumber beetle

Spotted cucumber beetle

Colorado potato beetle larvae and adults

Potato flea beetle and damage

Potato leafhopper (greatly enlarged) and leafhopper damage

Squash vine borer and damage

Squash bug nymphs and adult

From Anon 1968

FIG. 4.3. COMMON INSECTS ON VEGETABLE CROPS

Hornworms.—Hornworms overwinter as a dark-brown pupa in the soil. In the late spring, a hawk or sphinx moth emerges. It lays a single greenish-yellow egg on the lower surface of leaves of tomato, pepper, eggplant and potato plants. The larvae which hatch are bright green with diagonal white stripes on the side. They contain a slender horn at the rear end of the worm, hence the name hornworm. These worms eat large amounts of plant foliage for three or four weeks and grow quite large. Frequently a parasitic wasp will inject her eggs into a hornworm. The eggs hatch and the wasp larvae eat the inside of the hornworm. When the larvae are fully grown they emerge from the hornworm and spin a small white cocoon attached to the back of the hornworm. Hornworms with cocoons attached should not be destroyed as any damage to the vegetable plant has already occurred and the wasps should be encouraged.

Mites.—Mites are not true insects but are very small eight legged animals. They appear as tiny specks, frequently under a webbing. Mites suck the juices from the underside of leaves causing them to turn yellow, then brown and finally to fall off. Many generations can occur in a single season and large populations can occur rapidly. Mite buildup is encouraged by dry conditions.

Bean beetles.—The adults of the bean leaf beetle overwinter in plant debris near where beans were grown the preceding year. In the spring, these adults emerge and eat the new bean plants. They then lay eggs at the base of the bean plants. The eggs hatch into slender white larvae which eat the roots, nodules and stems of the plant just below ground. These larvae develop into adults which emerge a month or so later and eat irregular holes in the leaves of the plant. These adults also eat bean blossoms and pods.

Adults of the Mexican bean beetle overwinter in plant debris in the garden, fencerows, wooded areas and roadsides. The adults move to snap beans and lima beans in the spring. Here they lay eggs on the lower surface of the leaves. The larvae hatch and both larvae and adults eat the underside of the leaf. This gives the leaf a lacelike appearance. Larvae also eat the bean blossoms and pods.

Thrips.—Thrips are small insects which eat the leaf surface by rasping away small areas. This causes white streaks to appear on the leaves. The leaves wither, turn brown and fall to the ground. Thrips damage beans, onions and vine crops and are particularly a problem under drought conditions.

Root maggots.—There are several different species which eat the roots of different vegetable plants. They overwinter as pupae in the garden soil.

In the spring, the adult fly emerges and lays eggs near the stems of the vegetable plants. The eggs hatch into small maggots which eat the roots and may tunnel into root crops. Different species of maggots can be a problem in beans, broccoli, carrots, cabbages, cauliflower, onions, radishes, sweet corn and turnips.

Cucumber beetles.—The striped cucumber beetle overwinters as an adult in sheltered areas. In the spring, they move to the vine crops (cucumbers, gourds, pumpkins, squash) and eat the leaves. They lay eggs near the plants which hatch into larvae. The larva eats the roots of the plants. The spotted cucumber beetle is really the adult southern corn rootworm. It is similar in life cycle and damage to the striped cucumber beetle. Cucumber beetles do little damage by eating the leaves of vine crops. However they carry bacterial wilt and mosaic and infect the plants with these diseases. The plants then die from these diseases.

Colorado potato beetle.—The beetles overwinter as adults in the soil. In the spring they emerge and lay orange-yellow eggs on the lower surface of the leaves. The eggs hatch into larvae and both larvae and adults eat the potato leaves. The beetles may eat enough leaves to prevent the potato tubers from being formed.

Leafhoppers.—Leafhoppers suck plant juices from the leaves. They secrete a toxin into the plant which causes browning of the leaf tips and edges of the leaf (called 'hopperburn'). Leafhoppers migrate from the south to the north and may suddenly appear in the summer in large numbers. Other years they may not be found at all. Leafhoppers can completely destroy potato plants.

Flea beetles.—Flea beetles are a group of small beetles with enlarged hind legs. They jump readily when disturbed. The adults overwinter and appear on plants in the late spring. The beetles feed on the leaf surface. Potatoes and eggplant are quite susceptible to flea beetle damage.

Squash vine borers.—These insects overwinter as pupae in the soil. In late spring the moths emerge and lay single brown eggs on the stems of vine crops. The eggs hatch into larvae which bore into the stem and eat the inside. They must be controlled before the larvae tunnel into the stem. Fortunately they are seldom a problem in most home gardens.

Squash bugs.—The adults overwinter under old squash vines and move to new plantings in the spring. Here they lay brownish-bronze eggs on the lower surface of the leaves. The eggs hatch into nymphs. Both nymphs and adults suck the plant juices from the leaves, often killing the plants.

Cutworms.—There are many different species of cutworms. Cutworms may overwinter in the soil as larvae, pupae or adults. The larvae begin feeding in the spring and change in the soil into pupae and then adult moths. The adults lay their eggs on the stems of many weeds and grasses, and different species may have several generations during the growing season. The larvae are plump, soft skinned worms which attack nearly all garden vegetables. They eat the stem of the plants just at the soil surface at night. The plants can be found cut off and wilting on the soil. The worms are usually located in shallow holes in the soil near the stem of the plants. When the worms are disturbed they roll up into a tightly coiled spiral.

Slugs.—Slugs are not insects; they resemble snails without shells (Figure 4.4). Slugs frequently cause damage in mulched gardens which provide excellent living conditions for them (Judkins 1977). They eat most vegetables and can be a major problem on lettuce leaves and radish roots. Slugs range in size up to two inches long. Slugs are seldom seen in the daytime but leave shiny mucous trails.

From Judkins 1977

FIG. 4.4. SPOTTED GARDEN SLUG

Beneficial Insects and Biological Controls.

Biological control is the direct or indirect use of living organisms to reduce the number of damaging insects below a level of economic importance (Fletcher *et al.* 1972). It has been investigated by the U.S. Department of Agriculture since 1888 (Sailer 1972). A number of weeds and insects are presently controlled biologically but once the pest is no longer economically important, it is soon forgotten as a problem. Gardeners, however, may wish to control present insect populations biologically. The insect population may be controlled with parasites, predators and pathogens.

Parasites normally complete their life cycle on or in a single host and are smaller than the host. Frequently, a number of parasites live on the same host and may or may not result in the death of the host. Parasites cannot be depended upon to control insects in the garden but if they are present they should be encouraged.

Predators are usually larger than their prey and require several hosts to complete their development. They eat the pest and cannot be depended upon to control garden insects.

Pathogens are bacterial agents, fungi and viruses that are used for biological control. One pathogen that is effective as a biological control agent and is effective when needed is *Bacillus thuringiensis*, a microbial preparation sold in several commercial formulations.

Parasites and predators are most effective when the insect population is relatively low. When the insect population is expanding rapidly, these forms of biological control have little effect. Pathogens are most effective when pest populations are high.

There are several advantages in favor of biological control (Fletcher *et al.* 1972): 1) once established, it is a relatively permanent method of control; 2) there are few undesirable side effects as compared to chemical and botanical insecticides; 3) once established there is no additional cost.

There are also several disadvantages in the use of biological control methods: 1) many parasites and predators are not present in early spring when insects can easily destroy young plants; 2) many predators are poor searchers for food and eat beneficial insects instead of destructive ones; 3) many destructive pests have no known biological control agents; 4) destructive insects must be present to support the biological control methods, meaning some insect damage to plants will occur; and 5) most control agents are not easily handled and lady beetles shipped in bottles usually die from lack of food.

Biological control agents should be encouraged. Home gardeners should learn to recognize the various beneficial agents. Some of these are given below.

Assassin bug.—These bugs are about one inch long. They are sometimes called the 'kissing bug' as they bite painfully when handled or when they fly against a person's face at night. Assassin bugs (Figure 4.5) eat the eggs, larvae and adults of many destructive insects.

Bacillus thuringiensis.—*Bacillus thuringiensis* or B.T. is a natural occurring microbial preparation. It acts as a pathogen and is an extremely effective biological control agent. As any material which kills insects is an insecticide, B.T. is an insecticide. It is sold as Thuricide, Dipel and Biotrol among others. B.T. is effective on various cabbage worms, hornworms, fruitworms and bagworms, regardless of the worm's size. When eaten by the worm, B.T. disrupts and paralyzes the worm's gut. Then it infects the worm with a highly specific disease bacterium (Anon. 1978). The worms stop eating within minutes but it takes three or four days before the worms die. Therefore expect to still see cabbage worms for several days after spraying. B.T. is a biological control agent and as such has no tolerance requirements and is not restricted in its uses. It can be used on tender plants and is not harmful to bees, beneficial insects or fish.

Birds.—Many species of birds are helpful in controlling insect pests. They are more important in preventing insect problems than in control-

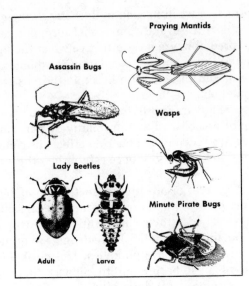

From Erhardt and Littlefield 1973
(USDA figure)

FIG. 4.5.   SOME COMMON BENEFICIAL INSECTS IN THE HOME GARDEN

ling the insect once it is established. To use birds as a biological control agent, those species which feed largely on insects must be encouraged. If all species are encouraged, damage to fruit trees, sweet corn and peas frequently result. Insect-feeding birds can be encouraged by 1) providing cover to hide and nest; 2) by supplementary feed, including the growing of sunflowers for bird use; and 3) preventing various predators, particularly cats, from entering the area. Such insect-feeding birds can be attracted to your home by growing the following ornamentals which provide food and cover (Taber *et al.* 1974): Bittersweet, Cherry, Cotoneaster, Crabapple, Dogwood, Elderberry, Firethorn, Hawthorn, Highbush Cranberry, Holly, Mountain Ash, Red Cedar, Russian Olive, Sumac and Wild Plum.

Brown creepers, kinglets, nuthatches and titmice (Erhardt and Littlefield 1973) will eat ants and ant eggs. Juncos, ruby crowned kinglets swallows, and sparrows will eat scale insects. Barn swallows, flycatchers, gnatcatchers, phoebes, red-eyed vireos and scarlet tanagers will help control all types of moths. Gnatcatchers and many warblers will control leafhoppers. Bluebirds, brown thrashers, catbirds, flycatchers, meadowlarks and mockingbirds, will eat grasshoppers. Juncos and towhees eat various insects which live in the soil. Downy woodpeckers eat snails.

Damsel bugs.—Damsel bugs are predators about one-half inch long (Figure 4.6). Both nymphs and adults eat eggs, larva and adults of many

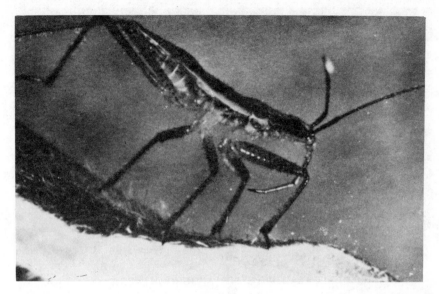

From Johansen et al. 1972

FIG. 4.6. NYMPH DAMSEL BUG

destructive insects including aphids, caterpillars, leafhoppers and mites. The adults are very fast and aggressive insects with enlarged front legs used to catch and hold their prey. They are one of the few predators which can catch lygusbugs.

Lacewings.—There are many types of lacewings found through North America. The adults (Figure 4.7) are filmy-looking insects with long hairlike antennae (Johansen *et al.* 1972). The name lacewing comes from their large membranous wings which have a netlike venation. The adults feed on honeydew and nectar and attach their eggs with a long silken stalk to stems and leaves of plants. The eggs hatch into larvae which are about one-half inch long when full grown. The larva is called an 'Aphis lion' and look somewhat like an alligator (Figure 4.8). These larvae eat large amounts of aphids, mealybugs, scale, insect eggs, spider mites and some small insects. The larvae are the beneficial form for insect control in the garden. They grab their prey with the two hollow mandibles and completely suck the body dry.

Lady beetle.—Lady beetles are the best known predator insect (Figure 4.5). The common species seen in the garden are red, brown or tan; and they usually have black spots. A few species are black, sometimes with red spots. The different species are known as the red lady beetle, convergent lady beetle (Figure 4.9) (red with black and white markings),

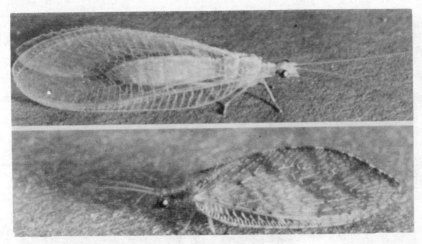

*From Hoy et al. 1978 (U. Calif.
Div. Ag. Sciences*

FIG. 4.7.   ADULT GREEN LACEWING (TOP) AND BROWN LACEWING (BOTTOM)

From Johansen et al. 1972

FIG. 4.8.   LARVA STAGE OF A LACEWING ("APHIS LION") EATING AN APHID

transverse lady beetle, twice-stabbed lady beetle (black with red spots), the two-spotted lady beetle, the nine-spotted lady beetle, the thirteen-spotted lady beetle, the fifteen-spotted lady beetle, the spotted lady beetle (pink with black spots), the glacial lady beetle and the parenthesis

From Johansen et al. 1972

FIG. 4.9. CONVERGENT LADY BEETLE FEEDING ON AN APHID

lady beetle. All lady beetles and their larvae eat aphids (Figure 4.10) insect eggs, scale insects, mites and mealybugs. One convergent lady beetle can eat 2,400 pea aphids and can lay 1,700 eggs in her lifetime (Johansen *et al.* 1972). Lady beetles eat about 100 aphids before they are ready to lay eggs and need a minimum of two aphids per day for each egg produced. Lady beetles do not kill grubs, Japanese beetles, caterpillars or other large insects. If there is not an ample supply of live aphids on the plants, the beetles will eat each other or leave the area. Lady beetles should be encouraged but are undependable as an effective biological control measure to quickly reduce a pest population (Vandemark *et al.* 1973).

Pirate bugs.—Pirate bugs are small predator insects. The minute pirate bug (Figure 4.5.) is about one-eighth of an inch long. They are black and white or brown and white as adults. Pirate bugs eat eggs, larvae and adults of small insects such as aphids and mites.

Praying mantids.—Praying mantids (Figure 4.5) are large predators. They commonly rest with the front part of the body upraised, and their enormous front legs are in an attitude of prayer (hence their common name). Mantids are exclusively carnivorous, eating only other insects. Their wings are fully developed but mantids are poor searchers for food and they wait for their prey to come to them. Praying mantids prefer grasshoppers, crickets, bees, wasps, and flies and may destroy more beneficial insects than destructive insects. In addition to destroying few garden insects, most mantids hatch in the middle or late part of the growing season. Thus, they are seldom present in sufficient numbers to

From Johansen et al. 1972

FIG. 4.10.   LADY BEETLE LARVA FEEDING ON AN APHID

suppress a pest population, particularly in the early part of the growing season. The eggs are laid in large masses about one inch long. They are contained in a frothy, gummy substance which hardens and fastens them to twigs of trees. These egg masses, containing about 200 individual eggs, are frequently available for sale. The first mantids hatched usually eat the subsequent mantids as they hatch from the egg mass and few nymphs survive the first week of life (Fletcher et al. 1972).

Syrphid flies.—Syrphid flies are also known as flower flies, sweat flies and hover flies. The adults are bright yellow or covered with long yellow and black hair and are often confused with wasps and bees. The adults feed on pollen and nectar (Figure 4.11) and pollinate many flowers. The adults lay their white eggs among aphid colonies. These eggs hatch into maggots as the larva stage. The larval stage is the predator stage and these larvae equal lady beetles and aphis-lions (green lacewing larva) as important biological control agents. Learn to recognize these brown, green or bright orange larvae about one-fourth inch long. Aphid colonies usually have at least one syrphid fly larva preying upon it. These larvae eat aphids at the rate of one a minute. They grasp the aphid with their pointed jaws (Figure 4.11), raise it in the air, suck and pick out the body contents and then toss the shell aside.

Wasps and flies.—The two most important parasite insects are ich-

From Johansen et al. 1972

FIG. 4.11.   ADULT SYRPHID FLY ON A FLOWER (TOP) LARVA STAGE FEEDING ON AN
APHID (BOTTOM)

neumon wasps (Figure 4.5) and tachinid flies. Ichneumon wasps vary in
size from one-eighth inch to two inches in length. They usually have a
long egg-laying structure at the tip of their abdomen (Johansen *et al.*
1972). These wasps parasitize various cutworms and caterpillars.
Tachinid flies resemble a large housefly. They can be identified from
houseflies because of their entirely bare bristle on the antenna. The
adults eat leaves and flowers. Tachinid fly adults lay eggs which are
glued to the skin of the host; or lay eggs on the leaves where the host
insect will swallow them whole while feeding; or deposit already
hatched larvae directly into the host insect. Usually only one fly develops per host insect. The larvae eat non-essential fat and muscle of
the host and the host caterpiller usually forms a cocoon before it dies.
However a tachinid fly not a moth or butterfly emerges from the cocoon. Tachinid flies attack caterpillers, cutworms and some beetles.
Chalcid wasps contain species which are both beneficial and harmful to
humans. One species parasitizes the imported cabbageworm. Braconid
wasps parasitize various caterpillers and beetles. One species attacks
the tomato hornworm (Figure 4.3). This species injects the eggs into the
hornworm where the eggs hatch. The larvae eat the inside of the hornworm and when fully grown eat a hole through the back of the hornworm. Here they spin small white cocoons and attach these to the host
(ANON. 1968). A very small braconid wasp parasitizes aphids, and may
completely control an aphid population (Metcalf *et al.* 1951).

Other predators.—Gardeners usually think of predators of destructive insects as other insects. However, geese, garden snakes and box turtles help control insects and slugs. Insects move from the plants to the ground at night and can be eaten by these predators. If the garden area is fenced to keep out dogs, box turtles are quite beneficial and seldom seen.

MECHANICAL AND CULTURAL CONTROL MEASURES

These methods are the oldest methods used to control insects (Erhardt and Littlefield 1973). These methods use direct or indirect measures to 1) destroy the insect directly; 2) modify the environment or planting conditions to make it undesirable for the insect; or 3) prevent or disrupt the normal life processes of the insect. These methods are used in many parts of the world and some of them are particularly effective in gardens. However, some of them require considerable time and effort.

Crop rotation.—Rotate the garden plot if possible. If this is not possible, the sequence of plants grown in the garden can be changed (Taber et al. 1974). Do not grow the same vegetables in the same place year after year. Soil insects build up into large populations. Do not plant on recently plowed sod or lawns as these usually contain various grubs. If soil insects such as wireworm, maggots, or grubs are a problem, avoid rootcrops such as carrots, potatoes, radishes, and turnips; and avoid broccoli, cabbage and cauliflower as these are also susceptible to soil insects. Beans, chard, peas and spinach are more tolerant of these insects.

Sanitation.—Many garden insects overwinter on old plant debris and weeds near the garden. The weeds and plant debris should be removed and composted or spaded under as soon as the harvest of annual vegetables is completed (Reed and Webb 1975). Unused or unwanted vegetables should also be removed as many insects continue to use them to reproduce. Manure and compost should be spaded under or used sparingly to prevent a build-up of grubs, slugs, snails, pillbugs and millipedes. If the garden is in an area infested with Japanese beetles, roses, raspberries and grapes should not be grown as these plants harbor the beetles.

Planting practices.—The garden should be well-maintained. Adequate fertilizer and water should be used to provide good plant growth. Healthy plants can withstand some insect damage. Plant crops that are adapted to your climate and best suited for your soil.

By paying attention to the planting dates, an early crop of sweet corn can be grown in northern areas without damage by corn earworms (Vandemark et al. 1973). Corn earworm moths are blown from the south to the north by the prevailing winds and the moth must lay the eggs on the fresh corn silk. By planting sweet corn by the middle of May, the silks will be produced and have dried up before the moths arrive. Late season corn frequently has an earworm problem.

Grow your own or use purchased transplants. The longer time that a plant is grown in the garden, the greater is the time available for the plant to be destroyed by insects. A small plant just developing from a planted seed is less able to withstand as much insect damage as a larger transplanted plant. This is particularly true for cool season crops which are planted from seed early in the growing season, such as cabbage.

Plant warm season crops when the soil is warm. The seeds will germinate quickly and the plants will grow rapidly. This will reduce maggot damage in beans and sweet corn.

With the exception of sweet corn, do not plant solid plantings of a given vegetable. If the plants are isolated from each other, there will be less insect damage. Use interplantings if possible.

Mechanically cultivate the garden to kill weeds and to work the soil. When the soil is worked, some insects will be injured or killed and some others will be exposed for birds to feed on. Plowing or spading in the fall in northern climates exposes many buried insects to cold temperatures. Many insects cannot withstand low temperatures or freezing and thawing winter conditions.

Resistant varieties.—All gardeners should use resistant varieties, or at least, varieties that are tolerant to certain insects. Sometimes a resistant variety will be susceptible to some other condition or disease and offer little advantage. Your own experience with several varieties will tell you which ones are best suited to your specific area.

Physical barriers.—Hot caps, paper collars, light roofing paper or used milk cartons can be placed around plants for some types of insect control. For cutworm control, the collar should extend one inch into the soil and at least two inches above the soil about one inch from the plant stem. For root maggot control on cabbage, broccoli and cauliflower, the collar should fit snugly around the base of the plant. Hot caps can be placed over cucumber, squash and pumpkin seedlings in the early part of the growing season to prevent cucumber beetle damage.

Traps and reflectors.—Aluminum foil has been shown to repel aphids (author's research, unpublished) and reduce Mexican bean beetle damage to garden beans (Topoleski 1972). Aphids feed on the underside of the leaf and are attracted to this area because of their orientation away from the sun. Sunlight from the aluminum foil is reflected to the underside of the leaf, disorienting the insects.

Slugs can be trapped in a shallow pan filled with beer and sunk to ground level. The pans need to be checked frequently to remove the dead slugs and replenish the beer. Slugs and other insects can be trapped under boards placed on the ground. The slugs and insects hide under them at night and can be collected and destroyed the next morning.

Various adhesive materials can be applied to cardboard sheets or screens which will trap the insects, similar to 'fly-paper.' The adhesive recommended by Erhardt and Littlefield (1973) is a mixture of hydrogenated castor oil, natural gum resins and vegetable wax. The sheets or screens can be placed on the ground or on the plants to trap leafhoppers, flea beetles and other insects.

Light traps have been recommended to trap destructive insects. Black light traps will collect a wide variety of insects, some of which will be destructive insects. These traps are a good way to determine which insects are in the area but they have little effect upon the garden insect population (Fletcher *et al.* 1972). Do not expect light traps to collect soil insects, daytime feeding insects and various worms. Light traps will also attract insects into the area which were not present originally. These insects frequently remain and cause plant damage.

Hand-picking.—Tomato hornworms are usually few in number and hand-picking is the recommended control. Colorado potato beetles and bean beetles may be shaken off the plants into a pail containing kerosene, diesel fuel or cooking oil.

Hand-picking requires the gardener to recognize the egg masses and injurious stages of the pest. It is impractical to hand-pick many small insects such as mites and aphids.

Soap and plant part sprays.—Washing house plants with warm soapy water to remove aphids and mites is usually successful. This method of aphid control in the home garden has been recommended since 1787 (Taber *et al.* 1974).Vegetable or plant-derived soaps are more effective than soaps derived from petroleum (Taber *et al.* 1974, author's research unpublished). Commercial soaps vary widely in purity and composition, and their effectiveness as an aphid control agent varies widely.

Some gardeners suggest boiling or grinding up plant parts in water to use as an insect spray. Boiling rhubarb leaves or soaking tobacco stems in water, for example, releases toxic materials into solution. These toxic materials are more toxic to humans than most chemical insecticides. Home-made sprays made from plant parts cannot be recommended.

CHEMICAL CONTROLS

Despite all precautions against insects, pest epidemics may become a threat and an insecticide is then needed to reduce the pest population to a tolerable level. The gardener should check the crops every two or three days and examine the plants for signs of an insect infestation such as egg masses, insect droppings and damaged leaves or fruit. In this way, most insect problems can be discovered and control measures taken before the problem becomes serious. The gardener should identify the insect and be sure it is causing damage before applying an insecticide. Sometimes lady beetle larva (see Figure 4.5) are not recognized and are intentionally killed with an insecticide, often resulting in an aphid problem. On the other hand, if the gardener recognizes two or three cabbage moths in the garden, broccoli, cabbages, cauliflower and some greens will soon be infested. Table 4.3 lists two chemical or man-made insecticides (Sevin and Malathion), one biological control agent *(Bacillus thuringiensis)*, and one mechanical method. Although these latter two methods of insect control are not chemical controls, they are the best control method for gardeners.

Bacillus Thuringiensis.—This microbial preparation is not a chemical control but is a biological control agent. (See Beneficial insects and biological controls, page 117). It is repeated as many gardeners do not recognize it as a non-chemical method. For those uses listed in Table 4.3, it is the safest and most effective control for gardeners.

Diazinon.—Diazinon is a moderately toxic insecticide. It is not listed in Table 4.3 as it is used to control soil insects of all types on all vegetable crops. The dust formulation is really a granule and label directions should be followed. For a spray formula, two tablespoons of 25% diazinon should be added per gallon of water. Both formulations should be applied to the soil at the beginning of the season and raked or rototilled into the soil.

Malathion.—Malathion is a widely used man-made insecticide that exhibits activity on a wide range of insects. It degrades very rapidly and disappears completely in about a week. Many parasites and predators can tolerate its use without major disruption. It has a low toxicity on birds but is highly toxic to fish and bees. It has been approved by the Environmental Protection Agency (Fletcher *et al.* 1972) for use on most vegetables. To give the reader some indication of the safety of malathion, one ounce of the 1% dust formulation per adult is recommended as the control for human lice (ANON. 1976).

Carbaryl or sevin.—Carbaryl is the common name and Sevin is a trademark of this widely used man-made insecticide. It exhibits activity on a wide variety of insect pests. Carbaryl has a low toxicity and degrades quite rapidly. About 50% disappears within three days with nearly complete disappearance in two weeks. It has a low toxicity to animals and birds, a slight toxicity to fish and is highly toxic to bees. Sprays

TABLE 4.3. COMMON GARDEN INSECTS AND THEIR CONTROL

Insect	Crop	Dust Formula	Spray Formula	Remarks
Aphid	Cabbage Cucumbers Melons Peas Potatoes Tomatoes	5-percent malathion	2 Tsp. 50-57-percent emulsifiable malathion	Apply on foliage when aphids appear. Repeat weekly as needed.
Blister beetle	Potatoes Corn Tomatoes Beans	5-percent Sevin	2 Tb. wettable Sevin in 1 gal. water	
Cabbage worms	Broccoli Cabbage Cauliflower Greens		*Bacillus thuringiensis;* follow label directions	Thorough treatment is necessary. Repeat weekly as needed. Begin treatment when worms are small.
Corn earworm (⅔ nat. size)	Sweet corn Tomatoes	5-percent Sevin; *Bacillus thuringiensis* (Thuricide, Dipel, Biotrol) on tomatoes	Inject ½ medicine dropperful of mineral oil into silk channel as silks start to dry *or* 2 Tb. wettable Sevin in 1 gal. water	Dust or spray silks with Sevin every other day for 10 days. Dust or spray tomatoes with Sevin 3 to 4 times at 10-day intervals; begin when first fruits are small.
European corn borer	Sweet corn	5-percent Sevin *or* 5-percent Sevin granules	2 Tb. wettable Sevin in 1 gal. water *or* 2 Tb. 25-percent diazinon in 1 gal. water	Apply insecticide four times at 5-day intervals beginning with egg hatching near mid-June. Avoid early spring plantings. On late corn dust as for corn earworm.
Striped cucumber beetle	Cucumbers Melons Squash	5-percent Sevin	2 Tb. wettable Sevin in 1 gal. water	Treat as soon as beetles appear. Repeat when necessary.
Cutworm	Most garden crops		2 Tb. 25-percent diazinon in 1 gal. water	At transplanting, wrap stems of seedling cabbage, pepper, and tomato plants with newspaper or foil to prevent damage by cutworms.

Insects are about natural size except where otherwise indicated. Where two drawings are shown, the smaller one is natural size. One pound of dust or 3 gallons of spray should be sufficient to treat 350 feet of row. Tb. = tablespoon. Tsp. = teaspoon.

(Table is concluded on next page)

TABLE 4.3. (*Continued*)

Insect	Crop	Dust Formula	Spray Formula	Remarks
Flea beetle	Most garden crops	5-percent Sevin	2 Tb. wettable Sevin in 1 gal. water	Apply as soon as injury is first noticed. Thorough application is necessary.
Grasshopper	Most garden crops	5-percent Sevin	2 Tb. wettable Sevin in 1 gal. water	Treat infested areas while grasshoppers are still small.
Hornworm (½ nat. size)	Tomatoes	5-percent Sevin *or* *Bacillus thuringiensis* (Thuricide, Dipel, Biotrol)	2 Tb. wettable Sevin in 1 gal. water	Ordinarily hand-picking is more practical in the home garden.
Leafhopper	Beans Carrots Potatoes Cucumbers Muskmelons	Use Sevin dust or 5-percent methoxy-chlor dust	2 Tb. wettable Sevin in 1 gal. water	Spray or dust once a week for 3 to 4 weeks, beginning when plants are small. Apply to underside of foliage
Mexican bean beetle	Beans	5-percent Sevin	2 Tb. wettable Sevin in 1 gal. water	Apply insecticide to underside of foliage. Also effective against leafhoppers on beans.
Potato beetle	Potatoes Eggplant Tomatoes	5-percent Sevin	2 Tb. wettable Sevin in 1 gal. water	Apply when beetles or grubs first appear and repeat as necessary.
Squash bug	Squash	5-percent Sevin	2 Tb. wettable Sevin in 1 gal. water	Adults and brown egg masses can be hand-picked. Trap adults under shingles beneath plants. Kill young bugs soon after they hatch.
Squash vine borer	Squash	5-percent Sevin	2 Tb. wettable Sevin in 1 gal. water	Dust or spray once a week for 3 to 4 weeks beginning in late June when first eggs hatch. Treat crowns of plants and runners thoroughly.

SOURCE: Vandemark *et al.* (1977).

should be used when bees are not in the garden. The dust formulation presents less of a problem to bees than the spray formula. The Environmental Protection Agency has approved (Fletcher *et al.* 1972) carbaryl for use on most vegetables. To give the reader some indication of the safety of carbaryl, one ounce of the 5% dust formulation per adult is recommended as the control for human lice (ANON. 1976).

Time to wait between application and harvest.—Gardeners must insure that the insecticide is not applied and the vegetable then immediately harvested and eaten. There is an established time the gardener must wait between application of the chemical and harvest of the vegetable (Table 4.4). These waiting times are designed to protect the consumer. The federal government and most states have laws which require pesticide containers to state the directions for rate and time of application of the material. By following these directions, the gardener is assured of producing vegetables which are safe and meet the tolerances established by the Food and Drug Administration.

BOTANICAL CONTROLS

Despite all other methods of natural pest control, pest epidemics will sometimes occur. Most organic gardening magazines recommend, and organic gardeners use, botanical insecticides as a last resort. Botanical insecticides are derived from plant sources and are not synthethic or man-made. Contrary to popular opinion, botanical insecticides are not non-toxic. Rather, some are more toxic (Table 4.2) to humans than their synthetic counterpart. Thus, many insect control recommendations do not list these botanical insecticides. Table 4.5 gives some common garden pests and their botanical control. The table lists three botanical insecticides (nicotine sulfate, pyrethrum and rotenone); one biological control agent (*Bacillus thuringiensis* and one natural occurring deposit (sulfur). The latter two methods of control are not botanical methods but are accepted organic methods and are included to make the table more complete.

Botanical insecticides such as rotenone are sold as a 1% or 2% dust. Nicotine sulfate is sold as 40% liquid which is diluted and applied as a spray. Pyrethrum is normally combined with rotenone and sold in a pressurized container. If you read the label on many insecticide containers for homeowners, you will note that many of them are botanical insecticides.

Diatomaceous earth —This material is a natural deposit composed of finely ground skeletons of various diatoms. It is sometimes reported as an insect control agent but its effectiveness is questionable. It is not registered by the Environmental Protection Agency for use on any vegetable

TABLE 4.4. DAYS TO WAIT BETWEEN APPLICATION OF THE CHEMICAL AND HARVEST OF THE VEGETABLE.[1]

Chemical	Vegetable											
	Collards, kale, and other leafy crops	Beans	Lettuce	Cabbage and related crops	Sweet Corn	Onions	Vine crops[2]	Tomatoes	Pumpkins	Eggplant	Peas	Potatoes
carbaryl	14	0	14	3	0	—	0	0	0	0	0	0
diazinon	10	7	10	7	1	—	3	3	—	—	0	0
malathion	7	1	14	7	5	3	1	1	3	3	3	0

[1]Bacillus thuringiensis has no time limit.
[2]Apply insecticide late in the day after blossoms have closed to avoid the bee kill.

SOURCE: ANON. (1976)

TABLE 4.5. SOME BOTANICAL INSECTICIDES AND THE VEGETABLE INSECTS THEY CONTROL

		Insecticide[1]			
Pest	B.T.	Nicotine sulfate	Pyrethrum	Rotenone	Sulfur
Ants	0	0	X	0	0
Aphids	0	X	X	X	0
Bean Beetles	0	0	X	X	0
Beetles and true bugs	0	0	X	X	0
Cabbage worms	X	0	X	X	X
Caterpillars	X	0	X	X	X
Cucumber beetle	0	0	X	X	0
Leafhoppers	0	0	X	X	X
Mites	0	X	0	0	X
Moths	X	0	0	0	0
Potato beetle	0	0	X	X	0
Thrips	0	X	X	X	0
White fly	0	0	X	X	0

[1]B.T. = Bacillus thuringiensis; X indicates the insecticide will control that particular pest; 0 indicates little or no control.

crop (Fletcher *et al.* 1972) and it is illegal to use this in the home garden.

Nicotine sulfate.—Nicotine sulfate is not the same as nicotine extracted by soaking tobacco in water. Nicotine is eight times more toxic to humans than nicotine sulfate (Table 4.2). Only the commercial formulation should be used.

Nicotine sulfate is a moderately toxic insecticide and has largely been replaced by malathion which has a lower toxicity rating. Nicotine sulfate controls aphids, thrips, and some soft-bodied sucking insects. It is usually sold as a 40% liquid concentrate such as Black Leaf 40. The material is then diluted with water and used as a spray. Dusts are not used because of their toxicity to the applicator. Nicotine sulfate is most effective when applied during warm weather. Nicotine sulfate degrades rapidly and has a short residual. It can be used within several days of harvesting of the vegetables. The Environmental Protection Agency has approved registration of nicotine sulfate for use on a large number of vegetables.

Pyrethrum.—These insecticides are obtained from dried flowers of *Chrysanthemum cinerariaefolium* from Ecuador and Kenya. Pyrethrum has been used for centuries as an insect control agent. They provide a rapid knockdown of a wide range of insects but will not control mites. Pyrethrum is very expensive and has a very short residual. Therefore it is usually used in combination with another insecticide such as rotenone, and with an activator or synergist such as piperonyl cyclonene or piperonyl butoxide.

Pyrethrum degrades extremely rapidly and can be used around parasites and predators although it is toxic to them while being used. Pyrethrum is a contact insecticide and kills those insects it touches.

Pyrethrum is not hazardous to birds and wildlife but is slightly toxic to fish. Pyrethrum is registered for use on most vegetables.

Rotenone.—Rotenone is probably the best general purpose botanical insecticide available for home gardens. It is derived from *Derris* roots from East Asia or *Cube* roots from South America. Rotenone is effective against bean and cucumber beetles and controls many sucking and chewing insects but will not control mites. It acts both as a contact and stomach poison. It will control some sucking insects such as aphids, which feed on the underside of the leaf and escape sprays of pyrethrum. Rotenone is a slow acting insecticide and frequently does not control insects which are rapid feeders such as caterpillars and cabbage worms.

Rotenone usually degrades within a week. After using rotenone the gardener must wait one day before harvesting the vegetables. The potency of rotenone declines with time and new material should be purchased each growing season.

Rotenone has a low toxicity to birds and wildlife but is extremely toxic to fish. In South America the natives use this material to stun and kill fish and it is still used in North America to kill unwanted fish in ponds and lakes. Rotenone is registered for use on most vegetable crops.

Ryania.—Ryania is derived from stems and roots of *Ryania speciosa* which is native to the Amazon River area and Trinidad. This material has frequently been recommended as a botanical insecticide in gardens. However, the Environmental Protection Agency has not approved its use on vegetables (Fletcher *et al.* 1972) and it controls few insects found in the home garden. Ryania should not be used and it is illegal to do so.

Sulfur.—Sulfur is a natural deposit rather than a botanical insecticide. The finely ground yellow powder can be used as a dust or spray and elemental sulfur should be used. Sulfur controls spider mites but should not be used on vegetables which will be canned. Sulfur creates an off-flavor in the canned vegetable and is converted to sulfur dioxide. This production of sulfur dioxide will cause the container to explode. Sulfur can be used on vegetables which are eaten fresh, frozen or dried. Sulfur is very safe and is an essential plant nutrient. Applications of large quantities of sulfur to the garden soil will cause the soil to become acid.

COMPANION PLANTING AND THE USE OF HERBS

Companion planting is based on the theory that certain kinds of plants will specifically prevent insect damage to certain other plants when grown nearby. For this technique to be successful, the major garden pests should be repelled such as cabbage worms, flea beetles, bean beetles, and cucumber beetles. Other insects are a problem only occasionally in most gardens. The author and others (Gessell *et al.* 1975) have examined this approach on several soil types and at different locations and climates for a number of years. The reported repellant plants such as wormwood, hyssop, thyme, catnip, rosemary, petunia and marigold were used. These were planted in the garden the same day as the vegetables were planted; or the 'repellant' plants were grown in the greenhouse and when six or eight weeks old were transplanted into the garden and the vegetables then planted. The transplanted 'repellant' plants were large enough to insure that any protection or repellant qualities were fully present when the vegetable plant began growth in the garden. The garden design was such that every vegetable plant had a 'repellant' plant on all four sides of it. None of these 'repellant' plants prevented insect damage from the major garden insect pests. Cucumber beetles killed many of the cucumber plants and injured the rest. Potato beetles and leafhoppers severely damaged potato plants reducing yields. For three consecutive years this author noted that bean beetles completely devoured the green bean seedlings so that only the stems remained, and when they finished with the bean plants, the beetles completely devoured the marigolds and petunias which were transplanted to protect the bean plants. In other studies conducted by this author, bean plants were dusted with rotenone to prevent bean beetle damage, and the beetles then ate the 'repellant' marigold plants. A lack of insect control by 'repellant' plants was also noted for cabbage worms on cabbage and flea beetles on eggplant and potato. In other studies leeks were planted with cabbage, snapbeans with potatoes, radish with snapbeans, onions with carrots and tomatoes at the edge of the asparagus bed. As with the above studies, no major insect pests were repelled. It can only be concluded that companion planting is not effective in preventing insect damage from the major garden pests. Gardeners should be aware that there are many vegetables which are resistant or tolerant to insects, or have few insect problems in the garden. The use of companion planting to 'repel' these 'phantom' insects is nearly always successful.

Another form of companion planting is to plant those vegetables together that require no special care or plant those that require similar care together. Many of the plants of the *Brassica* family such as cabbage, collards, kale, broccoli, Brussels sprouts and cauliflower are recommended to be planted as companion plants. The bacteria control agent, *Bacillus thuringiensis*, is extremely effective on cabbage worms and other main pests. In addition, we sometimes plant green beans and chinese cabbage side by side.

Diseases

Diseases often cause serious vegetable losses. Some diseases cause the seed to decay or the seedling to die before or at emergence. Others attack roots, stems and fruits. In contrast to insect control, vegetable disease control measures must begin before the disease is noted in the garden. There is no control once the disease is present. Nearly all materials which will control the disease on an infected plant will injure or kill the plant as well. Vegetable diseases are caused by many different types of 1) fungi; 2) bacteria; 3) nematodes; 4) viruses and 5) mycoplasma. Diseases develop only when 1) a susceptible plant is present; 2) the disease organism is present; and 3) a suitable environment occurs to allow development of the disease. Without all three requirements present, the disease will not develop. The gardener can use control measures to eliminate one of the three requirements and prevent many vegetable diseases without fungicides.

Most plant diseases are too small to be seen. Some virus particles must be magnified 100,000 times before they can be seen easily.

Nematodes are small wormlike animals which attack plant roots. Rootknot nematodes burrow into the roots of plants and cause small, knotlike or rounded swellings, or galls, in older, larger roots. They are easily seen in root crops such as carrots. Plants with severe root galling grow slowly, look unhealthy and tend to wilt in hot, dry weather and may die prematurely. Galls are swellings within the root in contrast to beneficial bacterial nodules, which are attached loosely to the roots of beans and peas. Gardeners who suspect nematodes are damaging their vegetables should contact their local county agent or Agricultural Experiment Station (see Appendix).

Mechanical and cultural controls.—Disease control measures are aimed at preventing the disease from occurring. In general, mechanical and cultural control measures are sanitation practices and good gardening methods. If these methods are used vegetable diseases should not be a major problem in the garden. Most good gardeners do not experience disease problems and chemical controls are rarely needed.

Crop rotation.—Always practice a rotation of vegetables within the garden area. Many soil borne diseases become a major problem when the same or related crops are grown in the same area each year. The cabbage group (broccoli, cabbage, cauliflower and others) are susceptible to clubroot, yellows, black leg and black rot and should not be grown in the same area each year. Eggplant, peppers, potatoes, and tomato are in the same family and have similar diseases.The cucumber family includes cucumber, gourds, melons, and squash and should be rotated in the garden area.

Sanitation.—Sanitation is most important in preventing vegetable diseases. Most diseases survive on infected plants between growing seasons. Crop debris should be spaded under after harvest or composted. Diseased plants should not be composted and should be removed and discarded as soon as they are observed. If diseased plants are added to the soil, the disease is added also. Some diseases live a long time in the soil, even though susceptible plants are not grown. Clubroot disease of the cabbage family survives at least seven years and verticillium wilt of the tomato family lives in the soil at least 10 years.

Gardeners should not smoke around tomato plants. The smoke may contain unkilled tobacco virus which infects tomato plants.

Weeds often serve as the initial sources of several vegetable diseases in the spring and should be destroyed. Dense weeds in the garden create an ideal microclimate for the growth of fungal and bacterial diseases.

Planting practices.—Locate the garden in a sunny area with good air and water drainage. Some diseases are encouraged by wet soils, and a sunny location will hasten the drying of dew and rain. Many diseases are most serious when plants remain wet for long periods of time. Cultivating or touching the plants when they are wet will spread some plant diseases, particularly bacterial wilt of beans. Avoid watering plants in the evening. If the soil surface stays damp all night, disease organisms can thrive (Vandemark *et al.* 1973).

Some diseases are carried in the seed, such as many cabbage, tomato and bean diseases. Hotwater treated seed should be purchased as this treatment kills the disease but not the seed. Bean seed should be certified, western-grown seed which is free of bean leaf diseases. Do not save bean seeds from east or midwest locations. Under these hot humid conditions, virtually all bean seed is infected. Potatoes should be certified seed potatoes to prevent scab diseases on the tubers.

Vegetables should be planted at the proper time in a garden with optimum fertility and pH. Excessively weak or vigorous plants are more susceptible to some diseases than similar plants grown under optimum conditions. Warm-season crops, such as beans, gourds, cucumbers, melons and squash should be planted when soil temperatures are warm. These crops require high germination temperatures and if planted into cold soil, the seeds rot. Under warm conditions the seeds germinate and the seedlings grow rapidly, preventing many diseases and damping-off fungi. Damping-off fungi occur in most soil worldwide and attack the seed when planted. The fungi are stimulated to grow and infect the seed or seedling by nutrients released from a germinating seed. Frequently, germinating seeds are killed before they emerge from the ground, accounting for poor stands in many crops. Older plants are usually not killed by damping-off fungi because the stem tissue has developed a protective barrier which limits fungal entry. Many purchased seeds will be treated with a fungicide such as thiram or captan to prevent damping-off fungi. However many seed suppliers sell untreated seed. Watering in the evening produces cool, wet conditions which favor damping-off fungi.

Vegetable plants should not be planted closely together. Dense stands of plants increase the humidity around the plants and encourage plant diseases. Various mildews, blights and white mold of beans are encouraged by high humidity. Applying water to the leaves of some plants also encourages mildews. Correct plant spacings allow for adequate air circulation and drying of the plants and soil.

Tomato fruit rots can be controlled by preventing the fruit from coming into contact with the soil. This can be achieved by using a three to six inch layer of mulch around the plants or growing the tomatoes in wire cages (Figure 4.12). Cages can be made of 10-gauge 6x6 inch mesh concrete reinforcing wire. The wire can be cut into four foot lengths, two and a half feet wide. The center wires can be cut out so the ends of the horizontal wires can be used as hooks to fasten the cage into a cylinder; and the ends of vertical wires can be pushed into the soil to support the cage. This forms a cylinder about two and a half feet high and 15 inches in diameter. These cages can be placed over the plants two weeks after transplanting and left for the growing season. The fruits are kept off the ground and fruit rots are controlled.

FIG. 4.12. TOMATO PLANT GROWING IN A WIRE CAGE TO PREVENT FRUIT ROTS

Mulches can be used to help control potato scab. If eight inches of straw mulch is applied when the plants are six inches high, the potato tubers will form in the straw. This will keep them out of the soil where scab diseases are present.

Fall plowing or spading to bury diseases is also helpful. Plant debris will be partially decomposed during the growing season and eliminate food sources for disease-carrying insects.

Resistant varieties and disease-free transplants.—All gardeners should use disease resistant varieties. Varieties are available for nearly all vegetable crops which are resistant to one or more diseases. Table 4.6 gives 'plant resistant varieties' as the control measure for a number of diseases which infect specific vegetables.

Grow your own or purchase disease-free transplants. Transplants should be grown from disease-free seed and grown in a disease-free soil. Many diseases are brought into the garden in diseased plants and soil. This is particularly a problem with transplants of the cabbage and tomato families.

Disease-carrying insects.—Several different kinds of insects carry virus, mycoplasma and bacterial diseases in their body and transmit the disease from infected plants to disease-free plants. It is easier to control the insect than to control the disease. These insects carry the disease overwinter, from wild to cultivated plants and from diseased to healthy plants. Diligent insect control will reduce such damage. This is particularly a problem with cucumber beetles which spread bacterial wilt, leafhoppers which spread yellows and various other insects which spread virus diseases.

Natural controls.—Roots of several plants contain chemicals which are leached out or released upon decay which are toxic to some diseases. Asparagus roots contain a material which is toxic to several types of nematodes (Erhardt and Littlefield 1973). French and African marigolds reduce the populations of lesion nematodes. Various mints destroy the disease organism which causes clubroot of the cabbage family. These plants have this effect regardless of what vegetable plant they are growing near.

Elemental sulfur has been used to control fungus diseases. The material can be applied as a dust or spray to control powdery mildew, rust and leaf spot. Sulfur should not be used on vegetables for canning. Sulfur forms sulfur dioxide in the container causing it to explode. Sulfur is very safe to humans.

Chemical controls.—About 90% of the plant diseases can and should be controlled by mechanical and cultural practices (Utzinger *et al.* 1973). However some plants are attacked by diseases which are not easily controlled by these methods.

Most fungicides have a low level of toxicity to humans (Table 4.2). To be effective, they (Table 4.6) must be applied at the right time. Applications should start before the disease appears, all above ground parts of the plant must be sprayed or dusted and the applications must be repeated at 10 day intervals during humid or wet weather.

Sometimes cucumbers, onions, potatoes and tomatoes need a mild fungicide during humid weather to prevent leaf blights. Asparagus beans,

TABLE 4.6.   COMMON DISEASES OF VEGETABLES AND THEIR CONTROL
MEASURES.

Crop	Disease	Control measure
Asparagus	Rust	Apply fungicide containing zineb after harvest. Make 5 applications at 10-day intervals.
Beans	Mosaic	Plant resistant varieties
	Leaf and pod diseases	No fungicide recommended. Do not cultivate, weed, or harvest beans when plants are wet. Plant certified, western-grown seed.
Beets, Swiss chard, Spinach	Leaf diseases	Apply fungicide containing maneb or zineb at 10-day intervals. Start when plants are 6 to 8 inches high.
Cabbage, Broccoli, Brussels sprouts, Cauliflower, Chinese cabbage, Kale, Collards, Kohlrabi, Mustards, Rutabaga, Radish, Turnip	Yellows	Plant resistant cabbage varieties
	Blackleg	Buy only hot-water-treated seed.
	Black rot	Buy only hot-water-treated seed.
	Clubroot	Apply one cup of transplanting solution containing pentachloronitrobenzene (Terraclor, PCNB) around the roots of each plant. The solution is made by mixing 3 level tablespoonsful of 50-percent wettable Terraclor in 1 gallon of water.
Carrots and Parsnips	Leaf diseases	Apply fungicide containing maneb or zineb when spots first appear.
	Yellows	Control leafhoppers, which transmit the mycoplasm Destroy infected plants.
Cucumbers, Pumpkins,	Bacterial wilt	Control cucumber beetles, which spread the bacteria from plant to plant
Squash, Gourds		Remove infected plants.
	Scab	Plant resistant cucumber varieties Buy hot-water-treated seed.
	Mosaic	Plant resistant varieties
	Leaf and fruit diseases	Apply fungicide containing zineb , or maneb at 7- to 10-day intervals. Begin after vines start to spread. If control is needed before vines start to spread, use ziram or captan .
Eggplants	Fruit rot	Apply fungicide containing maneb , zineb , or ziram at 7- to 10-day intervals. Begin when the first fruits are 2 inches in diameter.
	Verticillium	Plant resistant varieties
Muskmelons (Cantaloupes), Honeydew melons, and Watermelons	Fusarium wilt	Plant resistant varieties
	Bacterial wilt	See Cucumbers.
	Leaf and fruit diseases	See Cucumbers.
Onions, Garlic, and Chives	Leaf diseases	Apply fungicide containing maneb or zineb at weekly intervals. Begin when leaf spots are first noticed. Add 1 tablespoonful of powdered household detergent or 1 teaspoonful of liquid detergent to each gallon of spray solution.
	Smut	Plant disease-free onion sets. Smut only attacks onions grown from seed. Treat seed with thiram before planting.
Peas	Fusarium wilt	Plant resistant varieties
	Root rots	Plant early and use a seed treatment.
Potatoes	Tuber diseases	Buy certified seed potatoes. Plant uncut tubers. Grow varieties resistant to scab and late blight
	Leaf diseases	Apply fungicide containing maneb or zineb at 5- to 10-day intervals. Start when plants are 10 inches high.

(Table is concluded on next page)

TABLE 4.6 (*Continued*)

Crop	Disease	Control measure
Sweet potatoes	Black rot, Scurf, Foot rot	Buy certified plants. Use 3- or 4-year rotation.
	Wilt, Root-knot, Soil rot	Plant resistant varieties.
Tomatoes, Peppers	Fusarium wilt, Verticillium wilt	Plant immune or resistant varieties
	Leaf and fruit diseases	Apply fungicide containing maneb or zineb at 5- to 10-day intervals. Begin when the first fruits are 1 inch in diameter.

Zineb fungicides such as Dithane Z-78, Stauffer Zineb, Ortho Zineb 75 wettable, Chipman Zineb, Niagara Zineb, Penwalt Zineb, Black Leaf Zineb, etc., contain zinc ethylenebis (dithiocarbamate).

Maneb fungicides such as Manzate, Manzate D, Dithane M22, Dithane M-22 Special, Kilgore's Maneb, Black Leaf Maneb, and Penwalt Maneb contain manganese ethylenebis (dithiocarbamate).

Ziram fungicides such as Zerlate Ziram Fungicide, Karbam White, Corozate, Orchard Brand Ziram, Ortho Ziram, Stauffer Ziram, etc., contain zinc dimethyldithiocarbamate.

Captan fungicides such as Orthocide 50W, Captan Garden Spray, Captan 80 Spray-Dip, Orthocide Garden Fungicide, and Captan 50W contain N-(trichloromethylthio)-4-cyclohexene-1, 2-dicarboximide.

SOURCE: VANDEMARK *et al.* (1977).

beets, carrots, lettuce, peas, peppers and radishes do not (Topoleski 1972).

BIRD AND ANIMAL CONTROL

Animals such as toads and snakes and most birds eat large numbers of insect pests. However, at times and particularly in new housing developments and rural areas, animals and birds can become a nuisance.

Most chemical repellants are not suggested for use on food crops, although Thiram fungicide (one tablespoon per gallon), applied to the area, repels rabbits and a number of other animals.

Rabbits, squirrels and other animals are game animals and District Game Wardens should be consulted before trapping. Live trapping can be an effective means of removing the individual animals causing damage to the garden. The period of greatest activity for rabbits is just before sunrise and just after sunset; for squirrels it is just after sunrise and during late afternoon. Traps, other than live traps, must be used with caution, particularly around children or pets whose curiosity might result in serious injury.

Birds.—In many areas, some precautions are necessary to protect young seedlings and transplants from bird damage. A favorite method is to hang reflectors or fluttering objects over the area to discourage the birds. This method is only partially effective. Plastic bird netting, aluminum fly screen, nylon net, or cheesecloth can be used to make a shield that will completely protect a new planting of corn, cucurbits, peas and beans. These shields can be made of scrap lumber and need only be six to eight inches high. Once the plants are established, birds do little damage and the shields may be removed.

Gophers.—Gophers make elaborate tunnels 6-18 inches underground. Many gardeners who live in areas where gophers are abundant place a fence made of one inch galvanized wire about two feet in the ground around the garden area to prevent gopher damage.

Gophers frequently follow a person's footprints down a row of newly seeded corn, beans, squash and pumpkins, eating the seeds on the way. Damage can be prevented by raking the area lightly to remove the footprints or by the use of shields, similar to those used to control bird damage.

Moles.—Moles make mounds of dirt from their main tunnel and make ridges or raised and cracked soil just above their shallow feeder tunnels. The base of children's pinwheels can be placed into their tunnels and they are frightened away by the vibrations produced when the pinwheels turn in the wind. Good insect control measures will eliminate grubs which the moles feed on, and with no food available the moles will leave the area.

Rabbits.—Rabbit-proof fences two feet high made of one and a half inch galvanized wire, will prevent rabbit damage. The bottom of the fence should be buried in the ground six inches to prevent rabbits from digging or crawling under. Dried blood sprinkled around the edge of the garden also discourages rabbits. Many avid gardeners use mothballs. A mothball is tied with a piece of string and the string run through a small inverted cup (such as a disposable bathroom drinking cup). The string is then attached to a wire loop which holds the mothball off the ground five to six inches. The paper cup prevents the mothball from being dissolved by water and the rabbits are repelled both by the movement of the cup swaying in the breeze and the odor of the mothball. These will frequently last for one or two months.

Raccoons.—Raccoons are a serious problem in sweet corn as they eat the ears about two days before they should be harvested for optimum quality. The ears can be covered with a paper bag to prevent damage. Pumpkins, gourds or winter squash can also be planted among the corn plants. The spiney vines hurt the raccoon's feet and discourage them from entering the area and eating the corn.

SELECTED REFERENCES

ANON. 1968. Common vegetable insects. Ill. Agr. Exp. Stn. NHE-125 picture sheet No. 9.
ANON. 1976. Insect control guide home, yard and garden. Ill. Agri. Exp. Stn. Circular *900*.

ANON. 1978. One bite and the worm's a goner. Agrichemical Age. May.

BEVER, W. *et al.* 1975. Illinois pesticide applicator study guide. Ill. Agri. Exp. Stn.

BINNING, L.K. 1975. Vegetable gardens without weeds. *In* Weed control in the home garden. G.R. Miller and F. McGourty, Jr. (Editors). Brooklyn Botanic Garden, Brooklyn, N.Y.

COURTER, J.W. and VANDEMARK, J.S. 1973. Growing tomatoes in wire cages. Ill. Res. *15(1)*:14-15.

ERHARDT, W.H. and LITTLEFIELD, L.E. 1973. Natural gardening. Maine Agri. Exp. Stn. Bulletin *567*.

FLETCHER, R.F. *et al.* 1972. Extension agents guide to organic gardening, culture and soil management. Penn. Agr. Exp. Stn.

GENTRY, D. 1978. Proper storage methods curb pesticide poisoning. *Cited in* The Morning Courier, Champaign-Urbana. June 24 page 19.

GESSELL, S.G., PRECHEUR, R.J. and HEPLER, R.W. 1975. Companionate plantings-do they work. Brooklyn Botanic Garden *31(1)*:24-28.

HOPEN, H.J. 1972. Controlling weeds in the home garden. Ill. Agri. Exp. Stn. Circular *1051*.

HOY, M.A., ROSS, N.W., and ROUGH, D. 1978. Impact of NOW insecticides on mites in northern California almonds. Calif. Ag. *32(5)*:10-12.

JOHANSEN, C., EVES, J. and RETAN, A. 1972. Beneficial predators and parasites found on Washington crops. Wash. Agri. Exp. Stn. Bulletin *646*.

JUDKINS, W.P. 1977. Organic gardening-think mulch. *In* Gardening for food and fun. J. Hays (Editor) USDA Yearbook of Agriculture.

LINN, M.B., SLIFE, F.W. and BUTLER, B.J. 1966. Prevent 2,4-D injury to crops and ornamental plants. Ill. Agri. Exp. Stn. Circular *808*.

METCALF, C.L., FLINT, W.P., and METCALF, R.L. 1951. Destructive and useful insects. McGraw-Hill Book Co. Inc. New York.

REED, L.B. and WEBB, R.E. 1975. Insects and diseases of vegetables in the home garden. USDA Bulletin *380*.

SAILER, R.I. 1972. A look at USDA's biological control of insect pests:1888 to present. Agri. Sci. Rev. *Fourth Quarter*:15-27.

TABER, H.G., DAVISON, A.D. and TELFORD, H.S. 1974. Organic Gardening. Wash. Agri. Exp. Stn. EB*648*.

TOPOLESKI, L.D. 1972. Growing vegetables organically. New York Agri. Exp. Stn. Bulletin *39*.

UTZINGER, J.D. *et al.* 1973. Let's take a look at organic gardening. Ohio Agri. Exp. Stn. Bulletin *555*.

VANDEMARK, J.S., SPLITTSTOESSER, W.E. and RANDELL, R. 1973. Organic gardening can be successful if you follow sound practices. Ill. Res. *15(2)*:5.

VANDEMARK, J.S., JACOBSEN, B.J. and RANDELL, R. 1977. Illinois vegetable garden guide. Ill. Agri. Exp. Stn. Circular *1091*.

5

Harvest and Storage of Vegetables

Vegetables should be harvested at peak quality and are often eaten fresh from the garden. However, most gardeners have a surplus of some vegetables during the season. The different vegetables differ widely in how long they can be stored fresh. Potatoes can be stored for months while eggplants can only be stored about a week. Some of these vegetables may easily be frozen or canned and provide a year-round supply of vegetables.

HARVEST

Vegetables should be harvested at the proper maturity to obtain maximum quality for immediate use or for use as a stored product. Vegetables picked at the peak of maturity and used promptly are almost always superior in nutritional content, flavor and appearance. The difference in vegetable quality is mainly due to freshness of the produce.

Vegetables should be harvested all through the growing season rather than all at once. By harvesting the most mature vegetables first, the specific crop can be used as a fresh vegetable for an additional two or three weeks. To maintain quality, the vegetables should not be cut or bruised when harvested. After harvest, vegetables should be handled carefully for injury will encourage decay. Unless used immediately, vegetables such as sweet corn, peas, asparagus and leafy crops should be cooled to 40°F as soon as possible.

FREEZING VEGETABLES

Freezing is a most satisfactory method of preserving many vegetables. More of the original flavor, color, texture and nutritive value is usually retained during freezing than when foods are preserved in any other way. Freezing, however, does not add anything to the original quality of the vegetable. Vegetables for freezing should be harvested at peak flavor and texture; the kind you would choose for immediate use. When possible, they should be harvested in the cool part of the morning and processed as soon as possible. If processing is delayed, the vegetables should be cooled in ice water or crushed ice, and stored in the refrigerator to preserve flavor and quality and to prevent vitamin loss. Table 5.1 gives some suggestions on how to prepare vegetables for freezing.

Not all varieties of vegetables freeze equally well. In general, varieties that excel as fresh products have been found to be suitable for freezer storage.

Vegetables should be washed thoroughly in clean, cold water. All injured, bruised or sub-standard material should be discarded. This will remove dirt particles and reduce the number of bacteria.

Vegetables that are to be frozen must first be blanched (scalded) to inactivate enzymes, otherwise flavor and vitamins will be lost during storage. Rhubarb is satisfactory when it is frozen without blanching. Beets and winter squash are easier to handle if they are pre-cooked rather than blanched before freezing. For tomato juice, the fruits are simmered before the juice is extracted. For tomato paste, the fruits are ground and then simmered until most of the water has evaporated and the product is paste-like in consistency.

One gallon of water for each pound of vegetable is needed for blanching, except for leafy greens which need two gallons per pound. The water should be boiling and the blanching time counted from the moment the vegetable is placed in the boiling water. See Table 5.1 for blanching times for various vegetables. As long as the blanching water is clean and not too discolored, it may be used more than once.

TABLE 5.1.   HOW TO PREPARE VEGETABLES FOR FREEZING

Vegetable	Preparation[1]
Asparagus	Wash and sort medium and large stalks. Leave whole or cut in 1-or2-inch lengths. Blanch medium stalks 3 minutes, large stalks (½ to ¾-inch diameter) 4 minutes. Cool.
Beans (Green Podded)	Wash, snip off tips, and sort for size. Cut or break into suitable pieces or freeze small beans whole. Blanch 3-½ minutes. Cool.
Beans (Yellow Podded)	Process same as green podded beans.
Beans, Lima	Wash, shell and sort. Blanch 3 minutes; Cool.
Beans, Snap (Italian)	Wash, snap off ends, and cut or break into 1-or 1-½ inch lengths. Blanch 3-½ minutes. Cool.
Beets	Select small-or medium-sized beets. Remove tops and wash. Cook until tender. Chill. Remove skins. Slice or dice large beets.

TABLE 5.1. (*Continued*)

Beet Greens	Use tender, young leaves. Wash thoroughly and blanch 2 minutes. Cool.
Broccoli	Discard off-color heads or any that have begun to blossom. Remove tough leaves and woody butt ends. Cut stalks to fit container. Cut through stalks lengthwise, leaving heads 1 inch in diameter. Soak ½ hour in salt brine (½ cup to 1 quart water) to drive out small insects. Rinse and drain. Blanch 4 minutes in water. Steam-blanch 5 minutes. Cool. Pack heads and stalk ends alternately in container.
Brussels Sprouts	Wash and trim. Soak ½ hour in salt brine (see broccoli). Rinse and drain. Blanch medium sprouts, 4 minutes; large sprouts, 5 minutes. Cool.
Carrots	Use tender carrots harvested in cool weather. Top, wash, and scrape. Dice or slice ¼ inch thick. Blanch 3-½ minutes. Cool.
Cauliflower	Trim and wash. Split heads into individual pieces 1 inch in diameter. Soak ½ hour in salt brine (see broccoli). Rinse and drain. Blanch 4 minutes. Cool.
Sweet Corn	Husk, remove silks, and trim ends. Use a large kettle (12 to 15 quart capacity). Blanch whole kernel corn to be cut from the cob 4-½ minutes. For corn-on-the-cob, 14 small ears 1-¼ to 1-½ inches in diameter should be blanched 8 minutes, and cooled 16 minutes. 10 ears over 1-½ inches should be blanched 11 minutes and cooled 22 minutes.
Dandelion Greens	Use only tender, young leaves. Wash and blanch 3 minutes. Cool.
Eggplant	Precooked eggplant is usually more satisfactory for freezing than blanched eggplant. Peel, cut into ¼ to ⅓ slices, or dice pieces immediately into cold water containing 4 tablespoons salt per gallon. Blanch 4-½ minutes in the same proportion salted water. Cool and package in layers separated by sheets of locker paper.
Garden Herbs	Wrap sprigs or leaves in foil or seal in plastic bags and store in a carton or glass jar. Wash, but do not scald leaves.
Onions	Peel onions, wash, and cut into quarter sections. Chop. Blanch 1-½ minutes. Cool. (They will keep 3-6 months).
Peas, English Peas, Southern	Shell small amount at a time. Blanch 1-½ to 2 minutes. Blanch Southern peas 2 minutes. Cool.
Peas (Edible-Podded)	Wash. Remove stems, blossom ends, and any string. Leave whole. Blanch 2-½ to 3 minutes. Cool.
Peppers, Green	Wash, cut out stem, and remove seeds. Halve, slice or dice. Blanch halved peppers, 3 minutes; sliced or diced ones, 2 minutes. Cool. You can freeze chopped peppers without blanching them.

TABLE 5.1. (*Continued*)

Peppers, Pimiento	Oven roast at 400°F for 3 to 4 minutes. Cool, skin, and pack dry without additional heating.
Pumpkin	Cut or break into fairly uniform pieces. Remove seeds. Bake at 350°F, or steam until tender. Cool, scoop pulp from rind, and mash or put through dicer. You can prepare pie mix for freezing, but omit cloves.
Potatoes	Wash, peel, remove deep eyes, bruises and green surface coloring. Cut in ¼- to ½-inch cubes. Blanch 5 minutes. Cool. For hash brown: Cook in jackets until almost done. Peel and grate. Form in desirable shapes. Freeze. For french fries, peel and cut in thin strips. Fry in deep fat until very light golden brown. Drain and cool.
Rhubarb	Remove leaves and woody ends, wash, and cut in 1-inch lengths. Do not blanch. For sauce, pack in sugar syrup using 2-½ cups sugar to 1 quart water. For pies, pack in dry sugar using 1 cup sugar to 4 cups rhubarb, or pack without sugar for a few months storage.
Soybeans	Blanch 5 minutes in pods, cool and then hull.
Spinach and other Greens	Sort and remove tough stems. Wash. Blanch most leafy greens 2 minutes. Blanch collards and stem portions of Swiss chard 3 to 4 minutes. Blanch very tender spinach 1-½ minutes. Cool.
Summer Squash	Wash, peel and cut in pieces. Blanch ¼ inch slices, 3 minutes; 1-½ inch slices, 6 minutes. Cool.
Winter Squash	Prepare same as pumpkin. You can blend two or more varieties or blend squash with pumpkin.
Tomato Juice	Wash, quarter and simmer for 10 minutes. Strain off juice and add ½ teaspoon salt for each pint.
Tomato Paste	Wash, grind or blend entire fruit and simmer until most of water has evaporated. Roma types produce about ⅔ more paste.

[1]Blanching times given are counted from the time the vegetable was placed in boiling water.
SOURCE: Adapted from Brill and Munson, (1975) and Van Duyne (1970).

After blanching, the vegetable should be cooled in cold running water or ice water for the same time used for blanching. The vegetable should be drained, packed into containers, and immediately frozen. If vegetables are to be taken to a locker plant, they may be stored in the refrigerator, but not more than three hours should elapse between preparation, packaging and freezing.

Containers that are easy to fill, empty and occupy little freezer space are best. The more nearly moisture-proof and vapor-proof a container is, the better will be the frozen product.

Vegetables should be kept frozen until ready to use. Once frozen foods have thawed, the bacteria in them multiply and the food deteriorates in flavor, texture and nutritive value. All vegetables may be cooked from the frozen condition, except corn on the cob which should be partially defrosted. The frozen vegetables should be cooked in about ½ cup of boiling, salted water. They should be cooked until tender which is about half as long as if the same vegetable was fresh. Vegetables which were frozen in a solid mass such as greens and spinach should be broken into smaller pieces as they are boiled.

CANNING VEGETABLES

As in freezing, vegetables for canning must be picked at their peak flavor and color. Vegetables should be washed thoroughly in cool running water and sub-standard vegetables discarded. Successful home canning depends on the destruction of food spoilage agents by heat and exclusion of air from the jar. Enzymes, yeasts, molds and bacteria cause spoilage in canned foods. These agents are inactivated by temperatures of 212°F (boiling water) or higher. Some heat-resistant bacteria and bacterial spores of *Clostridium botulinum,* which causes food poisoning, are destroyed only at temperatures of 240°F or higher. A pressure canner is needed to reach these temperatures.

For home canning purposes, tomatoes and pickles are high acid foods, even so-called low-acid tomato varieties. The higher levels of acid inhibit the growth of botulism-producing bacteria but does not inhibit the growth of yeasts, molds and some bacteria. These high acid foods must still be canned in a boiling water bath at 212°F (or a pressure canner) to destroy these other spoilage agents. All other vegetables must be processed in a pressure canner (Anon. 1972). Process directions are included with canning equipment or may be obtained from a State Agricultural Experiment Station (see Appendix for addresses).

After canning, the seal on the jars should be checked after the containers have cooled. The self-seal lids are sealed if the lid is down and does not move when pressed with a finger. A ringing metal sound should be heard when the lid is gently tapped with a knife, indicating that there is a vacuum inside the jars.

Proper heating and correct sealing are absolutely essential for successful canning. Canned foods should be examined before using. The food should not be tasted if the container is leaky, the lid bulges, the seal is faulty, liquid spurts when the container is opened, the food has a peculiar odor, or mold is present. The food should be discarded. As a safeguard against botulism, all home-canned, low-acid vegetables should be boiled at least 10 minutes (spinach and corn 20 minutes) before tasting. If the material has an unusual odor or becomes foamy, it should be discarded.

FRESH STORAGE OF VEGETABLES

Vegetables may be stored fresh in a number of different storage facilities. All storage facilities should be above freezing temperatures during winter storage and most vegetables are stored under cool conditions. Cool temperatures retard respiration of the vegetables; slows down aging due to ripening which results in softening and color changes; prevents moisture loss and wilting or shrivelling; retards spoilage due to various fungi, bacteria and molds; prevents sprouting of potato tubers, onion bulbs and their relatives.

A well-ventilated basement under a house with central heat may be used for short-term storage of potatoes, sweet potatoes and onions, and for ripening tomatoes. For long term storage, an unheated basement is preferable. If the basement is heated, a well-ventilated area may be partitioned off and insulated to keep it cool.

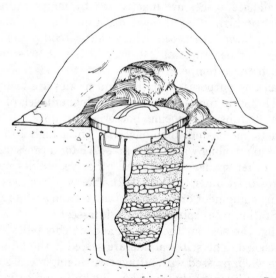

From Herner 1975

FIG. 5.1.   A LARGE GARBAGE CONTAINER PACKED WITH ALTERNATING LAYERS
OF STRAW AND VEGETABLES FOR OUTDOOR STORAGE

Outdoor storage cellars can be constructed partly or entirely below ground. Cellars constructed below ground are preferable because they maintain a more uniform and desirable temperature longer. Storage of vegetables in above ground buildings is practical only where the climate is consistently cold. A thermostatically controlled heater is necessary on cold nights to prevent the vegetables from freezing.

Many vegetables will keep for a short time in cold storage but others require warm temperatures as shown in Table 5.2. Gardeners can harvest small amounts of vegetables and keep many of them in the refrigerator. Most refrigerators are set at 35-40°F. If a high humidity is required, the vegetables can be placed in plastic bags or containers, and sealed to prevent water loss and wilting. Cucumbers particularly, shrivel badly if kept under dry conditions. If a large amount of vegetables is to be stored under, cold, or cool and moist conditions, an older model refrigerator without an automatic defrosting device may be used. Automatic defrosting devices remove water from the refrigerator resulting in lowered humidities and wilted vegetables. Small amounts of many vegetables can be stored fresh in these refrigerators for several weeks, but many gardeners will harvest more vegetables than the refrigerator will hold, and they may wish to store them for several months. In this case a basement room, outdoor pit, or above ground building may be constructed. Various plans are available from USDA and the Cooperative Extension Service.

TABLE 5.2. STORAGE RECOMMENDATIONS AND THE APPROXIMATE LENGTH OF THE STORAGE PERIOD

Vegetable	Temperature (°F)	Humidity (%)	Approximate length of storage period
Cold, Moist Storage			
Asparagus	32-35	85-90	2-3 weeks
Beets, topped	32	95	3-5 months
Broccoli	32-35	90-95	10-14 days
Brussels Sprouts	32-35	90-95	3-5 weeks
Cabbage, Late	32	90-95	3-4 months
Cabbage, Chinese	32	90-95	1-2 months
Carrots, Mature and Topped	32-35	90-95	4-5 months
Cauliflower	32-35	85-90	2-4 weeks
Celeriac	32	90-95	3-4 months
Celery	32-35	90-95	2-3 months
Collards	32-35	90-95	10-14 days
Corn, Sweet	32-35	85-90	4-8 days
Endive, Escarole	32	90-95	2-3 weeks
Greens, Leafy	32	90-95	10-14 days
Horseradish	30-33	90-95	10-12 months
Kale	32	90-95	10-14 days
Kohlrabi	32	90-95	2-4 weeks
Leeks, Green	32	90-95	1-3 months
Lettuce	32-35	90-95	2-3 weeks
Onions, Green	32-35	90-95	3-4 weeks
Parsnips	32-35	90-95	2-6 months
Peas	32-35	85-90	1-3 weeks
Potatoes, late crop	35-40	85-90	4-9 months
Radish	32-35	90-95	3-4 weeks
Rhubarb	32-35	90-95	2-4 weeks
Rutabagas	32-35	90-95	2-4 months
Spinach	32-35	90-95	10-14 days
Turnips	32	90-95	4-5 months

TABLE 5.2. (*Continued*)

Cool, Moist Storage			
Beans, Snap	40-45	90-95	7-10 days
Beans, Lima	32-40	90	1-2 weeks
Cantaloupe	40	85-90	15 days
Cucumbers	40-50	85-90	10-14 days
Eggplant	40-50	85-90	1 week
Okra	45	90-95	7-10 days
Peppers, Sweet	40-50	85-90	2-3 weeks
Potatoes, Early	50	90	1-3 weeks
Potatoes, Late	40	90	4-9 months
Squash, Summer	40-50	90-95	5-14 days
Tomatoes, Ripe	40-50	85-90	4-7 days
Tomatoes, Unripe	60-70	85-90	1-3 weeks
Watermelon	40-50	80-85	2-3 weeks
Cool, Dry Storage			
Beans, Dry	32-40	40	Over 1 year
Garlic, Dry	32	65-70	6-7 months
Onions, Dry	32	65-70	1-8 months
Peas, Dry	32-40	40	Over 1 year
Peppers, Chili Dry	32-50	60-70	6 months
Shallots, Dry	32	60-70	6-7 months
Warm, Dry Storage			
Pumpkins	55-65	40-70	2-4 months
Squash, Winter	55-65	40-70	3-6 months
Sweet Potato	55-60	70-85	4-6 months
Tomatoes, Unripe	55-70	85-90	1-3 weeks

SOURCE: Adapted from Wright *et al* (1954).

SELECTED REFERENCES

ANON. 1972. Ball Bluebook. Ball Corporation, Muncie, In.

BRILL, G.D. and MUNSON, S.T. 1975. Freezing fruits and vegetables. Minn. Agri. Exp. Stn. Extension Folder *156*.

HERNER, R. 1975. Research on ethylene yields storage tips. *In* Michigan science in action. Mich. Agri. Exp. Stn. Science and the home garden No. *28*.

VAN DUYNE, F.O. 1970. How to prepare fruits and vegetables for freezing. Ill. Agri. Exp. Stn. Circular *602*.

WRIGHT, R.C., ROSE, D.H. and WHITEMAN, T.M. 1954. The commercial storage of fruits, vegetables and florist and nursery stock. USDA Handbook No. *66*.

6

Growing Individual Vegetables

This section contains an alphabetical listing of various vegetables and a discussion of each. This includes some of their history and a few specific helpful aids on how to grow each one successfully in the garden. Included are some common problems encountered with each vegetable. Suggestions for control of pests can be found in the section on Pest Control.

Courtesy of Vincent Rubatzky

FIG. 6.1. ARTICHOKE WITH EDIBLE BUDS

ARTICHOKE

The globe artichoke (*Cynara scolymus*) is a thistle-like vegetable. It was eaten fresh and preserved for year around use by the Romans centuries

151

before Christ. The globe artichoke declined in importance as a vegetable with the fall of the Roman empire. However during the reign of the Medicis in Italy it was rediscovered and introduced into France as a gourmet item. When French and Spanish colonists settled in America they brought the globe artichoke with them.

Plant Characteristics.—The artichoke is a perennial which grows to about five feet in height with a five to six feet spread. If the buds are not harvested, six inch bluish flower heads appear.

Culture.—The globe artichoke grows best where cool, mild climates occur. It is very sensitive to frost and in these areas may be grown as an annual with a short harvest period in the fall. However, under warm or hot temperatures yields are reduced and the bud scales become tough. As the bud scales are the edible part, the artichokes are not very palatable. Thus artichokes are primarily grown along some sections of the California coast, in the south atlantic, and gulf coast regions.

Rooted offshoots or divisions from mature plants are planted in early fall. They are planted about three feet apart in rows with five feet between rows. As they are a perennial they should be planted at one edge of the garden in a sunny location. They will live and produce for five or more years.

After harvest, the plant is cut off at the soil line and removed. It is not watered for several weeks so that it is dormant during part of the summer. Fertilizer, particularly nitrogen, is added after the dormancy period and the plant irrigated. Rapid growth occurs and new stems with new buds develop for fall production.

Green Globe is the variety usually grown.

Harvest.—In a normal production cycle, new bud production begins in the fall, and reaches a maximum in the spring when warmer temperatures occur. The terminal bud is always the largest one and may be five inches in size. Auxiliary buds develop also and after the initial year, 40 buds per season may develop.

The buds are harvested before the bud scales begin to spread. This spreading is due to the growth of the flower parts within the bud, reducing the edible part of the plant. If the buds are harvested when small, yields are reduced but the buds are more tender. The bud is harvested by cutting the stem of the plant about two inches below the base of the bud. This small length of stem is also edible and tender.

Common problems.—Various types of aphids attack artichokes. These may be controlled with various chemical and botanical insecticides. Slugs and snails may also be a problem.

From Garrison and Ellison, 1977

FIG. 6.2. HARVESTING ASPARAGUS BY SNAPPING THE STEM AT GROUND LEVEL

ASPARAGUS

Asparagus (*Asparagus officinalis*) is a member of the lily family. It originated near the Mediterranean Sea and was considered a delicacy by the ancient Greeks. Methods for growing this vegetable were described in 200 B.C. and cultivated asparagus has changed little since. It was cultivated in England by the time of Christ and brought to America by the early colonists (Garrison and Ellison 1977).

Plant characteristics.—Asparagus is a perennial vegetable that can be grown in the same area for 20-30 years. It has an underground network of fleshy storage roots and underground stems called rhizomes. These roots store food and produce the asparagus spears. The root system is referred to as an asparagus crown. When temperatures are warm, buds develop on the rhizomes which become the edible spears. If the spears are not harvested, they develop into a green fern-like bush about four to six feet tall. This foliage produces the food material which is stored in the storage roots to be used to produce next years spears.

Asparagus has separate male and female plants. Bees transfer the pollen from the male plants to the flowers on the female plants which then produce red berries in the fall. The female plants use some of their energy in the production of these berries which contain the seeds. Female plants do not produce as well or live as long as male plants.

Culture.—Asparagus is a cool season crop and does best in climates where the soil freezes at least a few inches. In many southern locations and along the gulf coast the temperatures are too warm for asparagus. The plants do not store much material in the roots and few spears are produced. However asparagus is grown from southern California where temperatures reach 115°F in the summer to places where the winter temperature reaches 40°F below zero.

Asparagus should be planted with other perennial crops on the north or east side of the garden so as to not shade other vegetables. It can be planted along a fence in full sunlight. Asparagus can be planted in the spring as soon as the soil can be worked. About 1-2 pounds of 5-10-10 fertilizer or organic fertilizer equivalent per 100 square feet should be worked into the soil before planting. Asparagus grows poorly at an acid pH below 6.0 so the soil should be tested and pH adjusted if needed.

Healthy one year-old crowns should be planted in a furrow eight inches deep. The crowns should be placed a foot apart within the row and four feet between rows. If only one row is planted, at least three feet should exist between the asparagus and the rest of the garden. The roots should be spread so the crowns lie flat. The crowns should then be covered with two inches of soil and during the season the furrow should slowly be filled in the remaining six inches, being careful not to cover the asparagus foliage.

The plants should be watered weekly to wet the soil about eight inches deep during the first growing season. After a year, the plants have developed an extensive root system and about two inches of water every two weeks is sufficient during dry weather.

The second season after planting, the asparagus bed should receive 1.2 pounds of 5-10-10 or organic fertilizer equivalent per 100 square feet both in early spring and late summer. In subsequent seasons, the asparagus bed can be fertilized the same as the garden.

It is important to maintain good foliage growth of the plants after harvest. Allow the asparagus tops to grow until frost. The tops can then be removed or ground and left as a mulch. It is preferable to remove the tops and compost them to decrease problems with asparagus rust.

Most asparagus varieties came from the Martha Washington and Mary Washington varieties developed by the USDA. Mary Washington is the common variety grown in the south and the most important variety in the USA. In northern areas, Viking may be grown. On the west coast Mary Washington and various numbered California strains have been recommended. In the midwest and east, Rutgers Beacon and various Washington types, such as Waltham Washington are frequently grown in home gardens. The above varieties are all resistant to asparagus rust.

Harvest.—Asparagus crowns must grow for two full growing seasons before harvesting the spears. This allows the plants to develop an adequate root storage system to produce the spears. Damage or harvest of the plants before two years may reduce yield for the life of the bed.

When the spears emerge in the spring, all spears should be harvested. The spears should be seven to ten inches long. The spears can be cut at the ground surface or snapped off. Except in the cool central valleys of California, asparagus should be harvested for a two week period the third year after planting the crowns; four weeks the fourth year and eight weeks thereafter. In the cool valleys of California, spears may be harvested for four weeks the third year, eight weeks the fourth year and 12 weeks thereafter.

To harvest white spears, the row should be covered with a ridge of 8-10 inches of soil in the spring when the spears emerge. When the spears break through the top of the ridge of added soil, some soil can be removed from around the spear and a long knife used to cut the spear about eight inches below the tip.

Asparagus should be eaten immediately. However it may be washed and the cut ends placed in a small amount of water and immediately stored in the refrigerator for use a day later.

Common problems.—The asparagus bed must be kept free of weeds and clean cultivation is preferred to reduce rust and beetle problems.

Asparagus rust is a common fungus disease in the east, midwest and some areas of California. Water or dew left on the plant for 10 hours helps spread the disease. Resistant varieties should be planted.

The asparagus beetle may be a serious pest. The adult beetle overwinters in organic material and does not thrive in hot weather. It is not usually a problem in the south. The beetles can be controlled by hand picking, rotenone, malathion or carbaryl (such as Sevin).

BEANS, SNAP, AND OTHER

The common bean (*Phaseolus vulgaris*) includes a large number of different types and is called many names. Those beans grown for the immature pod are known as snap beans, Romano or Italian beans, garden beans, green beans, string beans, French Horticultural beans, French beans, wax beans or yellow beans. Those grown for the immature seed are known as green shell beans. Those grown for the mature seed, such as kidney beans are called dry beans. The requirements for growing these beans in the garden are similar.

The common bean originated in Central America and was widely distributed by the Indians of North and South America (Meiners and Kraft 1977). The Indians ate the beans primarily in the green shell or dry bean

Courtesy of Harris Seeds

FIG. 6.3. SPARTAN ARROW SNAP BEANS

stage. The original snap beans were stringy, hence the name string bean. Early American settlers introduced the snap bean into Europe. Within the past 25 years, the common bean has almost entirely been redesigned by plant breeders and few varieties available in 1950 are available today (ANON. 1975).

Plant characteristics.—Garden beans may be bush or pole types. The bushbean is a short erect plant one or two feet in height. They are used for quick production and successive plantings every two weeks are needed for a continuous supply.

Pole beans develop vines which must be supported by a fence, stakes, or grown on a trellis. Pole beans grow slower than bush beans but produce more beans per plant and only one planting of pole beans is needed.

Culture.—Snap beans are a warm season crop and are grown in all parts of the USA. They should not be planted until the soil is warm. In the south and southwest, snap beans may be grown during the fall, winter and spring. In the extreme south, snap beans are grown throughout the winter. During excessively hot, dry or wet weather the plants frequently lose the flowers or pods. Snap beans grow best between temperatures of 70° to 80°F and require about one inch of water each week.

To reduce diseases, western-grown seed should be used. Snap bean seed should not be soaked before planting as this injures many bean varieties. The seeds should be planted one inch deep in loam soils and one and one half inches deep in sandy soils.

Beans are legumes and as such enjoy an association with bacteria which convert nitrogen from the air into a form the bean plant can use. These bacteria may be purchased in a pea and bean inoculant, available at garden centers and through catalogues. If the area has never grown beans or peas before, some of this inoculant can be dusted onto the *moistened* (not soaked) seed. If the area has grown beans before, it is usually of little value to add additional inoculant. Beans therefore, require less nitrogen than some vegetables and if they are planted after some other early vegetable is harvested, the residual fertilizer is usually sufficient. Heavy applications of manure, or fertilizers high in nitrogen, may induce a large amount of vine or bush growth but frequently delay maturity and yield of the pods.

Bush type beans are planted one or two inches apart in 18—30 inch rows. They are thinned to stand two to four inches apart. Pole type beans may be planted in rows two to four feet apart near some support. A trellis made of stakes and string may be used. Pole beans are also planted in hills three feet apart with six seeds in each hill. The hill is thinned to four or five plants. Three or four long poles are placed over the hill and tied at the top in wigwam fashion. The vines are then trained to climb around the poles, frequently in a clockwise direction.

Green, bush type snap bean varieties include Apollo, Astro, Blue Crop, Blue Lake, Commodore, Contender, Gallatin 50, Greencrop, Greensleeves, Harvester, Provider, Slinderwhite, Slim Green, Spartan Arrow, Tendercrop, Tenderette, Tendergreen and Topcrop.

Yellow, bush type wax beans varieties often recommended are, Resistant Cherokee Wax, Eastern Butterwax, Earliwax, Goldcrop, Kinghorn Wax, Midas, Moongold, Sungold and Surecrop Wax.

Green, pole type snap beans are Blue Lake, Dade, Kentucky Wonder, and McCaslan.

The Italian or Romano beans produce large, flat pods which have a distinctive flavor. Green Ruler, Roma and Romano 14 are bush types and Romano is a pole type.

Horticultural or French Horticultural beans are large seeded beans which produce colorful pods. The pods are striped and mottled in red. These beans are usually used as green shell beans. Bush varieties are Dwarf Horticultural, French Horticultural, and Horticultural. King Horticultural is a pole variety.

Dry bean varieties are the bush type. Cranberry, Great Northern, White Navy or pea beans, Pinto, White Kidney, Red Kidney and the Horticultural bean varieties are good for dry shell beans.

Royalty is a purple podded bush bean. This variety is a selection from seed handed down through the years by a family of New England gardeners (Bubel 1977). It will germinate and grow in cooler soil than regular beans and it is less bothered by bean beetles. Royal Burgundy is another purple podded bean.

Harvest.—Beans should not be handled or harvested when they are wet as this helps spread disease. Green and yellow snap beans should be harvested when the pods are still young. The seeds will be small, the pod interior will be firm but the fiber content of the pod wall will be low. Beans should be harvested every few days as mature pods are of poor quality. Frequent harvesting induces the plants to continue to produce new pods. Bush types usually produce three or four harvests while pole types produce numerous harvests.

Green shell beans, produced by the horticultural varieties, are harvested when the pods change from green to yellow or red. At this time the seeds are about fully grown but they have not yet dried and become hard.

Dry beans are harvested after the pods are mature. Either the pods are removed or the entire plants pulled up when the leaves have turned yellow. The beans are then dried in a clean area and when the pods are dry the beans are removed and stored.

Common problems.—Snap beans have a number of insect and disease problems. Virus diseases and root rots are serious in the west. In the east and south, bacterial diseases infect snap beans. Bacterial diseases and anthracnose can be controlled by using western-grown seed. Virus diseases and rust can be controlled by using disease resistant varieties. Bacterial disease can be controlled by not handling the plants when they are wet from dew or rain. Root rots can be reduced by rotating the beans to a different spot in the garden each year.

Bean beetles are the major insect pest. Hand-picking or various botanical and chemical insecticides can be used for control.

BEANS, LIMA

Lima beans (*Phaseolus lunatus*) are often called butter beans in the south. Lima beans are natives to the western hemisphere and probably originated in Central America (Meiners and Kraft 1977). There are two types, a small seeded, and a large seeded type. The small seeded type had been used by North American Indians long before the time of Christ. The large seeded types were developed in Peru about the same time. Large seeded lima beans were collected and imported into the USA and called lima beans after the capital of Peru.

Courtesy of Harris Seeds

FIG. 6.4. FORDHOOK 242 LIMA BEANS

Plant Characteristics.— Lima beans are large seeded and generally referred to as the Fordhook type, or they are small seeded and referred to as baby limas. Both types are grown as bush or pole plants. The bush-bean is a short erect plant one or two feet in height. They are used for quick production. Pole beans develop vines which must be supported by a fence, stakes, or grown on a trellis. Pole beans grow slower than bush beans but produce more beans per plant.

Culture.—Lima beans are a warm season crop and require warmer temperatures than snap beans. Lima beans need a minimum soil temperature of 65°F for quick germination and then require three or four months of warm days and nights. Thus, in the states of the USA near the Canadian border, lima beans are difficult to grow in a garden. Below this area, bush baby limas can be grown as they mature quicker than other lima bean types. Lima beans require such a long growing season that successive plantings are impractical except in the deep south.

Lima beans grow best in sandy, well drained soils. The soil should not bake or form a crust. If this occurs, sand, vermiculite or leaf mold should be placed over the beans instead of soil when planting.

To reduce diseases, western-grown seed should be used. Bean seed should not be soaked before planting as this injures many bean varieties. The seeds should be planted one inch deep in loam soils and one and one half inches deep in sandy soil.

Beans are legumes and as such enjoy an association with bacteria which convert nitrogen from the air into a form the bean plant can use. These bacteria are available in a pea and bean inoculant, availabʰ. at garden centers and throughout catalogues. If the area has never grown beans or peas before, some of this inoculant can be dusted onto the *moistened* (not soaked) seed. If the area has grown beans before, it is usually of little value to add additional inoculant. Beans therefore, require less nitrogen than some vegetables, but the area should receive an application of general garden fertilizer. Large amounts of manure or fertilizers high in nitrogen may induce a large amount of vine or bush growth but frequently delay maturity and yield of the pods.

Bush type beans are planted one or two inches apart in 18-30 inch rows. They are thinned to stand two to four inches apart. Pole type beans may be planted in rows two to four feet apart near some support. A trellis made of stakes and string may be used. Pole beans are also planted in hills three feet apart with six seeds in each hill. The hill is thinned to four or five plants. Three or four long poles are placed over the hill and tied at the top in wigwam fashion. The vines are then trained to climb around the poles, frequently in a clockwise direction.

During excessively hot, dry or wet weather the plants frequently lose the flowers or pods. Lima beans grow best between temperatures of 70° to 80°F and require about one inch of water each week.

Bush type varieties of lima beans which are small seeded are Allgreen, Dixie Butterpea, Henderson's Bush, Jackson Wonder, Nemagreen, and Thaxter. Large seeded bush varieties are Burpee's Improved Bush, Fordhook 242. Pole type lima beans include Florida Butter Speckled (adapted primarily for the south); King of the Garden (large white seed, butter bean type); and Sieva (small seeded butter bean well adapted to the south and west).

Harvest.—Beans should not be handled or harvested when they are wet as this helps spread disease. Lima beans should be harvested when the pods are filled and are light green in color (creamy white for butter bean types). The end of the pod should feel spongy when squeezed. By frequent harvesting more pods are produced. Bush types are harvested for about three weeks and pole types for about four weeks or until frost.

Common problems.—Lima beans are susceptible to mildew in the mid-atlantic states, and anthracnose and nematodes in the south. These can be controlled by using disease-free seed, rotating the beans in the garden area, using resistant varieties and not handling the plants when they are wet with rain or dew.

Bean beetles are the major insect pest. Hand-picking or various botanical and chemical insecticides can be used for control.

BEANS, FAVA

The Fava bean (*Vicia faba*) is often called broad bean, Windsor or Horsebean. It is not a bean but is a type of vetch. The broad bean is native to Europe and Asia and was used by ancient Greeks, Egyptians, and Romans. They introduced it into China in about 2800 B.C. It was brought to America by early settlers from southern Europe.

Plant Characteristics.—The plants are erect, medium tall and produce pods which are about seven inches long. The pods contain five or six large beans.

Culture.—Favabeans are grown under even, warm temperatures. In most areas, the summers are too hot, and the winters too cold for it to be planted in the autumn and overwintered. In some parts of the south and pacific coast areas it may be planted in the fall and grown through the winter for a spring crop. Other culture requirements are similar to snap beans.

Long Pod, Broad Long Pod, and Broad Improved Long Pod are varieties usually available.

Harvest.—Favabeans are harvested as green shell or dry beans. The pods contain five or six large, flat, oblong beans, and are harvested similar to green shell or dry snap bean varieties.

Common Problems.—Many of the problems are similar to snap beans.

BEANS, GARBANZO

The garbanzo bean (*Cicer arietinum*) is neither a pea nor a bean. It is also called Chickpea, Egyptian pea, Gram, Chestnut bean, and Ceci or Cece bean. It is a native of the Mediterranean area and was widely used by Greeks, Romans and Egyptians. Today the Gram is one of the important food sources in India. Ceci or Cece beans are important in Italy and in Spain they are called garbanzos. Settlers from these countries brought this plant to America.

Plant characteristics.—The garbanzo bean is an erect bush-type plant which grows about two feet high. It produces one, and at most three, beans in a puffy little pod. The bean has a chestnut-like flavor.

Culture.—Garbanzo beans require 100 days to mature and are grown in warm climates. The seeds are planted one inch deep in loam soils and one and one-half inches deep in sandy soils. The plants are thinned to stand three inches apart, in rows two feet apart. Other culture methods are similar to snap beans.

Seed catalogues usually do not list a variety. They are usually listed as Chickpea or Garbanzo.

Harvest.—They are harvested similar to dry beans (see page 158). The mature pods are picked and allowed to dry. These pods are hairy and often exude a substance which irritates the hands. Often gloves are used when picking. After the pods are dry the beans are shelled and stored in air-tight containers.

BEAN, MUNG

The mung bean (*Vigna radiata*) is widely known in the Orient. It is used primarily for bean sprouts, raw in salads, or as a cooked vegetable in Oriental dishes.

Plant Characteristics.—The mung bean is a bush type plant one or two feet tall. The bean pods are produced at or above the foliage level which makes harvesting easy.

Culture.—The mung bean has about the same climatic and soil requirements as the Southern pea, and is grown in a similar manner. They require 90-100 days to mature and are very susceptible to cold. They can be grown in the mid to deep south.

The seeds are planted one inch deep, about two inches apart in rows two feet apart. They are planted after all danger of frost has passed.

Most garden catalogues do not list a specific variety but Berken is sometimes given.

Harvest.—The plants are pulled when the pods have matured and allowed to dry in a clean area. The pods shatter easily and careful handling is needed to prevent loss of beans. When the pods are dry, the beans can be removed and stored in an airtight container.

Common Problems.—Mung beans are resistant to most of the insect and disease problems that are found on Southern peas, snap beans and soybeans.

Use as Sprouts.—The beans are soaked overnight and then placed in a container which has holes in the bottom for drainage. The container needs to be large enough to allow the beans to expand and swell as they sprout. The container is placed in the dark in a warm place. The beans are moistened three times a day in the summer and twice a day during the winter when it is cooler. Under warm conditions, the beans are ready for use in about five days. Under cooler winter temperatures it may require 10 days or more. The beans are usually used when three inches long. They are then stored in a cool, humid place until use.

BEANS, SOY OR EDIBLE SOYBEANS

Soybeans (*Glycine max*) are known as edible soybeans, and vegetable soybeans. It appeared as a cultivated crop in northern China in 3,000 B.C. (Metcalf and Burnham 1977). The cultivated type is not known in the wild but it is believed to come from a viny North Asia type. Soybeans were brought to North America during colonial times but it did not become a major crop until after World War II. It is used as an important food source in China, Korea, Japan and Manchuria.

Plant Characteristics.—Soybeans are a warm season crop with an erect bush type growth. They grow slower than most types of beans and require from 75 to 170 days for maturity. They produce flowers which are self-fertile and usually self-pollinated. Most soybean seed is yellow, but green, black, black and yellow, and black and green seed are known.

Culture.—The soil and cultural requirements are similar to snap beans. Field soybeans may be grown and harvested when the seeds are immature. The edible soybeans have larger seeds and are thus often preferred. Small early varieties may be planted in rows two feet apart but later maturing, larger varieties are planted three feet apart. The seeds are planted one inch deep about eight seeds per foot of row when the soil has warmed up (the time when tomatoes are transplanted).

If soybeans have never been grown on the soil, the seeds can be inoculated with bacteria which fix nitrogen from the air into a form the plants can use. This inoculum is available in various garden catalogues and at garden centers. Nitrogen fertilizer is seldom needed for soybeans in a garden.

Soybeans, as immature beans, should be ready to harvest from early varieties about two months after planting. The time to maturity depends upon the daylength of the area and the variety grown. As one goes from North to South, the summer daylengths become shorter; and soybean varieties are classified into 10 maturity ranges. Varieties in group O and I are the earliest in maturity and adapted to the northern USA and southern Canada. Group I and II are used in the northern areas of the USA. Group II and III are adapted to the southern corn belt. Group III varieties can be grown further south but the plants will mature about a month earlier. Group VIII are late maturing varieties grown near the gulf coast. The edible soybeans most frequently listed in garden catalogues are Giant Green and Kanrich.

Group O and I varieties include Disoy, Early Hakucho, Okuhara Early and Giant Green.

Group II and III varieties are Kanrich, Sodefuri, and Verde.

Field soybeans which are adapted to the area may also be used. These varieties may be purchased from a local elevator or farm supply store.

Harvest.—Soybeans are usually harvested as the immature seed. The pods are harvested when the seeds are fully grown but before the pods turn yellow. Pods are harvested over a 10 day span. Soybean seeds are difficult to remove from the immature pods. The pods are usually placed in boiling water and cooked for two minutes. The pods can be removed and the seeds squeezed from the pods easily. These seeds are eaten similar to green shell beans.

If dry mature soybean seed is desired, the pods are allowed to remain on the plant. When the pods have turned brown, the entire plant is cut and placed on a rack or hung up to dry. This prevents loss of beans in the garden. The beans are shelled when the pods are dry. The beans should be thoroughly dried before storage.

Mature dried beans may be used to produce bean sprouts (Adjei-Twum *et al.* 1976) similar to mung beans or lightly roasted as a snack food.

Common problems.—Soybeans are seldom bothered by Mexican bean beetles and can be grown where this pest prevents the growing of snap beans. In some parts of the USA, soybeans may be attacked by various worms, caterpillars, grasshoppers and mites.

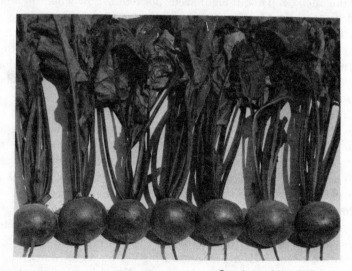

Courtesy of Harris Seeds

FIG. 6.5.   BOTH LEAVES AND ROOTS OF BEETS MAY BE USED AS A VEGETABLE

BEETS

Beets (*Beta vulgaris*) are also called garden beets and table beets. Beets originated in the Mediterranean area of North Africa, Europe and West Asia. Swiss Chard belongs to the same species as the garden beet and was probably the original wild beet without a fleshy root. Beets were first cultivated about the third century A.D. and were first used for their root in the 1500's. However it was not until the late 1800's that much interest was shown in beet varieties.

Plant Characteristics.—Beets are an annual which may be grown either for the roots or for the tops as greens. Various varieties have been developed which are classified according to the shape of the root and the time of maturity. Beet roots are most often round but may be flat or elongated. Their fleshy roots are usually red colored but golden colored varieties are available. The "seed" of beets is actually a dried fruit containing several tiny true seeds (Reynolds 1977).

Culture.—Beets are adapted to all parts of the country, being tolerant of both hot and cold temperatures. They will not withstand severe freezing and are grown in the spring, summer and fall in the north. In warm climates they are planted in the fall and winter for harvest in the spring. Temperatures below 50°F for two or three weeks may induce seed stalks to develop instead of the fleshy root.

Beets are planted one-half inch (loam soils) to one inch (sandy soils) deep in rows 12 inches apart. Heat, drought or crusting of the soil surface may interfere with seedling germination and emergence. The seeds can be covered with sand, leafmold or vermiculite instead of soil to prevent this problem. The beets should be thinned to stand two or three inches apart in the rows. Successive plantings, three weeks apart, are needed to insure a continuous supply of young beets.

Flat or globular early maturing varieties are Crosby Egyptian, Green Top Bunching, Ruby Queen, and Early Wonder. Explorer has only one seed per seedball. Medium maturing varieties are Detroit Dark Red and Perfected Detroit. Elongated late maturing varieties are Long Dark Blood, Long Smooth Blood and Cylindra. Golden Beet has a golden colored root which "bleeds" less when cooked than the red varieties.

For beet greens any variety can be seeded close together and not thinned. Varieties specifically developed for producing greens are Beets for Greens, Crosby Green Top and Early Wonder.

Harvest.—Beets are harvested when desired but have the highest quality when they are less than two inches in diameter. Beets left in the garden will withstand mild freezing. For storage, fall maturing beets should be used. The tops are removed one inch from the roots and stored at 95% humidity at 32°F.

Common Problems.—Beets have few insect and disease problems in the garden. In western areas a leaf hopper may transmit curly top virus disease. Beets should be planted early to allow them to mature before the virus develops in the summer.

In some areas, a lack of boron in the soil results in beets containing bitter black spots in the roots. Only small amounts of boron are needed and one-half teaspoon of household borax in 12 gallons of water per 100 feet of row is sufficient (Bubel 1977). Composted leaves of plants which accumulate boron may also be used, such as muskmelon (cantaloupe) and sweet clover.

Courtesy of Harris Seeds

FIG. 6.6. BROCCOLI IS GROWN IN ALL PARTS OF THE COUNTRY

BROCCOLI

Broccoli (*Brassica oleracea* var. *botrytis*) is a member of the cabbage family and its culture and problems are similar to cabbage. Broccoli is also known as Calabrese, Italian broccoli and green sprouting broccoli. Broccoli developed from various leafy cabbage forms in southern Europe. They were brought to America by early immigrants from that area.

Plant Characteristics.—Sprouting broccoli is the type grown in home gardens. The plant forms a loose flower head on a tall, green, branching stalk. The center flower head is from five to ten inches across and the plant may reach three to five feet in height.

Culture.—Broccoli is grown similar to cabbage. It can be planted as a transplant or from seed. Transplanting saves three or more weeks growing time but fall crops can be direct seeded.

Broccoli is adapted to all parts of the USA. In northern areas with short growing seasons, it can be planted in the spring for summer harvest or for early fall harvest. In areas with a longer growing season, it can be planted in early spring for a summer harvest and again during the summer for a fall harvest. Where mild winters occur, late summer and early fall plantings are made for harvest during the winter. Broccoli is hardy and will stand some frost.

In western areas broccoli is frequently grown on a raised bed. This is an advantage if drainage of water is slow during fall and winter seasons and furrow irrigation is used. The beds are formed several days in advance to allow the soil to settle. These beds are raised six inches and two rows one foot apart are planted on the beds.

Broccoli transplants are set in holes which are deep enough, so that the stem of the plant is slightly below ground level. Transplants should be four or five weeks old, and a starter fertilizer used after planting. Older plants have more food reserve and if they receive temperatures of 50°F for two weeks, they will produce a small flower stalk immediately. Small plants should be planted during cool weather.

For direct seeding, the seeds should be planted one-fourth to one-half inch deep about one inch apart. They are later thinned to stand one to two feet apart in the row. Broccoli must develop rapidly and requires adequate water. Once established, they require one to one and a half inches of water weekly.

Broccoli varieties are generally classified by the length of time it takes to mature. They mature in 50-85 days after transplanting, depending on the time of year planted and the variety. Depending upon planting date, De Cicco, Early One, Gem, Green Comet, Italian Green Sprouting, Premium Crop, and Spartan Early are early varieties. Calabrese, Costal, Bravo, Green Duke, Green Sprouting, Pacifica and Topper are medium maturing varieties. Waltham 29 is the most popular late maturing variety. Royal Purple Head is a type of broccoli which produces a compact purple head, somewhat like cauliflower. It turns green when cooked. This variety is frequently found listed as a purple cauliflower.

Green Comet, Premium Crop and Royal Purple Head are varieties which are resistant to fusarium wilt or yellows.

Harvest.—The central head together with six inches of stem is harvested. These flower buds and the attached stem is the edible part. It should be harvested before the flower buds begin to develop into bright yellow flowers. After the center head is removed, the smaller side shoots develop into new heads. This can extend the harvest a month or more.

Common Problems.—The insect and disease problems of broccoli are similar to cabbage (See page 172). Wilt, blackleg and black rot can cause severe damage. These can be controlled by using disease-free seed or transplants and by using resistant varieties.

Insect pests are rather local but aphids, cabbage worms and flea beetles are common through out the USA. They can be controlled with various botanical, chemical and biological control agents.

Courtesy of Harris Seeds

FIG. 6.7. BRUSSELS SPROUTS ARE A COOL SEASON CROP

BRUSSELS SPROUTS

Brussels sprouts (*Brassica oleracea* var. *gemmifera*) is a member of the cabbage family. It originated in Europe and has been grown near Brussels, Belgium (from where it received its name) for hundreds of years.

Plant Characteristics.—Brussels sprouts are a type of non-heading cabbage. It develops sprouts or small heads in the axils of the leaves (the upper area near where the leaf stem joins the main stalk). The plants grow slowly and require 80-100 days from transplanting for the first sprouts to mature.

Culture.—Brussels sprouts are a cool season crop and can withstand some frost. They are best transplanted during the summer or fall for a fall or winter harvest. In some areas they may be grown as an early spring crop.

Brussels sprouts for transplanting are seldom available when needed and gardeners will need to grow their own. The seeds can be planted in a protected area of the garden four to six weeks before they should be transplanted. If only a few plants are needed the seeds can be planted in peat pellets. Seeds are planted about one inch apart in rows three inches apart. At transplanting, they are placed in the garden, two feet apart in rows which are two to three feet apart. A transplant fertilizer should be used and additional nitrogen applied when the plants are a foot high to stimulate their growth. Brussels sprouts require good fertility and moisture. They should receive one to one and one half inches of water a week during dry weather.

Various selections of Catskill, Jade Cross and Long Island Improved are common varieties. Jade Cross is resistant to fusarium wilt or yellows.

Harvest.—The sprouts are harvested when they are one or two inches in diameter and plants may be harvested for a month or more. The leaf below the sprout is removed and the sprout is then cut or broken off. Sprouts are harvested upward on the stem until the sprouts are too small. These sprouts are left for future harvests.

In warm weather, the sprouts become loose and are not firm. When cool weather occurs the sprouts firm up and become milder in flavor. In areas where an early frost occurs, plants 15-20 inches tall, may be debudded. The top growing point is cut out in August or September to force all the plants' energy into the developing sprouts. All the sprouts will then be ready about the same time.

Some gardeners remove the lower leaves of Brussels sprouts as the sprouts develop. (The top leaves should not be removed). This practice makes harvest of the sprouts easier but it is not required.

Common Problems.—Brussels sprouts have insect and disease problems that are similar to cabbage (see page 172). They should not be grown where other members of the cabbage family (cabbage, cauliflower, Brussels sprouts and others) were grown last year. Most diseases can be reduced by using disease-free transplants and crop rotation.

Aphids, cabbage worms and flea beetles are common pests in all areas of the USA. They can be controlled by various botanical, chemical and biological control agents.

CABBAGE

Cabbage (*Brassica oleracea* var. *capitata*) developed from wild, leafy, non-heading types still found growing in Europe. Wild cabbage is found along the chalk coasts of England, Denmark, northwestern France and various other areas from Greece to Great Britain. Cabbage was in general use by 2000 B.C. It is said that the ancient Egyptians worshipped

FIG. 6.8. A GREEN CABBAGE VARIETY

cabbage. Cabbage was used throughout Europe by 900 A.D. but the head type was first described in 1536. Shortly thereafter, these types were brought to America by the settlers.

Plant Characteristics.—Cabbage types vary widely. They range in color from green to purple; in leaf character from smooth to savoy leaves; in head shape from flat to pointed; and in maturity from early (55 days after transplanting) to late (130 days or more after transplanting). The green, round headed types are most common.

Culture.—Cabbage is a cool season crop which tolerates frost but not heat. In the far South it can be grown in all seasons except summer. On the Pacific coast, it can be grown all year long. In areas with mild frosts, it can be planted in the fall and become one of the first crops harvested in the spring from the garden. Cabbage will adapt to cool temperatures and can withstand short periods of temperatures below zero. In the north it can be grown as an early summer crop or a late fall crop.

Quality in cabbage is dependent upon rapid growth. Cabbage responds to liberal application of nitrogen fertilizer. It should be fertilized before seeding and a starter fertilizer used when transplanting. Cabbage can be fertilized once or twice during the growing season at least three weeks apart.

For early spring planting, transplants should be used. If these transplants are hardened, they can be transplanted into the garden when the earliest vegetables are planted. As cabbage does not tolerate hot weather, varieties which mature before this time should be transplanted. Cabbage transplants are spaced 12-18 inches apart in rows about two feet apart. Fast growing vegetables such as green onions, early lettuce and radishes can be planted between the cabbage plants to utilize the space. These other plants should be harvested before the cabbage starts to spread out.

The stem of cabbage transplants should not be larger than the size of a lead pencil. Larger sized plants have more food reserve and if they receive a low temperature of 40°-50°F for three or four weeks, these plants will produce a seedstalk. Large transplants which receive a low temperature during the winter will flower in the spring. Heads from overwintered plants should be harvested early.

For late planting, seeds are planted one-fourth to one-half inch deep during midsummer. The plants should later be thinned. Summer plantings will produce the head during the cool fall weather. Late plantings may follow early potatoes, beets, peas or spinach. Frequently cabbage is planted before the potatoes are harvested to conserve space.

Cabbage requires adequate moisture. From one to one and one half inches of water a week are required.

To provide for a harvest over a long interval, different varieties with different maturity dates can be used. There are numerous varieties available and many are resistant to one or more diseases.

The following green varieties of cabbage are resistant to yellows: Defender (Blackrot resistant), Early Jersey Wakefield, Emerald Cross, Excell, Guardian (Blackrot resistant), Globe, Golden Acre, Gourmet, Greenback, King Cole, Marion Market, Market Dawn, Market Prize, Market Topper, Market Victor, Resistant Danish, Stonehead, Wisconsin Hollander, Wisconsin All Seasons, and Wizard.

Red colored cabbage varieties that are resistant to yellows include Red Danish, Red Head and Ruby Ball.

Savoy cabbage varieties include Perfection Drumhead, Savoy Ace (some plants are resistant to yellows) and Vanguard II (yellows resistant).

Harvest.—Cabbage heads are harvested any time after the head has become fairly firm. Heads from fall maturing varieties can be harvested and stored for several months at 40°F and high humidity.

Cabbage which is planted early for summer harvest will produce a second crop of small heads. The center head is cut, leaving as many leaves on the remaining plant as possible. Small heads will develop on the stem near the base of the leaves. These heads are quite edible and should also be picked when fairly firm (Minges 1977).

Common Problems.—The heads of early varieties frequently split in warm weather. This is caused by too much water moving into the mature head. To reduce this problem, cabbage should either not receive water once the head is mature or else the roots of the plant should be pruned (Doty 1973). To prune the roots, the plant can be twisted to break some of the roots or the roots can be cut with a shovel or knife.

There are several major diseases of cabbage. Fusarium wilt, commonly referred to as yellows, is a disease found in the upper south and the north. The lower leaves become yellow and turn brown. In areas where the disease is a problem, yellows resistant varieties should be grown.

Black rot and black leg are diseases spread by diseased seeds, transplants or by insects. Black rot causes yellowing of the leaves and blackening of the veins. Black leg causes dark sunken areas on the stem of young plants. The control is to use disease free transplants and to purchase hot water treated seed. Soaking the seed in water at 112°F for 27 minutes will destroy the organisms. Black rot resistant varieties should be grown if this disease is a problem. Once it infects the garden, no members of the cabbage family (cauliflower, broccoli, cabbage and others) should be grown on the area for three years. Crop rotation, destroying (not composting) diseased plants and insect control is recommended to help in disease control.

Club root attacks the roots of plants of the cabbage family. This causes the roots to become club-like in appearance. Once the fungus is established, it lives in the soil for 15 years or more. The disease is transmitted by diseased plants and infected soil.

The major insects of the cabbage family are cabbage worms of various types. The adults are grey, brown or white moths. The adult commonly seen is a white moth hovering over the plants in the garden. The worms are light green or dark green and can be controlled with chemical or biological control agents.

The cabbage aphid is a problem is some areas. The aphid has a waxy covering and a small amount of detergent is usually needed with the chemical or botanical insecticide for control. These aphids need to be controlled before the heads begin to form and serious damage has occurred.

CARROTS

Carrots (*Daucus carota*) are natives to the Mediterranean area. The wild carrot had a thin, tough root and roots resembling present day varieties were developed in France. Carrots were well established as a food in Europe by the 13th century. They were brought to America by the early settlers where they became a popular food among the Indians.

Plant Characteristics.—Carrot is a biennial that is grown for its root. A

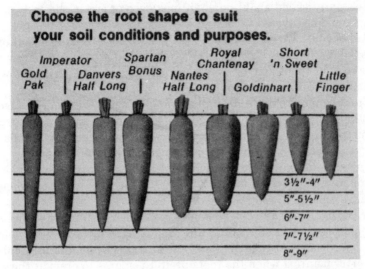

Choose the root shape to suit your soil conditions and purposes.

Imperator	Spartan	Royal	Short
Gold Pak	Danvers Bonus	Chantenay	'n Sweet
	Half Long	Nantes	Goldinhart	Little Finger
		Half Long		

3½"-4"
5"-5½"
6"-7"
7"-7½"
8"-9"

Courtesy of W. Atlee Burpee Co.

FIG. 6.9. CARROTS WITH SHORT ROOTS SHOULD BE GROWN IN SHALLOW SOILS

carrot root which is cut crosswise shows two distinct areas; an outer area and an inner area or core. High quality carrots are those with a large outer area compared to the inner one. The outer area contains more sugar and vitamins than the inner one.

Carrot produces a large root its first year of growth. During the second year, a large seedstalk two to three feet high is produced.

Culture.—Carrots are moderately frost tolerant. They are grown in the fall, winter and early spring in the south and Pacific southwest. In the north, they are grown from early spring to fall.

Carrots require a deep soil to produce a long root. If the garden contains a hardpan or if only the top three or four inches are worked, short rooted varieties should be grown. Long rooted varieties will be misshapen or forked if grown in poorly prepared soil. Carrots are easily grown in containers or in raised beds. A simple raised bed can be made from 2 x 8 lumber four feet or less wide. This bed is then filled with a container-type soil mixture containing fertilizer. Soil in this raised bed warms up quicker than the surrounding soil and carrots may be planted earlier in the spring. By being above the surrounding soil, the bed drains rapidly, preventing the accumulation of water from fall rains. This reduces root decay problems.

Unfinished compost or manure used as a fertilizer for carrots induces rough and branched roots. These materials should be well composted before being added to soil where carrots are grown.

Carrots are seeded about one-half inch deep or less in the early spring. They should be covered with sand, vermiculite, sawdust or fine peat moss instead of soil. Two to four seeds per inch are planted. About half of the seeds will germinate. Carrots can be planted in a bed, a wide row or in single rows one foot apart. Successive plantings about every three weeks will insure a continuous supply.

Carrots cannot tolerate deep planting or a dry seedbed. The seedbed must be kept moist during the germination period and this frequently means that the area is sprinkled lightly with water each day. Seeds may take two weeks to germinate. Gardeners often water the area after seeding and then cover the row with a clear plastic sheet. This will warm the soil and conserve moisture. The sheet should be removed when the seedlings emerge.

The top of the carrot root becomes green when exposed to sunlight. To prevent this, the plants should grow rapidly so that the leaves shade the roots. Gardeners frequently place additional soil around the roots 40 days after planting when the roots begin to enlarge to prevent the green areas from occurring.

Varieties need to be selected for the soil condition. All varieties grow well on deep sandy or loose soils. On heavy or impermeable soils, the short rooted varieties are best. Short rooted varietiés are easily grown in containers.

Short rooted varieties which are less than four inches long include French Forcing, Gold Nugget, Little Finger, Minipak, Oxheart, Sweet & Short and Tiny Sweet.

Short to medium rooted varieties, five to six inches long, includes Danners 126, Goldinhart, Gold King, Red Cored Chantenay and Sweetheart.

Medium rooted varieties, six to seven inches long, include Nantes Coreless, Nantes Half Long, Royal Chantenay, Scarlet Nantes, Target and Tuchon.

Medium long rooted varieties, seven to eight inches long, include Danvers Half Long, Hipak, Pioneer, Spartan Bonus and Trophy.

Long rooted varieties which are eight or more inches long include Gold Pak, Grenadier, Imperator, Spartan Delite, Spartan Fancy, Tendersweet and Waltham Hi-Color (resistant to carrot yellows).

Harvest.—Harvest of carrots can begin when they are pencil size to thin the plants in the row. The more space the remaining roots have, the larger they will become. Continued thinning and harvesting can continue for three to six months.

Carrots can be harvested, the tops removed and stored in a cool, moist place. They should not be washed until needed. However carrots are best left in the garden until a severe frost is expected. A heavy mulch can be placed over them and the roots harvested until the ground freezes. In areas where mild winters occur, they can be left in the ground until needed.

Common Problems.—The most frequent problem encountered is a poor stand. This can be solved by shallow planting, frequent light watering and preventing the soil from crusting during germination.

Carrots have few insect and disease pests in the garden. In the southeast, carrot yellows may be a problem. This is a virus disease carried by leafhoppers.

In the northeast and coast regions of the Pacific northwest, the carrot rust fly may cause damage. The larvae burrow into the roots. For control, carrots can be grown during cool weather and the plants should be grown to maturity as rapidly as possible. Carrots should be rotated within the garden area to reduce damage.

Courtesy of Harris Seeds

FIG. 6.10. THE LEAVES OF CAULIFLOWER ARE SOMETIMES TIED LOOSELY AROUND THE HEAD (BACKGROUND) TO PRODUCE A WHITER HEAD

CAULIFLOWER

Cauliflower (*Brassica oleracea* var. *italica*) is often called Heading Broccoli. It is a type of cabbage and originated with cabbage in southern Europe. Cauliflower is often called the aristocrat of the cabbage family due to its delicate growing requirements.

Plant Characteristics.—Cauliflower is grown for its white head, called the curd. The head is formed from shortened flower parts at the top of the plant.

Culture.—Cauliflower is a cool season crop which requires more attention than cabbage or broccoli, its close relatives. Too much heat prevents the cauliflower head from forming, and the plant is more sensitive to cold than cabbage. In the south and Pacific southwest, it is grown in the early spring, fall and winter. In the north, it can be grown as a spring or fall crop. At high elevations and a few other areas where the climate is favorable, it is grown during the summer as well.

Cauliflower must be grown rapidly through its entire life, from seedling to harvest. Anything which slows or delays its growth, such as insects, lack of water or excessive heat or cold will prevent development of the head.

To insure vigorous growth in the seedling stage, cauliflower is usually grown as a transplant for all planting dates. For spring crops, the plants are started indoors and are ready for use after 6-8 weeks. The plants are then transplanted to stand 15 inches apart in rows, which are 15-24 inches apart. They should be planted two weeks before the average frost free date. A starter fertilizer should be used when transplanting.

For fall plantings, transplants or direct seedings are used. For transplants, the seeds are planted one-fourth to one-half inch deep in a protected area of the garden. Seeds are seeded thick four weeks before they are to be used. In hot, dry weather the area is watered immediately and may require additional water to insure germination. Fall plantings are transplanted two feet apart in rows. For direct seeding, seeds are planted two weeks before the time cauliflower transplants are set in their permanent garden location. The fall crop must be planted so that it will form the head during cool weather. Direct seeded plants are thinned to two feet apart in rows 30 inches apart.

Cauliflower plants can be induced to produce the head prematurely. If the plants are large enough, and exposed to temperatures below 50°F for several weeks, a small head will form. This frequently occurs in areas with mild winters where the cauliflower is transplanted too early in the spring or too late in the fall. In the north, transplants are frequently set out in the garden too late and excessive heat causes the small head to form.

Adequate fertilizer and moisture are essential. The area should be fertilized before planting and the plants should receive additional nitrogen fertilizer when they are half grown. In dry weather, the plants should receive one to one and one-half inches of water each week.

When the head is two to three inches in size, it is often protected from sunlight. This keeps the head white, protects it from sunscald and frost injury and prevents the resulting off flavor. The top leaves are tied loosely over the head, being careful not to cramp the head. The heads are ready to harvest one to two weeks after covering. If the heads are produced under conditions where sunscald and frost injury are not a problem, slightly yellowish heads are produced. These heads are generally of a quality equal to the covered heads (Minges 1977).

Various types of Snowball varieties mature early and are most practical in the garden. Late maturing varieties take four to six months to mature and are difficult to grow in the garden.

Varieties which mature in about 60 days include Early Snowball, Perfected Snowball, Snowball, Snow Crown, Snow King, Snowball Y, Super Snowball and White Princess.

Self-Blanche is a variety reported to take 70 days to mature. However at hot temperatures it stops growing, unlike other varieties which produce a small head under these conditions. Thus Self-Blanche may mature fairly late. When grown under cool conditions, Self-Blanche produces leaves that curl naturally over the head. When grown at warm temperatures, tying may be necessary to produce a white head.

Royal Purple is often listed as a purple cauliflower. However it is a special type of broccoli and may be grown in place of cauliflower. See broccoli for its culture (page 167).

Harvest.—The heads are ready to use when they reach suitable size, usually six inches or more in diameter. Heads should be harvested before they are overmature and the flower parts separate. The heads are harvested by cutting the main stem and should be used soon after harvest.

Common Problems.—The most frequent problem is the production of small heads. This is induced by cold, heat, drought, plant damage, lack of fertility, hardening the transplants or other factors which interrupt the continuous growth of cauliflower.

Disease and insect problems are similar to cabbage (see page 172). Cabbage worms and black rot are most common. Cabbage worms can be controlled with a chemical or biological control agent. To help control disease, cauliflower should not be planted where members of the cabbage family (broccoli, cauliflower and others) grew the year before.

CELERIAC

Celeriac (*Apium graveolens* var. *rapaceum*) is also known as knob celery, celery root and turnip-rooted celery. It is a strain of celery which is native to most of Europe and parts of Asia. It originated as a form of celery which grows well in marsh areas.

Plant Characteristics.—Celeriac is a vegetable which somewhat resembles a beet. It is grown for its enlarged root which develops at the ground level. This root has a brown skin with white interior. It tastes similar to celery but is not stringy.

Culture.—Celeriac grows best on heavy, moist, well drained soils. It is less sensitive to heat and drought than celery but more sensitive than most garden vegetables. Celeriac requires a 120 day growing season and in most parts of the USA is grown from a transplant.

For transplants, the seed is planted indoors and grown for two months. It may require two or three weeks for the seed to germinate. When the plants are two to three inches high it is transplanted into the garden. It has good frost tolerance and may be planted early in the spring. Plants are spaced six inches apart in 18 inch rows. A starter fertilizer should be added to establish the plants.

In mild climates, celeriac may be direct seeded. It is planted one-fourth inch deep and the seed bed kept moist until the seedlings emerge. The plant and row spacing is similar to transplanted celeriac.

Celeriac requires adequate fertility and moisture. It should receive one to one and a half inches of water each week during dry periods. In low fertility areas, additional nitrogen should be added when the plant is half grown. If its growth is interrupted, small, poorly shaped roots are produced.

Few varieties are available but catalogues frequently list Alabaster, Giant Prague, Large Smooth Prague or Marble Ball.

Harvest.—Celeriac attains its full flavor after it has received a frost, but it may be harvested when the root has attained a diameter of two inches. When fully mature they will be two to five inches in diameter, depending on the growing region. In areas with mild winters, roots can be mulched with leaves or straw, left in the ground, and harvested as needed. Roots may also be removed and stored in moist sand in a cool place.

Common Problems.—Celeriac has few insect and disease problems in the garden.

CELERY

Celery (*Apium graveolens* var. *dulce*) is a native to marshy areas of Europe. It can be found growing wild from Scandinavia to Egypt, in parts of Asia and in the mountains of India. It was not grown for food until relatively recently, about 1600.

Plant Characteristics.—The first cultivated types were similar to the wild types. These plants had hollow, fibrous, strong flavored stalks. Modern varieties are of two types; the green types and the golden or self-blanch types. Celery is grown for its long fleshy edible petiole.

Courtesy of Harris Seeds

FIG. 6.11.   CELERY IS USUALLY GROWN BY EXPERIENCED GARDENERS

Culture.—Celery is a cool season crop and can be grown in most of the USA. It is grown during the winter in the Pacific southwest and the lower south. It can be grown as an early spring or late fall crop in the upper south and the north. Celery requires rich, moist soil and mild, even temperatures. Any condition which interrupts its growth causes problems. Celery requires 120 to 140 days to produce a crop. Because celery is slow growing and a delicate crop to produce, it is usually only grown by experienced gardeners who desire a challenge.

Celery is usually produced from transplants. At high temperature, the seed becomes dormant and will not germinate. Celery must be started four months before spring planting time. The seed requires 15-21 days to germinate, but soaking the seed overnight before planting reduces the time somewhat. The seeds are sown one-sixteenth of an inch deep in flats or peat pellets. They must be kept moist and at a temperature of 60°-70°F until the seedlings appear. The flat or peat pellets are covered with moist burlap.

Once the sprouts have appeared, the plants are moved into the sunlight at a slightly cooler temperature. Seedlings are transplanted or thinned to stand two inches apart and kept in full sunlight until danger of frost is past. The plants are then placed outdoors to harden them. If the plants receive several cold nights, they will produce seedstalks instead of the edible petioles.

Celery requires rich, moist, well drained, deeply prepared, mellow soil.

Large amounts of well composted material or peat can be added to the garden soil to simulate this condition. The transplants are spaced six to ten inches apart in rows which are two feet apart. If possible, they should be transplanted on a cool cloudy day to reduce water consumption. The plants should be watered after transplanting if the soil is at all dry.

Celery requires a continuous supply of fertilizer and water. It should be fertilized with a complete fertilizer every two or three weeks and plants should be watered thoroughly and often. When the plants become large, soil should be placed around the outside of the plants to keep them upright. If soil gets into the center of the plant, it will rot. About 120 days after transplanting, the plants will be ready for harvest.

Blanching to produce white petioles is usually not necessary with the self blanch varieties. However it can be done by excluding light from the petioles by wrapping them with paper or placing a drain tile around the plant. Blanching induces a change in petiole color but little change in flavor.

Varieties which are not easily induced to flower should be used for early spring planting such as Clean Cut, Golden Self Blanching or Summer Pascal. For late spring or summer planting where cold temperatures are not a problem, Florida 683, Fordhook, Giant Pascal, Tall Green Light or Utah 52-70 can be grown.

Harvest.—Celery is harvested by cutting the tap root below the ground. It is usually ready to harvest 90-120 days after transplanting. Overmature plants contain cracked and pithy petioles.

Celery may be left to overwinter and receive a cold treatment in mild areas. The plant then produces large amounts of celery seed which can be harvested and used in flavoring.

Common Problems.—A number of leaf eating worms and aphids attack celery. These can be controlled with a chemical or botanical insecticide. Blight and mildew can be controlled with a fungicide.

CHARD OR SWISS CHARD

Chard (*Beta vulgaris* var. *cicla*) or Swiss Chard is a type of beet which was developed for its large crisp leaves. It was first reported in the Mediterranean region and Canary Islands. Chard was popular as long ago as 350 B.C. It is a favorite crop of the people of Switzerland. Swiss settlers introduced it into the USA in 1806.

Plant Characteristics.—Chard is grown for its large green crinkly leaves and fleshy leafstalks. The leafstalks and mid-ribs are usually white but red varieties are available. Chard does not produce seedstalks during hot weather as do lettuce and spinach. Chard is frequently used in place of these vegetables during the summer.

Courtesy of Harris Seeds

FIG. 6.12. SWISS CHARD GROWS WELL DURING HOT WEATHER

Culture.—Chard is grown similar to beets. Seeds are planted in the fall to spring in the south and Pacific southwest. In other areas it is planted from early spring to midsummer.

Chard grows best in rich mellow soil. Seeds are planted one-half inch deep, one to two inches apart in rows about 18 inches apart. Plants emerge in 8-10 days. Each seedball of chard contains one to six seeds and the plants will need to be thinned until they are 12 inches apart. For rapid and continuous growth, additional nitrogen fertilizer can be applied about a month after planting.

Popular white ribbed varieties include Fordhook Giant, Large White Rib, Lucullus and Perpetual. Red ribbed varieties include Burgundy, Rhubarb Chard and Ruby.

Harvest.—The small chard plants can be harvested when the row is thinned and used as greens. Large leaves and stems are harvestable 50-60 days after planting. The outer leaves are cut off an inch above the ground with a sharp knife, while they are still young and tender. Care should be taken not to injure young leaves or the center bud. Leaves should be harvested continuously to stimulate the production of young new leaves from the center bud. Just before the first hard freeze the entire plant may be dug up, placed in a pail and stored in a cool place. Plants are placed upright with roots still containing some soil. They should be watered lightly to prevent wilting. The leaves can then be harvested into the winter months.

Common Problems.—In the garden, chard is generally free of insect and disease problems. Occasionally cabbage worms, aphids, beet leaf miner and flea beetle are a problem. Worms may be hand picked, and on smooth leaved varieties, the aphids can be washed off with a spray of water from the garden hose. Various chemical, botanical or biological control agents may also be used. In some warm climates, curly top virus disease causes severe damage. This can be avoided by planting in late winter or early spring.

Courtesy of Milo Burnham

FIG. 6.13. CHAYOTE IS GROWN IN THE WARM AREAS OF THE SOUTH

CHAYOTE

Chayote (*Sechium edule*) is also known as mirliton and vegetable pear. It is indigenous to Central America and the West Indies. It was grown by the Aztecs before the Spanish conquest.

Plant Characterstics.—Chayote is a perennial vine that bears large fruit. The common variety produces light green, pear shaped fruit. The fruit is often used as a substitute for summer squash and is related to pumpkins, squash and gourds. Similar to these plants, chayote produces separate male and female flowers on the same plant.

Culture.—Chayote can be grown in the mild winter regions of the south Atlantic and Gulf Coast states and in parts of California. In the southern USA it is grown usually as an annual as freezing kills the plant. Heavy mulching will protect the plant roots so the plant will sprout and grow from the roots the following spring. It cannot be grown in the north due to the long daylengths which delay flowering until fall.

Chayote produces one seed per fruit and the entire fruit is planted when the soil is warm and all danger of frost is past. The fruit is placed, stem end up, on a slant in the soil. The plant grows rapidly in well drained soil rich in organic matter. Plants should be about 10 feet apart but one plant is usually sufficient as it produces 30-35 fruits. Chayote grows best with little nitrogen but requires potassium. Excess nitrogen stimulates vine growth but few fruits are produced.

A large vigorous vine is produced which requires some type of trellis for support. The vine requires large amounts of water during dry periods.

Chayote seed is seldom sold as the whole fruit is planted. It is usually available only in areas where it is grown. To save the fruit for planting, the fruit should mature on the vine but be harvested before the seed sprouts. Individual fruits are wrapped in newspaper and stored in a cool ventilated area.

Harvest.—Fruits are harvested about 30 days after the flowers are pollinated. Fruits are from four to six inches long and may weigh two pounds.

Common Problems.—Insect and disease problems are similar to pumpkin and squash. Common insect pests are cucumber beetle, squash bug and squash vine borer. Mildew is the common disease. Pests are controlled with various chemical and botanical pesticides.

CHICORY, AND FRENCH ENDIVE

Chicory (*Cichorium intybus*) is also known as Belgium Endive, French Endive and Witloof Chicory. It is a close relative of endive and is native to Europe and Asia. The leaves from plants growing in the wild were used as a salad vegetable since time immemorial. It was first listed as a cultivated vegetable in the thirteenth century.

Chicory has several uses. The leaves can be used for greens or a salad vegetable. The root can be used as a coffee adulterant. The root can also be harvested and forced to produce new shoots during the winter, and is then usually known as French Endive.

Culture.—Chicory grows best in rich, deep loam soil without too much organic matter. The seeds are sown one-fourth to one-half inch deep with 18 inches between rows.

For Greens.—For greens, seeds are planted in the spring as early as the soil can be worked. Successive plantings can be made every several weeks for continuous salad greens. The plants are thinned to stand eight inches apart in the row. Leaves will be curled, somewhat bitter and resemble dandelion leaves. They are ready for harvest 60 days after planting when they are six to eight inches long. To reduce the bitter taste and the green color somewhat, the leaves are sometimes gathered and tied loosely together at the top when 10 inches long. This process is called blanching. Leaves should be dry before tying to prevent leaf rots. The blanching process requires two or three weeks.

Varieties commonly listed for use as a salad green are Catalogna, Radichetta, San Pasquale and Sugarhat. Most varieties withstand the summer heat and light frost. If seedstalks are produced, they are tender and can be eaten also.

For Coffee Adulterant.—To grow the plants for roots, the seeds are planted at the time of the average date of the last frost in the spring. If seedstalks are produced, it reduces the size of the root. Plants are otherwise grown similar to greens; planted one-half inch deep and thinned to eight inches apart in rows which are 18 inches apart. Plants will be larger than those used for greens and will develop a large root 10 inches long. Some leaves may be harvested for greens during the summer. About 120 days after seeding the roots are mature. They should be dug before frost. Roots are then cleaned, peeled, cubed and roasted. After roasting they are ground for a coffee substitute.

Varieties, include Brunswick, Large-Rooted Madgeburg and Zealand.

For French Endive.—Most gardeners who grow chicory will use it for French Endive. Seeds are planted in warm soil one-fourth to one-half inch deep. If seeds are planted too early, the plants will be exposed to cold temperatures and produce a flower stalk. Such plants cannot be used to produce French Endive. Plants are thinned to stand four or five inches apart in rows 18 inches apart.

Roots are harvested before freezing weather in the fall about 110 days after seeding. Roots are washed and all the leaves are removed except the single center crown bud on top. If this bud is not easily identified, all the leaves may be cut off two inches from the top of the root. Roots are covered and stored in a cool, moist, frost free area.

Roots vary considerably in size. Large roots produce large heads but these are usually composed of several small divisions and are not of high quality. Medium sized roots, one to two inches in diameter produce the best French Endive.

During the winter and early spring, the roots are removed from storage and the root tip cut off so that all the roots are six to eight inches long. Roots are then placed in a box. Sand, fine soil or sawdust is added around the roots and the roots are covered to a depth of six to eight inches. This covering excludes light and forces the heads to be compact. The box is watered thoroughly and placed at a temperature of 60°F. One additional watering may be required. In three to four weeks, the tips of the heads will begin to break through the surface. The heads are harvested by cutting them from the root. Heads are creamy yellow with tightly folded leaves which have not yet uncurled. Additional boxes of chicory roots can be made up every three weeks for successive harvests.

The variety commonly listed is Witloof Chicory or French Endive.

CHINESE CABBAGE

Chinese cabbage is also known as celery cabbage. Two types are available: leafy type (*Brassica chinensis*) and a heading type (*Brassica pekinensis*). Both types probably originated in China where they have been used since the fifth century. Chinese cabbage is more closely related to mustard than cabbage or celery.

Plant Characteristics.—Chinese cabbage is an annual which grows 10-20 inches tall. The leafy type has thin, long, dark green leaves which resemble Swiss chard in growth habit. The heading type resembles Cos lettuce but produces a larger, more elongated, and compact head.

Culture.—Chinese cabbage is a hardy, cool weather crop. It is grown in the south as a winter crop and as a summer-planted fall crop in the north. If the plants are grown under long days, they produce seedstalks and spring plantings of Chinese cabbage are frequently unsuccessful.

Chinese cabbage requires a rich, well drained, moist soil. Seeds are planted one-fourth to one-half inch deep in rows 18-30 inches apart. Plants should be thinned to 8-15 inches apart. If planted during dry, summer conditions, additional water is required to establish the plants. It should be seeded 45 days before the first frost for leafy types and 75-85 days before frost for heading types. Chinese cabbage responds to nitrogen fertilizer and its growth will be stimulated by adding nitrogen when it is half grown.

Varieties of leafy types are Crispy Choy and Pac Choy. Varieties of heading types are Burpee Hybrid, Early Hybrid G, Michihli, and Wongbok. The latter variety is the one most commonly sold as fresh produce in food stores.

Harvest.—The heads are harvested by cutting the entire head off at the ground line. They should be harvested before hard freezing weather occurs. The leaves are crisp and the inner leaves are faintly green. It can be used as a substitute for lettuce and celery.

Common Problems.—Chinese cabbage has few pest problems in the garden. Aphids, cabbage worms, cutworms and flea beetles are a problem occasionally. These can be controlled with chemical, botanical or biological control agents.

COLLARDS

Collard (*Brassica oleracea* var. *acephala*) is sometimes called nonheading cabbage. It originated in the British Isles and Western Europe where it has been used for food for more than 4,000 years. The present cultivated form has changed little in the past 2,000 years. Collard was brought to America by early settlers and it was a common garden vegetable by 1670.

Plant Characteristics.—Collard is a nonheading type of cabbage. It forms a large rosette of blue-green leaves. Plants grow two to four feet in height.

Culture.—Collard is a hardy, cool season vegetable. It withstands summer heat and short periods of cold as low as 10°F. It is grown throughout the entire year in the south, and as a spring and fall crop in the north.

Collard may be transplanted or seeded. It can be seeded four to six weeks before the last spring frost for summer harvest; or in midsummer for fall harvest; or in mild climates, in the fall for winter harvest. Seeds are planted one-fourth inch deep, one inch apart in rows 30 inches apart. They are later thinned to 6-18 inches apart depending upon the type of harvest.

The plants require one to one and one half inches of water each week and respond to nitrogen fertilizer. They should be sidedressed with nitrogen one month after planting.

Common varieties are Georgia (also called Creole or Southern), Green Glaze, Louisiana Sweet, Morris Heading, and Vates.

Harvest.—Collards may be harvested by three methods. 1) The entire young plant may be cut off at ground level and used; 2) The entire mature plant may be cut off at ground level when the plant is six to ten inches high and used; or 3) small plants can be harvested to thin the row and used. The remaining plants are allowed to mature and the bottom leaves harvested beginning when the plants are 10-12 inches high. The bud will produce more leaves and the bottom leaves can be harvested continuously throughout the growing season. Successive plantings are not required for a continuous supply. The last harvest procedure produces a plant with a bare stalk containing a group of young succulent leaves at the top. These plants may require staking to keep them from falling over.

Frost improves the mild cabbage-like flavor.

Common Problems.—The common insect and disease problems are similar to cabbage. Cabbage worms, aphids and harlequin bugs are the common insects. Downy mildew and black leg diseases may also be a problem. See cabbage (page 172).

CORN, POP

Popcorn (*Zea mays*), like sweet corn, originated in North America and is a mutation of field corn. Archaeological evidence has shown (Anderson 1954) that popcorn was among the most primitive types of corn used for food and was used in 5,000 B.C.

Plant Characteristics.—Popcorn has very hard starch in the kernels. This starch explodes when heated, producing fluffy white popcorn.

The type used by the Indians of North America was called "rice corn" (Anderson 1954). These kernels are sharply pointed and are produced on a relatively small plant. The rounded or "pearl" kernels are produced on larger plants of more recent origin.

Culture.—Popcorn can be grown for its popping qualities or as an ornamental. It can be grown wherever sweet corn is grown, but early maturing varieties must be selected in northern areas.

Popcorn is planted about one inch deep, four seeds per foot, in rows 30 inches apart. Seeds are planted when the soil temperatures have warmed to 50°F or above. When the plants are established, they are thinned to stand six inches apart. Popcorn should be planted in three or four short rows to insure good pollination, and not in one long row. If popcorn is planted near field corn or sweet corn, it will be pollinated by these corns. This does not affect popping quality. Seeds from these cross-pollinated plants should not be saved and planted the next year as the popcorn produced seldom pops.

Popcorn, like sweet corn requires adequate fertility and moisture (See page 189 for culture requirements).

Varieties which produce small ears early and are sometimes used for ornamental purposes include Black Jewel (black), Fireside (red), Lady Finger, and Strawberry (red). Early season white and yellow varieties include Burpee's Peppy (yellow hulless), Faribo (white), Minhybrid (white hulless), and Japanese Hulless (white). Late season varieties produce large ears and include Creme Puff Hybrid (yellow), Golden Hybrid (yellow), and South American Mushroom Hybrid (yellow-orange).

Harvest.—Many varieties of popcorn produce two or three ears per plant, particularly the varieties which produce small ears.

The kernels should mature on the plant before frost to about 20% moisture. Unless the kernels contain 35% moisture, they will not be damaged by a light frost. Freezing does not damage kernels with less than 20% moisture.

The ears should be harvested, the husks removed, and the ears stored an additional three weeks in a sheltered dry place outdoors. The kernels will dry naturally to about 13% moisture which is ideal for popping. The kernels can be removed from the cobs with a moderately aggressive twisting motion. The kernels are then stored in air tight, sealed containers for later use. When popped, the corn should expand 20-40 times its original volume.

Common Problems.—Popcorn has many of the same pest problems as sweet corn.

Popcorn frequently fails to pop. If the popcorn has been stored in a heated area in an open container it will dry to about 7% moisture. This is too low for good popping. The moisture content can be increased to about two percentage points by adding a small amount of water to the dry popcorn. One tablespoon of water is added to one quart of popcorn, the container sealed, shaken, and allowed to absorb the water for a week.

CORN, SWEET

The word "corn" is applied to oats, wheat, barley or rye in Europe. In the Americas, it refers to Indian corn or maize. Corn was grown in North America before 2000 B.C. The type of corn known as sweet corn (*Zea mays* var. *saccharata*) is believed to be a mutation of field or dent corn. It was grown by the Indians and first collected and described by settlers in about 1780. By 1900 over 63 varieties were described. Today over 2000 varieties and hybrids are available.

Plant Characteristics.—Sweet corn is an annual grass plant. It differs from all other types of corn. Sweet corn produces and retains large amounts of sugar in the kernels, hence its name "sweet." The skin of the kernels is thinner, making them tender. The seed is wrinkled when dried and the plant has a tendency to produce "suckers" or additional shoots at the base of the plants.

The male part of the corn plant is the tassel and the female part is the ear. The ear is pollinated by pollen blown by the wind and sweet corn ears can be pollinated by other types of corn making them less sweet.

Some newer sweet corn hybrids (extra-sweet varieties) produce kernels that contain more sugar, and convert sugar to starch less rapidly, than standard varieties. These new hybrids are sweeter initially and remain sweeter for a longer period of time. They also contain less water-soluble polysaccharides than standard corn, and this is what gives sweet corn a

Courtesy of Harris Seeds

FIG. 6.14. INDIAN ORNAMENTAL CORN IS FREQUENTLY
GROWN FOR A FALL DECORATION

creamy texture. This lack of creaminess is not noticeable if sweet corn is eaten fresh but it reduces the quality of canned or frozen sweet corn.

Culture.—Sweet corn is a warm season crop. It is easily killed by frost and requires a soil temperature above 50°F for the seed to germinate. It can be grown successfully in all states. In the south, sweet corn is grown from early spring until fall. In the north and northeast, it is grown from late spring until fall. In south Florida, Texas and some parts of the southwest, it is grown in the fall, winter and spring. In the Pacific northwest, an early maturing variety will need to be grown during the summer.

Sweet corn requires a lot of space and sunlight and is frequently grown only in larger gardens. It is wind pollinated and should be planted in three or four short rows rather than a single row. If the prevailing wind is blowing across, rather than down this single row, the pollen will not land on the silks and few kernels will develop on the ear. Different types of corn should not be planted together. Pollen from field corn or popcorn will land on the silks of sweet corn, causing the kernels to be less sweet. The extra sweet and standard varieties should not be planted at the same time. The pollen will intermingle and the quality of sweet corn produced by both varieties will be reduced. Cross-pollination between standard yellow and white varieties will change the colors of the kernels produced but not affect the flavor or quality. Different types of corn should be separated by planting 400 yards apart in distance or one month apart in time.

Seeds are planted about one inch deep in moist soils and one to two inches deep in light sandy soils after the soil has warmed to 50°F or above. Seeds of many of the extra sweet varieties do not germinate in cool, wet soil, and should be planted when the soil is 65°F or above. Seeds should be planted about five or six inches apart in rows 30-36 inches apart. Once the plants are well established, they should be thinned to stand 10-16 inches apart. The greatest reduction in quality and ear size in gardens is caused by lack of thinning or planting the seeds too close together.

To conserve space, sweet corn is often planted next to vine crops, such as cucumber, pumpkins and muskmelons. The vines can be trained to grow between the corn plants and utilize this space.

Plant nutrients are especially important for growing sweet corn. Once the plant is stunted, it never fully recovers. Fertilizer is generally broadcast and worked into the soil before planting. Additional amounts are applied when the plant is half grown. The fertilizer is then applied three inches to the side of the row and worked into the soil about four inches.

On light, sandy soils, such as found in the great plains and near the Atlantic and Gulf coasts, 20 pounds of 10-10-10 fertilizer or equivalent is applied per 1,000 square feet over the entire area before planting. An additional one-half pound of actual nitrogen per 100 feet of row is added when the plants have produced six to eight leaves.

On soils of average fertility, such as found in the northeast, 15 pounds of 5-10-5 fertilizer or equivalent is added before planting. An additional three pounds per 100 feet of row of the same fertilizer is added beside the row at planting.

On fertile soils, such as the midwest, some western valleys, and the Pacific northwest, the fertilizer is added at planting time. About three pounds per 100 feet of row of 5-10-5 is applied beside the row.

Sweet corn needs a continuous supply of moisture. After the tassels are produced, sweet corn requires one to one and one-half inches of water each week. This insures pollination and production of the ear.

Successive plantings can be made to provide a continuous supply of sweet corn. The number of days to maturity is not a good index. Sweet corn responds to warm temperature, and the warmer it is, the faster sweet corn grows and matures (up to 100°F). Successive plantings are made when plants in the previous planting contain three or four leaves. An early variety and a full season variety may be planted at the same planting date to provide for a longer harvest.

The number of suckers a sweet corn plant produces depends upon the variety. These should not be removed. Their removal does not increase yields, and it may actually reduce yields.

Sweet corn varieties are affected by the length of day. Early maturing varieties grown in the north are adapted to long, cool summer days. These varieties do not grow well in the south. Varieties adapted for the south respond to short summer days. If these are planted in the north, these southern varieties will not flower (produce the tassel and ear) until short days occur in the fall. These plants may become 10 feet tall or more and are sometimes grown as a novelty. However, they seldom produce a satisfactory ear before they are killed by frost.

Courtesy of Harris Seeds

FIG. 6.15. SPRING GOLD SWEET CORN

There are now over 2000 sweet corn varieties. These include early, full season and late varieties; yellow, white and bi-color; and standard sugar and extra sweet types. There is a wide assortment for the gardener to chose from. Contact the State Agricultural Experiment Station in your area (See Appendix for address) for the varieties adapted to that location.

Harvest.—Each sweet corn plant should produce at least one large ear. Many varieties produce a smaller second ear which develops later. The ears should be harvested at prime maturity. This occurs 17-24 days after the silk has emerged from the ear. When grown under warm days and nights, prime maturity occurs 17-18 days after silking. If grown during cool weather, prime maturity may occur 22-24 days after silking.

Sweet corn of prime maturity is in the milk stage. The silks are brown and the ear has enlarged to fill the husk tightly to the tip. The kernels are plump, soft, tender and filled with a milky juice. Prime quality lasts only four or five days. It is not a good practice to remove part of the husk to determine if the ear is at prime maturity. Birds and insects then frequently attack the kernels. Placing a paper bag tightly over these disturbed ears usually prevents damage however.

Sweet corn is removed from the plant by snapping the ear from the stalk. The ear is bent downward, twisted to one side and pulled off; all in one quick movement.

Harvested ears should be eaten as soon as possible after harvest. The sugar content rapidly declines. The ears may be kept in a refrigerator for two or three days with only a small loss of quality.

Common Problems.—Diseases are usually not a serious problem in gardens. Corn smut is sometimes prevalent, particularly on white colored varieties. The smut is not poisonous and is characterized by large, fleshy galls on the stalks, tassel or ears. Smut can be controlled by avoiding injury to the plants, avoiding areas where smut occurred the year before and by removing and destroying the smut. The smut should be removed before the galls break open and release new spores to infect other plants. They should be destroyed and not left in the garden area.

Root rot frequently occurs on seedlings planted on cool moist soil. Most sweet corn seeds sold commercially have been treated with a mild fungicide to prevent this problem.

Stewart's bacterial wilt is sometimes a problem in the midsouth. Early infected plants wilt and die. Later infected plants are stunted and contain yellow streaks on the leaves. The disease is spread by the corn flea beetle and is more of a problem after mild winters have occurred. Most newly developed full season sweet corn varieties are resistant to Stewart's wilt.

Insects which attack sweet corn during its early growth include southern corn rootworm, cutworm, white grub, wireworm and flea beetle. See the section on Pest Control for control measures if these are a problem in the garden, page 124.

Once the sweet corn plant is established, it can withstand considerable insect damage. Corn borer damage is usually ignored in the garden as the crop is harvested before severe damage occurs.

Corn earworms can be a problem. Early plantings in the north are often not infested, but later plantings are usually affected. Corn earworm control must be timely. The corn earworm moth lays eggs on the silk. These eggs hatch in 24 to 48 hours and the small caterpillars move down the silk into the ear where they feed on the tip. Once inside, they cannot be controlled. Insecticides must be applied while the caterpillar is still on the silk and that means every two or three days. Thus most gardeners ignore the problem and just remove the damaged ear tip when the sweet corn is husked. Tightening the end of the husk around the ear to restrict the caterpillars entry is sometimes effective. Placing a rubber band around the tip after the silk has appeared may reduce damage.

CRESS

Cress is a native to Europe where it has been grown for over 2000 years. Cress is now extensively naturalized in many parts of the world and it was one of the first vegetables brought to America. Three major types can be grown as a vegetable.

Garden Cress or Pepper Grass.—Garden Cress (*Lepidium sativum*) or pepper grass is a hardy, cool season annual. It can be grown from as soon as the ground can be worked in spring, to fall. In the south and Pacific southwest it can also be grown during the winter. It is easily grown indoors during the winter.

Seeds are sown one-fourth inch deep, one inch apart in rows one foot apart. Plants are not thinned. At 65-70°F, they germinate in four to seven days and the leaves can be harvested in 10-14 days after planting. Successive plantings every few weeks must be made for a continuous supply. Leaves are harvested when they are three to five inches long. During hot weather the plants tend to produce seedstalks quickly and the leaves are reduced in quality.

Varieties available include Curleycress, Curled, Extra Fine Curled, Fine Curled, and Salad Cress.

Upland or Winter Cress.—Upland cress (*Barbarea verna*) is also called winter cress, spring cress and Belle Isle cress. It is a hardy biennial but grown as an annual or winter perennial.

Seeds are planted one-fourth inch deep in rows one foot apart. After the plants are established, they are thinned to stand four inches apart. They can be planted as soon as the soil can be worked in the spring (hence the name spring cress) or in mild climates, they can be planted in the late summer and grown through the winter (hence winter cress). The plants grow about five inches high and a foot across and can be harvested in 50 days. Plants require moist soil and can withstand fall frosts. It is frequently only listed in garden catalogs as upland cress or winter cress.

Watercress.—Watercress (*Rorippa nasturtium* var. *aquaticm*) is a cool season semiaquatic perennial widely distributed in Europe and western Asia. It grows naturally in clear, cold, shallow, slow moving streams; either as a floating plant or rooted to the bottom.

To grow high quality watercress requires a considerable effort. It can be grown in a container (with drainage holes) filled with potting mix. Seeds are covered with one-sixteenth of an inch of fine sand and misted. Cuttings of watercress purchased for a salad may also be used. Cuttings are placed in the container and rooted. The container must be kept moist and it should be placed in a tub of water and grown in partial shade. One plant per eight inch pot is grown.

When the plants have grown about six inches high, the leading shoot is pinched off to encourage branching. Flowers should not be permitted to form. When buds are observed, the plant is cut back.

It requires about 60-70 days for the plants to reach harvest maturity from seeds. Cuttings require a little less time. Plants are harvested by cutting about six inches of the leading shoots and side shoots.

Garden catalogues usually only list water cress instead of varieties.

Courtesy of Harris Seeds

FIG. 6.16. CUCUMBERS READY TO PICK FOR USE AS PICKLES

CUCUMBER AND GHERKIN

Cucumber (*Cucumis sativus*) and gherkin (*Cucumis anguria*) are natives of Asia and Africa where they have been grown for food for at least 3,000 years. They were introduced into China in 100 B.C. and into France in the ninth century. They were grown by the Indians before Columbus and other additional varieties were introduced by the early settlers.

The gherkin is well established in tropical central and south America and grown widely in the West Indies. The West Indian gherkin is also called burr cucumber.

Plant Characteristics.—The cucumber and gherkin plants are similar. They are vine plants with large leaves and long petioles. Some varieties produce short vines for growing in a small garden or containers. The vine contains separate male and female flowers with the first flowers produced being males. A tiny cucumber develops at the base of the female flowers and these produce the edible fruit.

Gynoecious cucumbers are special hybrids which have all female flowers. These plants usually produce fruit earlier than other varieties and are usually sold with a few seeds of a standard variety for use as a pollinator.

Special types are sold for production of fruits in greenhouses. These types are long, narrow, seedless, English cucumbers frequently seen in the produce market. These types are usually parthenocarpic; that is they produce fruit without pollination. However, in the garden, these flowers will cross with other cucumbers and produce fruits with seeds.

Cucumbers do not cross pollinate with muskmelons or watermelons. The flavor of the fruit is unaffected by pollen from these plants.

Cucumber fruit is usually green and warted. However, white and yellow varieties and smooth skinned, green varieties are available. Gherkin fruit is generally round, more warted than cucumbers and only one to three inches long.

Culture.—Cucumbers are a warm weather vegetable and are very sensitive to cold. They can be grown during the winter only in a few extreme southern locations.

Cucumbers grow best in a fertile mellow soil with large amounts of compost. The compost should not be made from cucumbers, pumpkins, melons or squash as these plants have similar disease problems.

Fertilizer should be added before planting and again when the plants begin to produce vines.

Cucumbers love warm soil and the use of plastic mulches is common. They may be started as transplants (see pages 45 and 46), particularly in the Pacific northwest and the Rocky Mountain states. In warm areas they are planted directly in the garden. Temperatures should be 60-75°F when the plants or seeds are planted.

Seeds are planted one inch deep in rows three or four feet apart. They may be planted and thinned to stand 12 inches apart as single plants, or three plants together in a hill every two or three feet.

Cucumber vines and fruit are light weight and they are easily trained onto a trellis, fence, or cage similar to that used to control tomato fruit rots (see page 137). When vines of the long fruited varieties are supported, the fruits hang free and are long and straight. When space is limited, or the plants are grown in containers, the various small vining varieties may be used.

Cucumbers are relatively shallow rooted and require irrigation in most parts of the country. If alternate methods of irrigation are available, sprinkler irrigation is not recommended. Moisture on the leaves from rain, dew or irrigation encourages diseases. If the plant does not receive adequate water, it stops growing but will resume growth when water is applied.

Cucumbers are generally used for slicing and pickling. The pickling varieties produce smaller fruits but all varieties may be used for both purposes. There are numerous varieties available.

Standard varieties commonly used for slicing include Burpee Hybrid (resistant to mildew, mosaic); Challenger Hybrid (resistant to mildew, mosaic); Lemon (produces small yellow fruit); Marketer; Marketmore 70 (resistant to mosaic, scab); Pacer (resistant to scab, mosaic); Poinsett (resistant to mildew, anthracnose, leaf spot-popular in the south); Saticoy (resistant to mosaic); Spartan Valor (resistant to mosaic, scab, mildew); and Triumph (resistant to mildew, mosaic).

Standard varieties commonly used for pickles include Liberty Hybrid (resistant to most diseases); Spartan Dawn Hybrid (resistant to mosaic, scab); and SMR 18 (resistant to mosaic, scab).

Gynoecious varieties used for slicing include Gemini (resistant to anthracnose, mildew, scab, mosaic) and Victory Hybrid (tolerant to mildew, scab, mosaic, leaf spot).

Gynoecious varieties used for pickles include Greenpak (resistant to scab, mosaic) and Pennant (resistant to scab, mosaic).

Burpless cucumbers produce long fruits with skin which is tender and free of bitterness. Varieties include Burpless Hybrid, Green Knight Hybrid and Sweet Slice Hybrid (resistant to mildew, mosaic, scab).

Small vined varieties for use in small gardens or containers include Little Minnie (24 inch vines); Tiny Dill; Patio Pik (24 inch vines-tolerant to mildew); Peppi Hybrid (tolerant to mildew, mosaic, scab); Pot Luck (18 inch vines-tolerant to mosaic) and Spacemaster (requires one third the space of standard-tolerant to mosaic).

Greenhouse varieties include Fertila (can be grown outdoors) and La Reine or the Queen (resistant to leaf spot, scab).

The gherkin most commonly listed in garden catalogues is West India Gherkin.

White Wonder is a white fruited cucumber. Armenian is a variety which produces light green, smooth skinned fruit with deep ridges.

Harvest.—Cucumbers are usually harvested immature before the seeds become hard. They are of highest quality when dark green, firm and crisp. The large burpless and greenhouse types should be about one and a half inches in diameter and less than 10 inches long. To force the plant to produce continuously, fruits should be picked every other day, even if the fruit is not needed.

Common Problems.—Cucumbers are susceptible to a number of diseases. Resistant or tolerant varieties should be used wherever these diseases are likely to be a problem. Do not handle or harvest the plants when they are damp to help prevent spread of disease.

Anthracnose.—This disease is particularly a problem in the southeast. It attacks cucumbers, muskmelons and watermelons. Small, round, water-soaked spots appear on the fruits. Infected leaves have a scorched appearance. To control, plant resistant varieties and treated seed. Remove all vines from the garden at the end of the growing season and rotate the crops in the garden.

Mildew.—Downy mildew is a fungus which grows rapidly under warm, moist conditions. It is particularly a problem in the Atlantic and Gulf states. Low humidity, high temperatures and lack of water on the leaves prevent its growth.

Symptoms appear on leaves as small, yellow spots with irregular edges. The tissue in the middle of each spot dies and spots appear in large numbers. The leaves die and curl upward. The problem develops about the time the plants begin to set fruit. Use resistant varieties if possible.

Powdery mildew is a problem with cucumbers, muskmelons and pumpkins but not watermelon. Small white spots develop on the underside of older leaves. The leaves then become covered with a white mold growth. The leaves die and leave fruit exposed to sunlight to become sunburned. In muskmelon, the fruit ripens prematurely and are of poor quality. This fungus requires high temperature and a lot of sun. Rain and low sunlight reduce its growth.

Mosaic.—This disease is caused by a virus. Watermelon mosaic is not seed borne and is carried by aphids from various ornamental plants around the home. Squash mosaic is seed borne and carried by cucumber beetles. Symptoms appear as light-green mottling of the leaves. The young leaves and flowers are malformed and small. The leaves are dwarfed and the vines fail to grow. Poor quality fruit is produced. Late infections are usually mild and do little damage. Control aphids, cucumber beetles and grow resistant varieties.

Scab.—Scab fungus attacks the fruit and is particularly a problem with cucumber. Sunken, dark brown spots, irregular in shape appear. A gummy material exudes from these spots. It is most serious in the northern states. Using resistant varieties and destroying vines after harvest usually controls this problem.

Aphids.—Aphids are a sucking insect on the underside of leaves (See pages 112, 128 and 132 for identification and control).

Cucumber Beetle.—Cucumber beetle spreads bacterial wilt. The eastern type has three black stripes down its wing covers. The western type has 12 black spots on yellow wing covers (see page 113). Bacterial wilt causes the plants to wilt and die. The beetles plug the water transporting system and when symptoms are noted it is usually too late for control of the wilt. Remove infected plants and see pages 128 and 132 for control of the beetle.

DANDELION

Dandelion (*Taraxacum officinale*) is a native to Europe and Asia and was brought to America by early settlers for use as greens and in salads. The plant is a perennial with jagged irregular dark green leaves.

Culture.—Dandelion is a hardy cool season plant which withstands freezing temperatures. It grows in any well drained soil in all parts of North America. Dandelion is a perennial and it should be planted to one side of the garden with the other perennial vegetables, such as rhubarb.

Seeds are planted one-fourth inch deep in spring in rows a foot apart. Plants are thinned to stand six to ten inches apart in the row. A good supply of fertilizer in the spring and moisture during dry periods is necessary for a quality product.

Wild plants may be used but the named varieties grow better and have a better flavor. Two such varieties are Improved Thick Leaf and Thick Leaf.

Harvest.—Leaves can be harvested in the fall by cutting a small piece of the root off with the leaves. The root will produce new leaves the next spring for next years harvest. Unharvested plants will produce a large amount of growth the next spring. These plants should be harvested in the spring before they produce flowers and the leaves become bitter.

The bitter taste may be reduced somewhat and the dandelion greens made to resemble endive. When the leaves are eight to ten inches long the outer leaves are gathered and tied together at the top, or a tarpaper collar placed over the plant to exclude light. The inner rosette of leaves become light green in color in about two weeks.

DASHEEN

Dasheen (*Colocasia esculenta*) is also known as taro and has been used as a food crop in Oriental countries for 2,000 years. It was brought into America from two separate continents. Some varieties were brought into the southern states from Africa with slaves who used it as food. Later, better varieties were introduced which originally came from China.

The dasheens look similar to and are easily confused with tanniers (Splittstoesser 1977). In southern Florida, tanniers are called cocoyam or malanga (*Xanthosoma caracu*) but are a different species from dasheen. They are all grown similarly however.

Plant Characteristics.—Dasheen is related to ornamental elephant's ear, jack-in-the pulpit, calla and caladium. The plant resembles elephant's ear but produces edible corms and tubers underground. Some tropical varieties grow well in wet areas and plants grow five feet tall.

Culture.—Dasheen requires a growing period of seven months under full sunlight. It is grown in the lowland coastal plains from South Carolina to Texas. In Hawaii, dasheen is grown to make poi.

Dasheen grows best in rich, loamy, well drained soil with ample moisture. Small tubers weighing two to five ounces are planted three inches deep, two feet apart in rows three to four feet apart. The tubers are planted about two weeks before the last frost occurs in the spring. Tubers may also be planted indoors and then transplanted into the garden after danger of frost is past.

Fertilizer should be applied before planting and again when the plants are two feet tall. Adequate moisture is required and mulching heavy will reduce water loss. Dasheen is shallow rooted and produces poor quality corms during drought followed by regrowth.

Varieties are seldom sold through garden catalogues. They are often available only in localities where the plant is grown.

Harvest.—The corms and tubers are harvested after seven months when the plant tops have died in the fall. They should be dug in dry weather to prevent injury to the corms. If the soil is well drained, the crop may be left in the ground and dug when needed. Each plant will normally have a large central corm surrounded by smaller tubers. Yields range from two to eight pounds and both corms and tubers are edible. The tubers should be stored at room temperature for several days to cure bruises and then at 45-50°F with good ventilation for long storage.

Young leaves which are just beginning to unroll can also be eaten. They are boiled 15 minutes with a teaspoon of baking soda to remove the calcium oxylate found in the leaves which is harmful to humans. This water is then discarded and the leaves boiled until tender in fresh water.

Common Problems.—Root knot nematode can be a major problem. Tubers free of nematodes should be planted.

The tubers rot if they are harvested when immature. Storage rots also occur if tubers are not stored at the correct temperature with good ventilation.

Courtesy of Harris Seeds

FIG. 6.17. EGGPLANT IS A WARM WEATHER PLANT

EGGPLANT

Eggplant (*Solanum melongena*) is probably a native of India where it grows wild. It was recorded as growing in China in the fifth century. Eggplant was introduced into Spain during the Moorish invasion where it spread throughout Europe. The Spanish explorers introduced purple and white varieties into America. The fruit of eggplants grown in the 16th century were small and were similar to the types now grown as an ornamental.

Culture.—Eggplant is grown in the late spring, summer and fall in most of the north and upper south. In the extreme south it can be grown in the winter. It grows poorly in many parts of the Pacific northwest.

Eggplant is a warm weather plant requiring 100-140 days from seeding to produce fruit. In most areas it is therefore grown as a transplant. Anything that stops its growth is detrimental to eggplant. See pages 45, 46 and 52 for growing transplants.

Eggplants should be fertilized before planting and grow best in well drained soil with ample organic matter. The plants should receive a starter fertilizer and be fertilized every six weeks over the season. If eggplant stops growing, inferior fruit are produced.

Plants are planted in the garden in direct sunlight two weeks after all danger of frost has passed. Eggplants grow best at 78°F day and 68°F night temperatures, and a common mistake is to set the plants out too early. If there is any danger of frost, the plants need to be covered with paper or plastic coverings or boxes. The covers should be removed during the day.

Plants are spaced 12 inches apart in rows 30 inches apart. Eggplants are easily grown in containers or minigardens. Plants grow best with one inch of water each week. They will tolerate dry weather once the plants are established, but they need water during extended dry weather. Eggplant grows well under all types of irrigation systems.

Over 30 varieties are available in different shapes and colors. Oval types include Apple Green (medium apple green fruit which do not require peeling); Albino (medium white); Black Beauty (large purple); Black Magic (large purple); Burpee Hybrid (large purple); Dusky (medium purple); Morden Midget (medium purple); White Beauty (large round white fruit); and White Italian (large white). Classic is a large slim type. Small slim varieties include Ichiban, Long Tom, Short Tom and Slim Jim.

Harvest.—Fruits are harvested about 70 days after transplanting when the fruits are one-third to two-thirds mature. Large varieties will be six to eight inches long. The fruit skin should have a glossy shine and fruit can be removed with a pruning shears or knife. Part of the stem should be left on the fruit. When the fruit skins become dull or brown they are mature and too tough for good quality. Fruits should be eaten soon after they are harvested.

Common Problems.—Phomopsis rot may be a problem. Symptoms are large sunken tan or black areas on the fruit. Canker-like lesions may appear on the stem. Leaf spots appear and enlarge, the centers die and the leaves turn brown. The disease is often carried over-winter by previously infected plants of eggplant. To control, remove and discard diseased plants, use resistant varieties and use clean seed.

Verticillium wilt is common in cooler areas. The fungus lives in the soil almost indefinitely and is also carried by tomatoes and peppers. Resistant varieties and crop rotation is the best control.

Insects which attack eggplant include flea beetles, aphids and sometimes Colorado potato beetle and red spiders. See pages 128, 129 and 132 for control procedures.

ENDIVE AND ESCAROLE

Endive and Escarole (*Cichorium endivia*) probably originated in East

India. It was used for food by the Egyptians and Greeks in 200 B.C. and later by the Romans.

Plant Characteristics.—Endive has finely cut, loose, narrow, medium green, fringed, and curly leaves. The leaves have a slightly bitter taste.

Escarole, sometimes called Batavian endive, is a selection of endive. These plants have broad, thick, smooth leaves which have a white midrib. The plant forms a loose head with partly blanched (white) inner leaves. Escarole has a milder flavor than endive.

Culture.—The culture of endive and escarole are similar and both are grown like lettuce. They are planted in the winter in the south and in the early spring, summer and fall in the north. The plants produce seedstalks with blue flowers in hot weather and a fall crop is best. They grow best at a temperature of 60-70°F.

Endive and escarole may be planted indoors for later transplanting. The seeds are planted one-fourth inch deep in flats or peat pellets six to eight weeks before planting in the garden. Plants are thinned to stand two inches apart and are transplanted when they are three inches high. A starter fertilizer helps establish the plants.

Seeds may be planted directly in the garden in early spring, two or three weeks before the frost free date. They are planted one-fourth inch deep. Both seeds and transplants are placed in rows 18-30 inches apart and thinned to stand eight to ten inches apart. Summer plantings produce a fall crop which matures in cool weather making the leaves milder in flavor. Summer plantings are frequently interplanted as transplants into other rows of vegetables.

Endive and escarole respond to fertile soil and a uniform supply of water. Summer plantings will require frequent irrigation during dry periods. The plants are hardy and withstand temperature of 28°F.

When the leaves are 10 inches long they can be gathered together and tied so the inner leaves or heart will become white (called blanching). For winter use, plants may be dug with a ball of soil and placed in a cold frame or cool place where they do not freeze. The leaves may be blanched and plants used as needed. Blanching requires two to three weeks.

Common varieties of endive include Deep Heart, Green Curled, Ruffic and Salad King. Common escarole varieties include Broad Leaved Batavian, Florida Deep Heart and Full Heart Batavian.

Harvest.—The entire head is cut at the base when leaves are partly or wholly blanched. The outer leaves are usually tough and bitter and discarded.

Common Problems.—Endive and escarole have few insect and disease problems. Slugs and snails sometimes are a problem.

Rotted centers sometimes occur. This is frequently due to over-crowding, water splashing in the center or by tying the leaves for blanching when the leaves are wet.

FIG. 6.18. FLORENCE FENNEL IS GROWN FOR THE LICORICE FLAVORED ABOVE GROUND BULB

FLORENCE FENNEL

The fennel commonly grown as a vegetable is called (ANON. 1975) florence fennel (*Foeniculum vulgare* var. *dulce*), finocchio or sweet anise. Fennel was used by the early Romans for food and medicinal properties. Florence fennel is related to celery and celeriac.

Plant Characteristics.—Florence fennel somewhat resembles celery. The plants are 24-30 inches tall with fine feathery leaves. The stalks overlap at the base to form a solid bulb with a licorice flavor. The plant is not to be confused with the common fennel which is used as an herb and does not form the large bulb at the base.

Culture.—Fennel is a cool season crop grown in early spring, planted in the summer for a fall crop, or grown in the fall and winter in the south.

Seeds are planted one-fourth inch deep two weeks before the last frost in the spring. Plants are thinned to six to ten inches apart in rows about 18 inches apart. Repeated plantings may be made. Plants withstand light frosts.

When the base of the leafstalks have reached two inches in diameter, soil may be mounded up around these forming bulbs. This blanching process is not necessary, but if done, the bulbs will become white.

Fennel grows best in well fertilized soil with plenty of water. It has few insect and disease problems.

The only variety usually listed is Florence Fennel or Finnochio. It is frequently listed in the herb section of garden catalogues.

Harvest.—Fennel should be eaten before they become tough and stringy, usually 80 days after planting. The compact bulb and petioles can be eaten like celery or cooked for its licorice flavor. The leaves are used in salads.

The plant will produce a seed stalk in midsummer if not harvested. Yellow flowers with a seed head resembling dill is produced. The seeds which form can be used similar to common fennel, the herb.

GARLIC

Garlic (*Allium sativum*) is a member of the onion family. It is native to southern Europe and has been in use for over 2,000 years. The Romans disliked the strong flavor of garlic but it was used by the laborers and soldiers who brought it to England in the sixteenth century.

Culture.—Garlic can be grown in any area where gardeners grow bulb or dry onions successfully. Garlic plants respond to daylength and form a bulb under long days, regardless of the plant's size. In addition, if the soil temperature is above 68°F, the plants produce poor bulbs. Thus, in many areas, garlic is poorly adapted to home gardens.

Garlic is planted in the south and southwest from fall till January. In the rest of the country, it is planted as soon as the soil can be worked in the spring, often six weeks before the frost free date.

Garlic is propagated by planting the small cloves which are divisions of the entire large bulb. The cloves are separated and planted separately. The larger the clove, the larger will be the size of the bulb produced for harvest. Cloves should not be separated until planting time. Separating them early and then storing them, reduces yield.

The cloves are planted in an upright position one-half to one inch deep, four inches apart in rows 12-24 inches apart. They should be planted in deep fertile soils with a high organic matter content. In order to produce large bulbs in areas outside the south and southwest, high fertility is required to produce large plants before they bulb. The equivalent of 30 pounds of 10-10-10 fertilizer per 1000 square feet is often recommended.

Elephant garlic is a popular home garden vegetable which may produce a bulb six times larger than regular garlic. In the south and southwest, it is fall planted and grown similar to regular garlic. In the north, it is planted in the fall, allowed to mature, mulched and then left to overwinter. The plants grow the next spring and when they mature during the summer they may be harvested.

Garlic needs ample water. If the soil becomes excessively dry, the bulb will be small. If the soil becomes compacted, the bulb will be irregular in shape.

Insect and disease problems are similar to onions.

There are a number of varieties, including California Early, California Late, Creole (adapted to the southwest), Extra Sweet, and the larger Elephant Garlic type. Many gardeners plant the variety available from their local seed supplier. These seed bulbs should be smooth, large and disease free.

Harvest.—Garlic is harvested when the top dries down. The bulbs are dug and cured for storage by placing them under cool, dry conditions for several days. The bulbs are then stored under dry conditions between 40-60°F.

Courtesy of Harris Seeds

FIG. 6.19. TURK'S TURBAN IS OFTEN CALLED A GOURD
BUT IT IS EDIBLE AND TASTY

GOURDS

The word gourd is commonly used to describe warm season vining crops which produce fruits for decoration, novelty items or household utensils. They are members of the same family and various types are found in *Cucurbita pepo, Cucurbita maxima, Lagenaria siceraria,* and *Luffa cylindrica.* The *Cucurbita* species originated in America and were widely distributed in North and South America long before Columbus. They were used for receptacles, household utensils and food. The *Luffa* species originated in tropical Asia and had spread into China by 600 A.D.

Plant Characteristics.—The gourds have sprawling vines with large leaves. The flowers are large and usually yellow. The bottle gourds have white flowers. The plant contains separate male and female flowers on the same plant and may cross pollinate with squash and pumpkin (See page 60). Any pumpkin, squash or gourd within the same genus and species can cross pollinate with each other. The *Lagenaria* and *Luffa* genus do not contain any pumpkins or squashes commonly grown in America and do not cross pollinate with the *Cucurbita* species found on page 60.

Culture.—Gourds are tropical or semi-tropical plants that are extremely frost tender. They are not able to grow below 60°F. They can be grown in all areas if planted during the late spring or summer. Plants may be transplanted similar to pumpkins or seeded directly. Plants are transplanted and seeds are planted after all danger of frost has passed. Seeds are placed two inches deep, six to twelve inches apart, in rows six to eight feet apart. The plants are thinned to stand three feet apart in the row. With ample water the vines grow rapidly and cover the entire area in two months. When garden space is limited, vines may be trained onto a fence or trellis.

Gourds grow on almost any good well drained garden soil, containing a generous amount of organic matter.

The *Lagenaria* species produce the best shaped gourds for dippers, birdhouses and rattles. They should be grown on a fence or trellis so the fruits hang free and the fruit is long and straight.

Cucurbita varieties of gourds are given on page 60. These gourds usually have thick shells and are difficult to cure. Their color usually begins to fade in three or four months. Some, like turks turban, appears in the catalogues as a winter squash.

Lagenaria varieties of gourds include Calabash, Cave Man's Club, Large Bottle, Dolphin, Dipper, Drum, Hercules Club, and Swan Gourd. One edible variety called New Guinea Bean, Guinea Bean or Italian Edible Gourd grows to five feet in length and weighs 15 pounds.

The *Luffa* variety is called Vegetable Sponge, Sponge Gourd or Dishrag Gourd.

Harvest.—The *Lagenaria* varieties can be eaten like squash or eggplant when immature. The fruits are harvested about one week after they blossom. The *Luffa* variety is eaten like cucumber or cooked like a vegetable when the fruits are four inches long or less. Turks Turban can be harvested mature and used as an ornamental or eaten like a squash. The large blossom end is cut where it joins the rest of the fruit. The seeds are removed, the cavity filled with rice, your favorite seasonings, and ground beef, the blossom end replaced and the entire fruit baked similar to winter squash.

Fruits which are not eaten are usually allowed to remain in the garden until frost kills the vines. The *Cucurbita* varieties will have brightly colored, hard, glossy shells. When harvesting, one or two inches of stem is left on these gourds. The gourds should be handled carefully as bruises discolor them and cause them to soften and decay. The *Cucurbita* gourds are cured for several days in the shade under warm dry conditions.

The *Lagenaria* varieties are thin shelled and are harvested after a frost or when the shells begin to harden, the fruits become lighter in weight and the tendrils on the vine nearest the fruit begin to dry and shrivel. These gourds may require six months in a warm, dry place to cure. Large dipper and bird house gourds may be made into wren houses. After harvest, the very thin skin is scraped from the shell of the gourd with a knife and the gourd then dried. A hole the size of a quarter is drilled into the dipper end for the wren and a small one at the stem end (for a hanging wire). The surface is painted with shellac or polyurethane.

Luffa or sponge gourd is harvested when the *Lagenaria* varieties are harvested. The fruit is placed in a tub of running water, and the outer skin is peeled off similar to an orange. This exposes the inner core or sponge. The sponge is squeezed to remove the inner contents.

Common Problems.—Weeds can be a problem late in the season. If weeds are controlled until the vines cover the ground, many weeds will be shaded. Late in the season the crop is mature and little damage is caused by weeds.

Gourds have insect and disease problems similar to cucumber (see page 197). Cucumber beetles should be controlled from the time the plants emerge.

The squash bug occasionally attacks gourds. (See pages 129 and 132 for control measures.)

HORSERADISH

Horseradish (*Armoracia rusticana*) is native to southeastern Europe and both the leaves and roots were eaten in Germany during the Middle Ages. The word horseradish first appeared in 1597 in an English herbal on medicinal plants. It was grown in gardens of the early American settlers and it is now well established as a wild plant.

Culture.—Horseradish is a hardy, cool season, perennial that produces a whorl of large, rather coarse textured leaves. Horseradish grows best in the northern regions of the USA and grows poorly in the south.

FIG. 6.20. HORSERADISH IS A PERENNIAL GROWN FOR ITS ROOTS

The plants grow on deep, rich, moist soils. The yields are reduced and the roots are malformed when grown on shallow, stony or hard soils. Organic matter or manure should be worked into the soil at least 10 inches deep the fall before planting. The manure should not be added in the spring.

As horseradish is a perennial, it is frequently planted at one edge of the garden with the other perennial vegetables. Either crown divisions or root cuttings are planted. Crown divisions are a piece of root and the crown buds. These are removed from the old plant and planted. Root cuttings are small side roots from the main root, that are the size of a lead pencil and 10-12 inches long. The part of the cutting which was attached to the main root is considered the "top" and is planted near the soil surface.

Root cuttings are planted as soon as the soil can be worked in the spring. Cuttings are planted on a slant, 18-24 inches apart in rows 30 inches apart. The top of the root cutting should be about three inches below ground level.

To produce a large main root, the plants are "lifted" when the largest leaves are 10 inches long and again about six weeks later. The soil is carefully removed from around the main root but the roots at the bottom end of the set are undisturbed. The small roots at the top or sides are rubbed off and only those at the bottom are left. The crown is raised and all but the best sprout or crown of leaves is removed. The plant is returned to its original position and the soil replaced.

If horseradish is growing in a soil high in organic matter, it should receive enough moisture from rainfall. However if the plant wilts during hot weather, it should be irrigated. Horseradish makes its largest amount of growth during the cooler weather of late summer and fall.

Horseradish varieties are few. The gardener usually purchases the variety available but Bohemian and Maliner Kren are sometimes listed. Once the plants are established, new root cuttings can be obtained from the harvested plants. Usually the roots remaining in the soil after harvest are sufficient to reestablish the plants.

Occasionally horseradish is attacked by root rot. Use disease free root cuttings and do not plant in the same area for three years.

Harvest.—Horseradish may be harvested anytime after a hard frost in the fall until the plants begin to grow again the next spring. Roots are dug with a shovel or spading fork using the tops as a handle to help pull the roots from the soil. Roots may be stored in an air tight, black plastic bag in the refrigerator.

To prepare horseradish, the root is washed, peeled and cut into small cubes. A blender is filled half full with the cubes and a small amount of cold water and crushed ice added. The roots are ground and two or three tablespoons of white vinegar (cider vinegar causes the root to turn brown), and one half teaspoon of salt per cup of horseradish is added. For extra hot horseradish, wait three minutes before adding the vinegar. The mixture is stored in tightly capped jars in the refrigerator between use. In about six weeks the ground horseradish darkens and looses some flavor and new horseradish may be prepared.

JERUSALEM ARTICHOKE

Jerusalem artichoke (*Helianthus tuberosus*) or sunchoke is a relative of sunflower. It has no relationship either to Jerusalem or to artichoke. It is a native of North America and was being grown for food by the Indians when the early settlers arrived. It was taken to Europe in the 1700's where it is now well established.

Plant Characteristics.—The plant resembles sunflower. It is a perennial which grows over six feet high and produces tubers similar to potatoes. These tubers may become four inches long and two or three inches in diameter. The principal storage carbohydrate in the tuber is inulin, rather than starch. When eaten, fructose is released from inulin rather than glucose as occurs with common starch. Inulin starch is a type of carbohydrate usually tolerated by diabetics (Gibbons 1973). The inulin content is greatest just after frost and decreases during the winter.

Culture.—Jerusalem artichoke can be grown in nearly all parts of the

USA. It grows on soil too dry or too infertile to grow beets or potatoes. However, it grows best on good soils and the tubers are easier to dig in sandy or loamy soils.

Jerusalem artichoke is planted where they will not shade other plants. The tubers are planted in the spring as soon as the soil can be worked, or in the fall at harvest time. Tubers or two ounce pieces of tubers are planted three inches deep, 24 inches apart in rows 36-40 inches apart.

Plants require irrigation and fertility similar to potatoes for best growth. They are seldom bothered by insects and diseases.

Several garden catalogues list Jerusalem artichoke or sunchoke and once grown the gardener can save tubers for seed. They are also found in the produce market and some "health food" stores.

Harvest.—Tubers are dug in the fall after the tops have been killed by frost. They may be harvested at any time until growth begins in the spring. Spring dug tubers have less inulin and taste sweeter.

Tops are removed before digging. The tubers are then dug with a fork or shovel. All the tubers should be harvested and tubers are located some distance from the plant. Unharvested tubers will produce new Jerusalem artichoke plants the next spring, creating a weedy condition.

Tubers may be used to start a new planting of Jerusalem artichoke or stored. The tubers do not store as well as potato tubers and should be harvested as needed until freezing conditions are approaching. Tubers are then dug, cleaned, washed and stored in air tight, black plastic bags in a refrigerator. Tubers may also be placed in damp sand and stored in a root cellar or vegetable pit.

KALE

Kale (*Brassica oleracea* var. *acephala*) or borecole is a member of the cabbage family. It is native to Europe and was recorded as being used for food as early as 200 B.C.

Culture.—Kale is a hardy, low growing plant well adapted to growing in the fall in both the north and south. It will live overwinter as far north as northern Maryland, southern Pennsylvania, and areas having similar winter climates. It withstands heat but is usually grown as a fall crop. Plants grow best on well drained, fertile soils with ample moisture. They are grown similar to collards.

Seeds are planted in early spring for a summer crop; in early summer for a fall crop; or in areas with mild winters, in late summer for a winter crop. Kale is frequently planted to replace vegetables harvested in midsummer. Seeds are planted one-fourth to one-half inch deep in rows 18-24 inches apart. Seedlings are thinned to stand 8-14 inches apart. Kale is easy to grow and has few insect and disease problems when spring or fall planted. Cabbage worms can be a problem during the summer.

FIG. 6.21. KALE IS A HARDY PLANT GROWN FOR ITS LEAVES

Courtesy of Harris Seeds

FIG. 6.22. KOHLRABI IS GROWN FOR ITS EDIBLE STEM

Common varieties include Dwarf Blue Curled Vates, Dwarf Curled (or Vates), Dwarf Green Curled, Dwarf Siberian and Tall Green Curled Scotch. Curled or Scotch types have very curled foliage which is grayish green in color. Siberian types produce leaves which are less curled and a bluish green color.

Harvest.—The flavor of kale is usually improved by frost. Kale is harvested two ways: 1) the entire plant is cut off at ground level 40 days after seeding; or 2) the lower leaves periodically stripped off. The inner leaves and bud are left to produce new leaves for a continuous supply. Leaves are harvested before they become old, tough, and stringy.

KOHLRABI

Kohlrabi (*Brassica oleracea* var. *caulorapa*) is a cool season vegetable. It is a relative of cabbage which developed in northern Europe about 1500. It was imported into the USA about 1800.

The plant develops an enlarged stem just above the ground line and the leaves grow out from this stem. It can be eaten raw or cooked like turnips.

Culture.—It is grown as a cool season vegetable in all parts of the USA. It can be grown in the early spring but is usually grown as a fall crop in the north and a winter crop in the south. Kohlrabi is normally planted for fall use after all the frost tender vegetables are gone. It grows easily in containers.

Seeds are planted one-fourth to one-half inch deep in rows 12-18 inches apart. Plants are later thinned to stand four inches apart.

Kohlrabi grows best in fertile soil with one inch of moisture each week, similar to cabbage. Seeds are frequently planted in midsummer between vegetables that are maturing or already harvested. The seeds will need frequent watering to establish the plants. Slow or checked growth of the plants results in tough, woody stems. Kohlrabi must grow rapidly in the spring before hot weather to be of good quality. Thus, most gardeners plant it for a fall or winter crop.

Kohlrabi may have insect and disease problems similar to cabbage. Early spring, fall and winter crops are usually not attacked severely by cabbage worms.

Common varieties are the white skinned Early White Vienna and the purple skinned (but white flesh) Early Purple Vienna.

Harvest.—Kohlrabi is ready to harvest in 50-60 days after planting. It has the best flavor when it is two to four inches in size and the flesh is still tender. Large kohlrabi have woody, stringy, tough stems. The leaves of young plants may be used like spinach.

LEEK

Leek (*Allium porrum*) is a biennial, native to the Mediterranean region. It has been cultivated for food since prehistoric times. Leek is a member of the onion family which does not form a bulb. The thick, fleshy stalk is the same diameter as the base and resembles a large green onion.

FIG. 6.23. LEEKS MAY BE HARVESTED THROUGHOUT THE WINTER WHENEVER THE GROUND IS NOT FROZEN

Culture.—Leeks can be grown in any garden that produces good onions. Leeks are grown as an annual from seed in all parts of the USA. It is either transplanted or seeded directly into the garden. Leek requires about 120 days from seeding to harvest or 80 days from transplanting to harvest. In areas with short growing seasons, seeds are planted in a hot-bed, two or three months before transplanting. The plants are set out in the fall in the south and southwest and in early spring in the north. Leek transplants are handled similar to onion transplants (see page 52).

Seeds are planted one-half to one inch deep, one inch apart, in rows 12-18 inches apart. The plants are thinned to stand four inches apart. When the plants are at least the size of a pencil, soil is placed around the edible portion. This makes the edible part whiter and longer at harvest. Placing soil around the edible part (leaf bases) when the leaves are small may cause the plants to rot and die.

Common varieties are American Flag, Broad London, Conqueror, Electra, Giant Musselburg, Large American Flag, London Flag and Tivi.

Leeks have few insect and disease problems. In hot, dry conditions, onion thrips may stunt the plants growth. The problem can be reduced by harvesting all affected leeks and onions and destroying weeds which provide winter protection for the thrips.

Harvest.—Leeks can be harvested whenever they are three-fourths of an inch in diameter, but they can be left to grow to almost two inches in diameter. Plants can be removed with a shovel or fork until the ground freezes. They may be mulched heavy and harvested during the winter whenever the ground is not frozen. Plants may also be left mulched or unmulched for spring harvest. Plants are removed in early spring, before the leeks begin spring growth and send up a seedstalk.

The roots and all but two inches of the green leaves are cut from the harvested leeks. Soil may be caught in the layers of the growing leek. The plant may be cut lengthwise and thoroughly washed to remove this soil.

LETTUCE

Lettuce (*Lactuca sativa*) is a native to Europe and Asia and has been grown for over 2,500 years. It was grown by Persian kings in 500 B.C. The various forms of head lettuce appeared in the 1500's. Columbus brought lettuce to America and it was one of the first plants grown by the early settlers.

Plant Characteristics.—Lettuce is extremely sensitive to high temperatures. When seeded at temperatures of 80°F, lettuce seed does not germinate and the seed becomes dormant. High temperatures induce a seedstalk to form in all types and results in internal tip burn of the leaves of crisp head types.

Courtesy of Harris Seeds

FIG. 6.24. DARK GREEN BOSTON LETTUCE IS A BUTTERHEAD TYPE

There are four general types of lettuce which are recognized as subspecies. Gardeners however generally recognize five types.

Butterhead.—Butterhead (*L. sativa* var. *capitata*) or bibb lettuce is a head type in which the leaves are loosely folded. The inner leaves are cream or yellow, and outer leaves green. Butterhead types bruise and tear easily. Varieties include Bibb, Buttercrunch (resistant to heat), Butter King, Dark Green Boston, Deer Tongue (also called Matchless), Summer Bibb (resistant to heat), Summerlong (resistant to heat), and White Boston. Tom Thumb is a small variety easily grown in containers.

Cos.—Cos or Romaine (*L. sativa* var. *longifolia*) lettuce is an upright plant which grows about 10 inches high. The outer leaves are smooth and green, the inner leaves whitish green. Leaves are more crisp than other heading types. Varieties include Paris Island, Paris White, Valmaine and White Paris. Sweet Midget is a small variety easily grown in containers.

Crisphead.—Crisphead (*L. sativa* var. *capitata*) or Iceburg is the common lettuce found in the produce market. Leaves are thin, crisp and frequently have curled and serrated edges. Heads are hard and durable. Varieties include Calmar, Fairton, Great Lakes types, Iceburg, Ithaca, Mesa and Pennlake.

FIG. 6.25. LEAF LETTUCE IS COMMON IN HOME GARDENS

Leaf.—Leaf lettuce (*L. sativa* var. *crispa*) is also called looseleaf or loosehead lettuce. Plants do not form a head and leaves may be serrated, deeply lobed, or crinkled. Leaf color varies from light green to red. Varieties include Black-Seeded Simpson, Grand Rapids types, Green Ice (resistant to heat), Oak Leaf, Prizehead, Salad Bowl, Slobolt (resistant to heat) and Walsmann's Green. Ruby is a red variety which grows well in containers during the winter.

Stem.—Stem (*L. sativa* var. *asparagina*) or asparagus lettuce can be used like celery and lettuce. The young leaves can be used like lettuce. The plant produces an edible seedstalk which is eaten raw like celery or cooked in Chinese dishes. The variety commonly listed is Celtuce and often indexed as such.

Culture.—Lettuce grows best at cool temperatures. It is grown in late fall, winter and spring in the south and Pacific southwest. In the north, lettuce is limited to spring and fall.

Lettuce is planted a quarter inch deep, one seed per inch, in rows 12-18 inches apart. It can be planted as soon as the soil can be worked in the spring. The plants are thinned to stand six to eight inches apart for Butterhead and Cos types, and four to six inches apart for Leaf types. Several spring plantings may be made.

All types of lettuce may be grown as transplants, and Crisphead types should be grown as such, particularly in the northern, central and mid-west areas. A fall crop of Crisphead types cannot be grown in these areas. Seeds are started indoors, in a coldframe or hotbed. (See section on Plant Growth-pages 45-52). Plants are hardened and planted in early spring. They may be planted up to a month before the frost free date as hardened lettuce is usually not harmed by temperatures as low as 28°F. The Crisphead types are set out 10-12 inches apart, in rows 18 inches apart. For fall crops, seeds are planted directly in the garden as transplanting does not save time.

Lettuce has a shallow root system and frequent watering causes the leaves to rapidly develop. On heavy soils, too much water may lead to burning at the edges of the leaves and disease. Summer and fall plantings will require frequent irrigation to establish the plants. All cultivation around lettuce should be shallow, due to its meager root system.

Harvest.—Leaf lettuce can be harvested whenever the leaves are large enough to use. Plants which have been thinned from the row are also eaten. The inner leaves of the leaf varieties are of high quality and the entire plant can be harvested in 50-60 days. If the plants are crowded, many plants are formed but the leaves are small and of low quality.

Butterhead and Cos types are usually ready to harvest in 60-70 days. Crisphead types are harvested when the heads are firm and full.

Lettuce may be washed, dripped dry and stored in an airtight container in the refrigerator.

Common Problems.—Lettuce produced in the garden is often free of disease and insect problems. In many areas, cabbage worms attack the

Courtesy of W. Atlee Burpee Seed Co.

FIG. 6.26.   CELTUCE

plants. If the plants are grown closely together, or mulched with organic material, garden slugs and snails will need to be controlled.

MUSKMELON OR CANTALOUPE

Muskmelon (*Cucumis melo*) is called cantaloupe in the south and produce trade. It probably originated in India although it has never been found growing in the wild. It was grown by the early settlers in the 1600's.

Plant Characteristics.—The fruit of all, except some later maturing varieties, have a musk aroma, and this character gave the plants their name. The plants have separate male and female flowers on the same vine and are cross pollinated by bees. Only garden plants within the same genus and species will cross pollinate and muskmelons will only cross pollinate with other muskmelons. They do not cross pollinate with cucumbers, gourds, watermelons, squash or pumpkins. The bitter flavor sometimes noticed is due to cloudy weather during ripening, too high temperatures or too much or too little water.

Culture.—Some types of Muskmelons may be grown in nearly all parts of the USA. The Casaba, Honeydew and other large maturing varieties may require 130 days to mature and grow best in the south and parts of

FIG. 6.27. GOLD STAR MUSKMELONS

California. Plants may be grown in the garden from transplants (see pages 45 to 53) or by seeding directly. Transplants must be grown in individual containers to prevent root damage.

The cultural requirements for muskmelon are about the same as cucumber, except that muskmelons are less tolerant of high humidity and rainy weather. In northern and midwestern states, the rain and humidity hasten disease problems, and resistant varieties should be used.

Garden soils should be well drained and contain large amounts of compost or well rotted manure. Sandy soils warm up quickly and are preferred for an early crop. In northern locations and on heavier soils, black plastic mulches (see section on Soils and Plant Nutrition-page 97) can be used to warm the soil. The mulch is installed before planting and holes made every two or three feet for the transplants or seed.

Seeds or transplants (a starter fertilizer should be used) are placed in the garden when all danger of frost has passed and temperatures have warmed to 60°F. Plants grow best at temperatures of 60-85°F. Muskmelons are of the highest quality when grown at these temperatures, when the vines remain healthy and when the weather is relatively dry when the fruits are ripening.

Seeds are planted one to one and a half inches deep, one foot apart in rows. Seeds may also be planted in hills, two plants every three feet or three plants every four feet. Rows are spaced at least five feet apart. The vines will fill in the space between rows. Crowding the plants results in a large leaf cover which reduces the opportunity for bees to pollinate the flowers, and yields are reduced. In gardens where space is limited, the vines can be trained on a fence or trellis. The fruit will need to be supported with a mesh bag or cheesecloth sling.

Muskmelons should receive an application of fertilizer about the time the plants begin to vine. Late maturing varieties also respond to a second application when the plants begin to set fruit. Vines require ample water when they are growing rapidly and the fruits are developing, and should not be irrigated when the fruits are ripening as this may cause them to split open. Furrow or trickle irrigation is best, as moisture on the leaves from any source encourages disease.

A large number of varieties are available. Very early maturing ones may be grown in the far north and the very late varieties grown in the south and far west. In areas of high humidity and rainfall mildew resistant varieties should be grown.

Extra early varieties which mature in under 80 days include, Farnorth, Minnesota Honey (fusarium resistant), Minnesota Honeymist and Minnesota Midget (small vines).

Varieties which mature in 80-90 days include Ambrosia, Burpee Hybrid, Delicious 51 (fusarium resistant-adapted to northeast and upper midwest), Early Crenshaw, Earlydawn (fusarium, mildew resistant), Edisto (alternaria, mildew resistant-adapted to south and southeast), Fordhook (green flesh-can be northern grown), Gold Star (fusarium resistant), Harper Hybrid (alternaria, fusarium, mosaic resistant), Harvest Queen (fusarium resistant, adapted to midwest, midatlantic), Jumbo Hale's Best (adapted to south, southeast), Queen of Colorado (also called Pride of Wisconsin-fusarium resistant), Saticoy (fusarium, mildew resistant) and Supermarket (fusarium, mildew resistant).

Late maturing varieties which require about 110 days to mature and are grown in the south and California include Casaba, Crenshaw, Golden Beauty Casaba, Honey Dew, Persian and Top Mark.

Harvest.—At maturity, the fruit changes from green to yellow or tan and an abscission layer forms between the stem and the fruit. The stem breaks away cleanly from the fruit with slight pressure and this is called the "full slip" stage. Muskmelons should not be harvested before this stage. They do not increase in sugar when picked green.

Casaba, Crenshaw, Honey Dew and Persian varieties do not develop an abscission layer and "slip." They are harvested when the fruits turn yellow and the blossom end of the fruit begins to soften. These melons can be stored for a short time.

Muskmelons should be harvested every other morning once they begin to ripen. At the peak season, they should be harvested daily. Harvesting when the plants are wet with dew or water helps spread disease and the plants should be dry.

Common Problems.—Insect and disease pests are similar to cucumber. In humid, wet regions, resistant varieties should be selected (see page 197).

FIG. 6.28. GREEN WAVE MUSTARD SHOWING LEAVES READY TO HARVEST

MUSTARD

Mustard (*Brassica juncea* var. *crispifolia*) originated in China and Asia and is used for its tender leaves. Black mustard is a different species grown to produce seed for table mustard. The Tendergreen variety is a mustard spinach (*Brassica perviridis*).

Culture.—Mustard is grown similar to collards and spinach and may be grown in all regions of the USA. It is grown in very early spring or fall in the north and in late fall and winter in the south. It grows at an optimum temperature of 60-65°F and forms a seedstalk under long, warm summer days.

It can be planted in the spring three to four weeks before the frost free date, or six to eight weeks before the first frost in the fall. Seeds are planted one-half inch deep in rows 15-24 inches apart. Seedlings are thinned to stand about four inches apart. Mustard responds to irrigation during dry weather.

Common varieties with curled leaves are Green Wave and Southern Giant Curled. Florida Broadleaf has smooth leaves and Tendergreen has large thick leaves. Aphids and cabbage worms may be a problem similar to cabbage (see page 172).

Harvest.—Mustard is ready to harvest in about 40 days when the leaves are six to eight inches long and before they become tough and woody. The entire plant may be harvested or young, lower leaves harvested continuously, similar to collards and kale.

Courtesy of W. Atlee Burpee Co.

FIG. 6.29. OKRA IS GROWN FOR ITS PODS

OKRA

Okra (*Hibiscus esculentus*) or gumbo is a perennial related to cotton. It probably originated in Africa or Asia and was in use by the Egyptians in the twelfth century. It was being grown in America by the early 1700's.

Plant Characteristics.—Okra is grown as an annual and varieties differ in their size from dwarf plants of three feet to tall plants of five to ten feet. Pod shapes range from round to ridged and short to long. The plant and pods may have small spines on them which create allergies in some people. Spineless varieties are available. The varieties vary in pod color, and flower color and shape, and may be grown as an ornamental.

Culture.—Okra is a warm season plant similar to cucumber and tomato. It may be grown in all areas of the USA. In the north, the growing season is short and yields will be reduced. In the south and Pacific southwest it withstands midsummer heat and produces when many other vegetables do not.

Before planting, the seeds are soaked in water overnight. The seeds which have swollen are planted after all danger of frost has passed. Seeds are planted one-half to one inch deep in rows three (dwarf types) to five (tall types) feet apart. Plants are thinned to stand one to two feet apart. It is usually planted in full sunlight at one edge of the garden where it does not shade other vegetables.

Okra grows well on any well drained garden soil. It needs an application of fertilizer high in phosphorus before planting. As okra has a long growing season, an additional application is beneficial at the time the pods begin to form. A fertilizer high in nitrogen should not be used as this stimulates the vegetative growth and reduces the number of pods produced.

When plants become too large in the south, they are sometimes cut off six to eight inches above the ground and allowed to regrow. These plants should receive some fertilizer high in nitrogen to stimulate vegetative growth.

Okra requires irrigation during dry weather; about one to one and a half inches of water per week.

The size of the garden area often determines the variety to choose. Dwarf plants are preferred in small gardens. Varieties usually under five feet tall include Clemson Spineless (green, smooth, ribbed pods), Dwarf Long Green Pod (green, ribbed pods), Emerald (green, smooth pods) and Perkins Spineless (also called Dwarf Green Early-green, smooth, ribbed pods). Large growing varieties include Louisiana Green Velvet (round, green pods) and Perkins Mammoth Long Pod (ribbed, green pods).

Harvest.—Pods are harvested by cutting them from the plant with a knife or shears. They are harvested four to seven days after the flower has opened and the pods are not fibrous (pods two to four inches long). Pods should be harvested every other day and mature pods should be removed and discarded as they reduce the plant's growth and decrease yield. The pods contain a mucilaginous material that makes some okra dishes seem slimy to some people. This is the material which is valuable in soups and gumbos.

Pods may be stored for several days in an airtight plastic bag in the refrigerator.

Common Problems.—Nematodes may be a problem in gardens that have been in the same location for several years. The corn earworm may eat into the pod and stink bugs cause damage late in the season.

ONION

Onion (*Allium cepa*) is probably a native of Asia. It has been grown for food since recorded history and mentioned in the Bible. There are over 300 species of onion, some of them native to North America. The domesticated types were brought to America by Spanish explorers.

Courtesy of Harris Seeds

FIG. 6.30.   ONIONS ARE GROWN OVER A WIDE RANGE OF CLIMATES

Plant Characteristics.—Onions can be grown under a wide range of soil and climate and are grown in nearly all parts of the USA. The production of the onion bulb is dependent upon daylength. Early or southern varieties require 12 hours of daylight to bulb while late or northern varieties require 15 hours. The bulbs begin to form regardless of the size of the plant. Onion varieties adapted to the south grow little and form small bulbs in the north. Some bunching varieties such as Evergreen, are used for green onions produced from seed. These varieties are a different species and do not form bulbs at all.

General Care.—Onions continuously produce new roots and develop best in cool, damp conditions. They produce the bulbs in warm weather. Onions require about twice as much fertilizer as other vegetables. Onions respond to additional fertilizer 40-60 days after transplanting or seeding. About one pound of 10-10-10 or equivalent, per 25 feet of row should be worked into the soil about two inches deep and three inches to the side of the row.

Onions develop best in loose, crumbly soil. Hard soils induce the bulbs to be small and irregularly shaped. One pound of compost per square foot of soil helps loosen the soil.

Onions grow in the south during the fall, winter and spring. In the north, they are grown from early spring to fall. Onions may be grown from seed, sets or transplants. Seeds are cheapest but require a longer time to grow.

Onions may be bothered by onion thrips. In the north, root maggots may burrow into the bulbs. Maggots can be controlled with a soil insecticide applied before planting. Onions are poor competitors and weeds must also be controlled.

Onions from sets.—Sets are small, dry onions which have been grown the previous year specifically for starting plants. They may be used to produce green onions or mature, dry bulbs.

Culture.—Sets are usually yellow or white but occasionally red sets are available. A variety is seldom listed. Sets should be purchased early while they are still firm and dormant. The round sets mature into flat shaped bulbs and elongated or tapered sets mature into round bulbs.

The sets should be separated into two sizes; sets smaller than three fourths of an inch (the size of a dime), and larger sets. The large sets are used for green onions as they frequently form a seedstalk instead of a bulb. The small sets are used for mature, dry bulbs.

For green onions, sets are planted one and one half inches deep, close enough to touch each other, in rows 12 inches apart. When the plants are four inches high, soil can be placed around the stems to produce long, white stems.

For dry onions, the sets are planted one inch deep, two inches apart in rows 12-16 inches apart. Soil is not placed around dry onions as this may induce the bulb to rot in storage.

Harvest.—Green onions may be harvested whenever the plant is six inches or more high. If a plant begins to produce a seedstalk, it should be harvested. It will not produce a bulb for storage. Green onions become stronger in flavor as they become older.

Dry onions are harvested when half or more of the onion tops have fallen over naturally. Tops should not be broken over early as this reduces bulb size and may introduce diseases, causing rots in storage. Mature bulbs are pulled, the tops placed over the bulb to prevent sunburn, and air dried in the garden for a day or two. Bulbs are air dried in a well vented place for an additional two to three weeks. Tops may then be cut off about one inch from the bulb and the bulbs stored under dry cool conditions in a mesh bag.

Onions from transplants.—Transplants are an easy way to produce an early crop of large, mature bulbs. Practically none of the transplants form seedstalks.

Culture.—Transplants are planted in the fall in the south and southwest and as soon as the soil can be worked in the north. Transplants are set four inches apart in rows 12-18 inches apart. Plants are set one to one and a half inches deep and a starter fertilizer applied. Plants also receive a side dressing of fertilizer similar to sets.

Transplants are not always available to the gardener at the correct planting time in the south. Transplants may then be grown from seed and planted. (See section on Plant Growth-pages 42-52). Varieties can be the same as those grown from seed in the south.

In the north, transplants are more readily available. Red transplants include Benny's Red, Red Burgundy and Red Hamburger. White bulbed varieties include White Bermuda, White Sweet Spanish, Yellow Bermuda and Yellow Sweet Spanish.

Harvest.—Mature dry bulbs are ready to harvest when the tops have fallen over, similar to those grown from sets. Bulbs from transplants usually do not store as well as bulbs from sets, and should be used by early winter.

Onions from seeds.—Onions may be grown from seed to produce both green (or bunching) onions and mature, dry bulbs. The bunching onions are a different species from the onions produced from sets or those used to produce bulbs. Most of the bunching onions do not form bulbs and are used only for green onions.

Culture.—For best results, seed for mature, dry bulbs should be sown indoors and transplanted (see section on Plant Growth-pages 42-52). Seed may also be planted directly in the garden. In the north, seed is planted as soon as the garden can be worked. In the extreme south, seed can be planted in late September to produce bulbs in June or planted in January for an August harvest. The seed of bunching onions is planted directly in the garden. There is no value in growing it as a transplant.

Seed is planted one inch deep, one seed per inch, in rows 12-18 inches apart. When the plants are four inches high, they are thinned to stand one inch apart for green onions, two inches apart for medium sized dry onions and four inches apart for large onions. The thinned plants are used as green onions.

Bunching varieties used for green onions include Beltsville Bunching, Evergreen, Southport White Bunching, White Knight and White Spanish Bunching.

Varieties planted from seed for dry onions in the south and southwest include: early varieties, Grano, Granex, Early Grand, Texas 502, White Grano and Yellow Grano; medium varieties, California Early Red, Fresno Red, Italian Red and Stockton Yellow Globe; and late varieties, Australian Brown, Crystal Wax, Excel, Fiesta and Yellow Sweet Spanish.

In the middle latitudes of the country Bronze, El Capitan, Golden Beauty, Perfection, Pronto S and San Joaquin are suitable varieties.

In the north, Abundance, Autumn Spice, Autumn Splendor, Benny's Red, Fiesta, Nutmeg, Red Globe, Ruby, White Globe, White Sweet Spanish and Yellow Globe are common.

Harvest.—Green onions can be harvested when desired. Mature, dry bulbs are harvested similar to those produced from sets. Bulbs produced from seed can frequently be stored until spring.

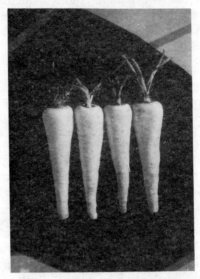

Courtesy of Harris Seeds

FIG. 6.31. PARSNIP

PARSNIP

Parsnip (*Pastinaca sativa*) is native to the Mediterranean area and was known to the ancient Greeks and Romans. It was introduced to America by the early colonists. Parsnip can be grown in all parts of the country. It does not grow well in midsummer in the south and is usually grown and used by early summer. In mild areas it can be planted in the fall and grown during the winter.

Culture.—For spring planting seed is planted one or two weeks before the frost free date. The soil and weather should be warm at planting time but seeds germinate poorly during the summer. Fresh seed should be used as old seed germinates poorly.

Seeds are planted one-half inch deep, two seeds per inch in rows 18 inches apart. The seed may be covered with sand, peat or vermiculite instead of soil to prevent crusting and poor seedling emergence. Plants are thinned to stand three inches apart in the row. Crowding the plants at this spacing forces the plants to produce smaller, more tender roots.

Culture is similar to carrots. Plants grow best in lighter soils and stony soils cause the plants to produce rough, forked roots. Parsnips have few insect and disease problems.

All American, Hollow Crown and Model are the three varieties normally available.

Harvest.—Parsnips are harvested before they mature and the root has become woody. They are harvested in midsummer in the south and after a frost in colder climates. Frost induces some of the starch in the roots to be converted to sugar, and plants have a sweet nut-like flavor. Roots left in the ground are remarkably resistant to freezing injury and rots and may be harvested and used at any time. Plants may be mulched with straw so roots can be dug throughout the winter. In areas with mild winters, the spring seeded plants continue to grow slower throughout the winter and the roots become woody. In these areas, the roots should be harvested in early winter and stored. Neither chilled nor non-chilled roots are poisonous as sometimes supposed.

FIG. 6.32. EDIBLE PODDED PEAS (ABOVE) ARE GROWN SIMILAR TO ENGLISH PEAS

PEA, ENGLISH AND EDIBLE PODDED

Pea (*Pisum sativum*) originated in eastern Europe or western Asia and was grown in the stone age. They were an important crop in England by the eleventh century. English peas are types which originated in England

and are called English Peas to distinguish them from southern peas which are really beans. The edible podded pea (*Pisum sativum* var. *macrocarpon*) is a special type grown for its pod rather than seeds.

Plant Characteristics.—The pea is a hardy, cool season, tendril climbing, annual. It is best grown in the garden on a trellis, fence or some other support to conserve space. Peas are related to beans and their roots will support nitrogen fixing bacteria. If peas or beans were never grown in the garden before, the seed should be inoculated with these bacteria. The inoculum is available in garden centers and catalogues. Once the bacteria are established in the garden, it is of little value to inoculate each year.

There are two types of peas the gardener may grow and their culture is similar. English peas (garden peas or sweet peas) are grown for the seed. Edible podded peas (sugar peas, snow peas, or Chinese peas) are grown for the long pod. The walls of the pod are brittle, succulent, tender and fiber-free.

Culture.—Peas grow and mature best in cool weather and can be grown in all parts of the country. In the south and lower California, they are grown during fall, winter and early spring. Further north they are grown as both spring and a fall crop. In the far north and at high elevations, they may be grown from spring to fall. Pea plants do not withstand summer heat and the seeds mature and become hard rapidly.

Peas grow in any well drained, moderately fertile soil. They grow poorly in wet or water soaked gardens. Excessive nitrogen causes the plants to produce large vines but fewer peas are produced. Inoculated peas on loam soils seldom respond to nitrogen fertilizer in a garden. They usually produce more on light, sandy soils when a light amount of a complete fertilizer is applied before planting.

Seeds are planted in the spring whenever the soil temperature is above 45°F. Fall crops are planted 60-70 days before the date of the first freeze. Seeds are planted one to one and a half inches deep in heavy soils and two inches deep in sandy soils. Peas are planted eight to ten seeds per foot in a single row 18 inches apart or in a double row eight to ten inches apart. A support can be placed between the double row.

There are now over 2,000 distinct varieties of peas (ANON. 1975). Smooth seeded peas have a starchy flavor, even when young. Wrinkled seeded varieties are sweeter and the sugar does not convert to starch rapidly and these types remain sweet past their prime quality. There are large vined, small vined, or bush types and include Mighty Midget, a variety for containers that grows vines only six inches long. Varieties vary in disease resistance and heat tolerance. Varieties should be chosen to fit the gardener's location and needs.

Edible podded varieties include Dwarf Grey Sugar, Giant Melting,

Melting Sugar and Oregon Sugar Pod. Sweetness and starch are unimportant in these varieties as they are eaten for the pod before the seed attains any size.

Harvest.—English peas and edible podded peas are harvested differently.

English Peas.—The pods are harvested when they are well filled but before they harden and fade in color. The peas should not be hard and starchy. Peas are best picked and shelled just before cooking as the sugar content decreases rapidly after harvest. Two or three pickings are made as all the pea pods do not mature at the same time. The pods should be carefully pulled from the vine to prevent the plants from being uprooted. At the last harvest, the plant may be pulled up and all the pods picked.

Edible Podded Peas.—These peas are picked when the pods are long and the peas just developing. Pods, three to five inches long, are produced five to seven days after flowering, and the pea seeds are slim and small. Pods need to be picked every other day to prevent them from developing large seeds and fibrous pods. If the seeds develop, they may be used similar to English peas.

Pea pods can be stored 10 days in plastic bags in the refrigerator without a loss in quality. Pods are stir fried or briefly steamed to prevent overcooking.

Common Problems.—Pea roots are easily damaged by hoeing and shallow cultivation should be practiced. Peas have few pests in a garden. On cold, wet, soils fusarium wilt may be a problem and resistant varieties should be grown. Pea weevil is a pest in the west which feeds on the blossoms and the larva enter the developing peas. Pea aphids may cause the plant to wilt. (see pages 128 and 132 for control measures.)

PEANUT

Peanut (*Arachis hypogaea*) also known as earth nut and goober pea originated in South America and was taken to Africa by the Portuguese. Peanuts were shipped to North America as on-board food for slaves. It was well established here by the year 1800.

Plant Characteristics.—Peanut produces bright yellow flowers above ground which are self-pollinated. The ovary, called a "peg", emerges and grows downward until it enters the soil. The peanut then develops in the soil. Peanuts are divided into several types. The Virginia type has two large seeds per pod and are better adapted to short growing seasons. Spanish types have two or three small seeds per pod.

FIG. 6.33. PEANUTS PRODUCE A YELLOW FLOWER ABOVE GROUND BUT A PEG
EMERGES AND ENTERS THE SOIL CAUSING THE SEED TO
DEVELOP BELOW GROUND

Culture.—Peanuts are popular in the south, southeast and southwest but can be grown in any area having 110-120 days of warm weather. They grow poorly under a long, cool growing season. As the "nut" develops underground, coarse textured sandy soils are best, particularly for Virginia types. Spanish types also grow well on fine textured or heavy soils. Soils should have a good supply of calcium to prevent the production of empty pods. If the soil is low in calcium, two pounds of gypsum per 100 feet of row should be applied when the plants begin to flower.

Individual seeds are planted one inch deep in heavy soils and two inches deep in sandy soils, two weeks after the frost free date in the spring. They can be grown as transplants in peat pellets if the growing season is short. Spanish types are placed six inches apart in rows 24 inches apart. Virginia types are spaced eight inches apart in rows 36 inches apart. Plants may also be grown in large containers.

Plants should be irrigated during dry weather when the plants are flowering and the "pegs" are entering the soil. Near harvest time they should not be watered as this may cause the peanuts developing underground to sprout.

The soil should be cultivated to control weeds and keep the soil loose to help the "pegs" penetrate the surface. Once pods develop in the soil, it is difficult to cultivate without harming the plants. Do not place soil around the plants or cover up the spreading branches.

Common varieties include Early Northern, Early Spanish, Jumbo Virginia, Large Virginia, Red Tennessee and Spanish.

Harvest.—When the leaves have begun to turn yellow, the plants may be harvested and should be dug before a hard freeze. The plants containing the peanuts are air dried in a warm, dry place for two weeks. The moisture content should then be about 15% and the peanuts can be removed from the plants. They can be shelled and roasted in a shallow pan at 350°F for 20 minutes. Unshelled peanuts may also be roasted. The oven is preheated to 500°F, the peanuts placed in the oven in a colander or wire basket and the oven turned off. They are roasted when the peanuts have cooled.

Common Problems.—Corn earworm, cutworms, armyworms and caterpillars may feed on the leaves. The white fringed beetle eats the below ground parts.

Stem rot may attack the stems, roots, pods and pod stems. Leafspots cause infected leaves to become yellow as though the plant was mature. To help control these diseases, peanuts should not be grown in the same garden location each year.

Courtesy of Harris Seeds

FIG. 6.34. BELL TYPES OF PEPPER (ABOVE) ARE A COMMON GARDEN VEGETABLE

PEPPER

Pepper is native to tropical America and was grown in North and South America over 2,000 years ago. The small hot peppers were taken back to

Europe by Columbus where they became popular. Pepper varieties used by gardeners are grouped in *Capsicum annuum* and are different from the red hot tabasco pepper and the household pepper.

Varieties.—There are many varieties available which may be classified as sweet, mild or hot depending on the amount of capsaicin present. This material gives pepper its hot or pungent taste.

Bell types.—Plants produce large, blocky fruits, three inches wide and four inches long. The dark green fruit usually turns red when mature but is usually eaten green. Varieties include Bell Boy (mosaic resistant), Bellringer (mosaic resistant), California Wonder, Canape, Keystone (mosaic resistant), Yolo Wonder (mosaic resistant), and Golden Cal-wonder (turns yellow at maturity). Fruits are stuffed or eaten in salads.

Perfection or Pimiento types.—Plants produce sweet, round slightly pointed fruit two inches wide and four inches long. Varieties include Bighart, Sunnybrook, Sweet Banana, and Pimiento. Fruits are canned and eaten in salads.

Cayenne Types.—Plants produce fruits that are slim, pointed and slightly curved. Fruits are two to twelve inches long and usually red when mature. Varieties include Anaheim (mild), Cayenne, Hungarian Wax (hot), Jalapeno (extra hot), Long Red Cayenne (hot), Red Chili and Serrano. Fruits may be used green or fully mature. Dried fruits are ground to make chili powder (hot types) or paprika (sweet types).

Celestial Types.—Plants produce small fruits (up to two inches) which are upright. Fruit color ranges from yellow to red and purple to orange. More than one color may appear on the same plant. Varieties include Floral Gem, Fresno Chili and Celestial. Plants are used as an ornamental but hot fruits may be ground for chili powder.

Tabasco Types.—Plants produce fruits up to three inches long. Fruits are long, slim and very hot. Varieties include Coral Gem, Chili Piquin, Japanese Cluster, Small Red Chili, Very Small Cayenne and Tabasco. Plants are used as an ornamental and fruits are pickled or ground for chili powder.

Cherry Types.—Fruits are cherry shaped and may be sweet or hot, large or small and orange to red in color. Varieties include Bird's Eye, Large Red Cherry (hot), and Sweet Cherry (mild). Plants are used as ornamentals, and the fruits for chili powder or pickled as a relish.

Tomato Types.—Fruits look like a very small tomato and are usually pickled immature. Varieties include Sunnybrook (mild), Topepo and Tomato.

Culture.—Peppers are a warm weather crop. Flowers fall off when night temperatures are below 60°F or above 75°F. Plants do not grow when night temperatures are below 55°F. Peppers are grown in most sections of the country as transplants (see Plant Growth-pages 42-52). They are easily container grown.

Transplants should be set out after all danger of frost is past and planted 18 inches apart in rows 24 inches apart. A transplant fertilizer should be used.

In areas with a long growing season, seeds may be thickly planted one fourth inch deep to insure a good stand. To prevent crusting, seeds may be covered with sand, peat or vermiculite instead of soil. Plant and row spacings are similar to transplants.

Peppers respond to a small amount of additional fertilizer when the plants have set several fruits. One to one and a half inches of water is needed during the growing season.

Harvest.—Fruits may be harvested 70-130 days after planting. Fruits are normally broken off from the plant with part of the stem attached to the fruit. Bell types are usually harvested when they are three or four inches long. Hot peppers are harvested when they are red and mature. The Jalapeno is usually harvested when it is green in color.

Common Problems.—Blossom end rot can be a problem. It is caused by drought stress and a deficiency of calcium (limestone or gypsum). Tobacco mosaic is a problem on peppers handled by gardeners who use tobacco. Mosaic resistant varieties should be grown.

Leaf miners, aphids, flea beetles, weevils, cutworms and root maggots can be a problem. They can be controlled with various insecticides.

PHYSALIS OR HUSK TOMATO

Physalis (*Physalis* spp.) is also called husk tomato, ground cherry, and poha berry. It occurs naturally in the Western Hemisphere and is common in Latin American and Hawaiian gardens. It should not be confused with chinese lantern plants which are also *Physalis* spp. but are perennial flowers used as ornamentals.

Culture.—Physalis is a warm season plant grown similar to tomato. It usually grows one to two feet high. Seeds are planted one-fourth inch deep in rows 24 inches apart after the soil has warmed in the spring. Plants are thinned to stand 18 inches apart. As the seed is small, transplants are easier to establish in the garden. Six week old transplants are set out a week after the last frost.

Physalis responds to fertility and irrigation similar to tomato. Physalis is listed in most garden catalogues as ground cherry or husk tomato. Once the plant is grown, the unharvested fruits left in the garden are sufficient to produce volunteer plants the next year.

Harvest.—The edible fruit is a berry enclosed in a thin husk. The husk turns from green to yellow to brown when the fruit is ripe, while the fruit turns from green to yellow. They are eaten fresh or made into jam or sauce.

FIG. 6.35. POTATOES CAN BE PRODUCED IN A STRAW MULCH
FOR EASIER HARVESTING

POTATO

Potato (*Solanum tuberosum*) originated in Peru and was used by the Incas. It was taken by Spanish explorers to Europe about 1540 and was a major source of food in Ireland from 1600 to 1845. Irish settlers brought it back to America in 1719 and thus is commonly called Irish potato. The potato is the only vegetable among the five principal world food crops (Splittstoesser 1977).

Plant Characteristics.—Potato develops the edible part, the tuber, underground. Long days, warm temperatures and high moisture and fertility promote vegetative growth. After the plants have reached a certain size, tubers are formed. Short days, cool temperatures between 60-70°F, lower moisture and less fertility promote tuber development. Tubers do not form when the temperature is above 80°F.

Potato plants often produce flowers and fruits or seed balls which resemble small tomatoes. These fruits are not edible and are not the result of cross pollination with tomatoes. Flowering has nothing to do with tuber formation. Non-flowering potato plants will form tubers.

Culture.—Potatoes are a cool season crop and do not grow well in the south during midsummer. They can be grown as an early crop in small gardens and vine crops (pumpkins, squash) later planted between the rows to utilize the space once the potatoes are harvested.

Potatoes are grown from seed pieces or small whole potatoes. For seed pieces, the potato is cut into one and one half to two ounce blocks, about the size of a hen's egg. Potato eyes, sold in some garden centers, frequently weigh less than an ounce and are too small to produce strong plants. The seed piece is planted immediately after cutting. Small whole potatoes are best for planting. They have less disease and decay and produce better plants.

Planting dates vary but potatoes are generally planted in early spring in the north and November to February in the south. They should be planted early for highest yields and light frost will not damage the tubers. Prolonged wet and cold weather may cause the seed pieces to rot however. Early maturing potatoes do not keep as well as those that mature later. Mid season and late varieties are frequently planted in late spring or early summer in the north for winter storage.

Potatoes are planted two or three inches deep, ten inches apart in rows 24 inches apart. Plants should shade the area and prevent high temperatures which inhibit tuber development. When the plants are five inches high, soil should be drawn around the plants in a ridge to cover the stems. This prevents green areas developing on the tubers.

Potato tubers develop in darkened areas and will easily produce tubers above ground in a mulch. This method reduces scab disease, keeps the soil 10° cooler, thereby increasing yields, and makes harvesting easier. The potatoes are planted at or one inch below ground level. When the plants are one inch high, the entire area is covered with a six inch layer of mulch, such as straw or pine needles. The tubers will be produced in the straw which can carefully be moved aside to harvest early potatoes. The straw can be replaced and the plants left to produce more potatoes until the vines die.

Potatoes grow best in fertile, well drained soil. Misshapen potatoes develop in hard, compact soil and organic matter should be added to such soils. Fresh manure increases the incidence of scab disease and well-rotted manure should be used.

Plants should be irrigated during dry weather at weekly interludes. If the soil becomes dry and then irrigated after a period, the tubers begin a second growth period and knobby potatoes are produced. Alternate wet and dry periods also cause potatoes to develop a cavity in the center of the tuber.

There are over 100 potato varieties available. Those commonly grown in North America have white flesh and light brown (called white) or red skins. Only certified seed potatoes should be used to reduce disease problems. Home grown potatoes may become infected in a single season. Potatoes purchased for eating often have virus diseases present and may have been treated with a material to prevent them from sprouting. Potato varieties are early, mid season and late maturing. Some early maturing varieties adapted to gardens include Anoka (white), Irish Cobbler (white), Norgold (red, scab resistant), and Norland (red, scab resistant). Mid season varieties include Superior (white, scab resistant), Red La-Sota (red, grows well in south), and Red Pontiac (red). Late maturing varieties include Katahdin (white, resistant to several diseases), Kennebec (white, resistant to several disease), Russet Burbank (also called Netted Gem and Idaho Russet-scab resistant but cannot stand moisture fluctuations or heat) and Sebago (white, resistant to late blight).

Harvest.—Potatoes may be harvested before the vines die but as long as the vines are alive the potato size will increase. The tubers are usually one or two inches in size when the plants are flowering. Potatoes are usually harvested when the vines die and should not be bruised or injured when dug. Potatoes are stored for a week at 65-70°F in the dark to help heal bruises. Tubers are then stored at 35-40°F at high humidity.

Common Problems.—Numerous insect and disease pests attack potatoes. Certified seed and resistant varieties should be used where the disease in question is prevalent. Crop rotation should be practiced.

Blights can be controlled with a fungicide. Colorado potato beetle, flea beetle and leaf hoppers may also be a problem (see pages 128 and 132).

PUMPKIN

Pumpkins originated in tropical America and were used by the Incas. Pumpkins belong in three species and are defined as the edible fruit of any *Cucurbita* species which is harvested mature and usually not used as a baked vegetable.

Plant Characteristics.—Pumpkins have large leaves on sprawling vines. The plant produces male and female flowers on the same plant and must be cross pollinated. The first flowers are males and do not produce fruit. Pumpkins do not cross with cucumbers, watermelons or muskmelons. They readily cross with any plant of the same species however. Page 60 gives the varieties of squash, pumpkins and gourds which freely cross pollinate within a given species.

Courtesy of Harris Seeds

FIG. 6.36. PUMPKINS ARE FREQUENTLY GROWN ONLY IN LARGE GARDENS

Culture.—Pumpkins are sensitive to cold and do not thrive in the south during midsummer. Pumpkins are transplanted (see Plant Growth-pages 42-53) or direct seeded, two weeks after the frost free date. They grow best between 65-85°F. Plants require a lot of space but can be grown near an early crop of corn or potatoes and utilize this space when the plants are harvested. The pumpkin vines may be trained on a fence or trellis but the fruits will need to be supported with a mesh bag or cheesecloth. Large pumpkins produce fruits which are usually too heavy to grow on supports.

The vining pumpkins are planted in hills, two inches deep. Large vining types are thinned to three plants every five feet with 10 feet between rows. Semivining types are thinned to two plants every four feet with eight feet between rows. Bush types are planted two inches deep, and thinned to one plant every three feet in rows six feet apart.

Pumpkins are grown similar to cucumbers and muskmelons. They grow best on well drained, fertile soil, with a large amount of organic matter.

There are many varieties available (see page 60). All pumpkin seeds are edible and pumpkins were originally grown for their seeds, not the flesh. Seeds are still sold like peanuts in Mexico. The naked seed varieties have a large seed without a seed coat. The flesh of these pumpkins is coarse in texture and flavor. (It can however, be baked, pureed and used to thicken soups.)

Harvest.—Pumpkins can be harvested whenever the rind is hard and they have developed a deep solid color. Some types have the best quality if they are harvested after the vines are senescent or have been killed by frost. When the pumpkin is cut from the vine, three or four inches of stem should be left attached to the fruit. Pumpkins without stems do not store well. All pumpkins should be harvested before they are injured by a heavy frost. They are stored in a dry, well-ventilated area between 50-60°F.

Common Problems.—Diseases and insects are described on page 197. Mildews can be controlled with a fungicide. Cucumber beetles should be controlled from planting onward. Any insecticide should be applied in the early evening when bees are not active. Bees are needed for pollination.

Pumpkins may also be attacked by the squash bug and squash vine borer, particularly east of the Rocky Mountains. If only a few plants are infected with the squash vine borer, the wound can be located on the stem just above the soil line. The stem can be slit with a sharp razor blade, puncturing the borer. Moist soil is placed around the stem to a height just above the wound. New roots will develop, compensating for the injury.

RADISH

Radish (*Raphanus sativus*) is a native of Europe or Asia and was being used by the Egyptians at the time of the Pharaohs. They are hardy to cold but cannot withstand heat. In the south, they are grown in fall, winter and spring. In the north, they are grown in spring and fall. In regions with cool summers, they can be grown throughout the growing season.

Soils should be prepared and fertilized before planting. Spring radishes grow rapidly and conditions must be favorable for rapid growth. Slow growing radishes have a hot or pungent flavor. Overfertilization can result in excessive top growth with no root enlargement.

Spring Radishes.—Spring radishes mature in 20-30 days and can be grown throughout the season in cool climates and all but the hottest months in warmer areas. Successive plantings are made every 10-14 days beginning in spring as soon as the soil can be worked and again a month before frost. In the south and Pacific southwest they are planted in the fall. Seed is planted one-fourth to one-half inch deep in rows 12 inches apart. They are frequently grown between slow maturing vegetables such as cabbage, pepper and tomato. Plants are thinned to stand one inch apart. Overcrowding results in poor root development. During hot weather the roots become pungent and plants produce seedstalks. Radishes

FIG. 6.37. SCARLET KNIGHT (ABOVE) IS A RED GLOBE TYPE OF RADISH

are pulled when they are one to one and a half inches in size. Mature radishes become pithy.

Radishes can be mixed with carrot, beets and parsnips to mark the row of these vegetables which grow slower.

Many varieties are available. The red globe types include Champion, Cherry Belle, Comet, Early, Scarlet Globe, Sparkler and Red Prince. Burpee White is a white globe type while White Icicle and Icicle are white types with long roots. French Breakfast has a globe root which has a red top and a white bottom.

Winter Radishes.—Winter radishes grow slower, are larger and keep longer than spring types. They require a 45-70 day growing period and are usually grown as a fall crop. The lower temperatures and shorter daylengths discourage the plants from forming seedstalks. The variety All-Season can be grown either early spring to summer or fall to winter.

Seeds are planted one-half inch deep, four to six inches apart, depending on the variety. They are usually planted in the space in which early corn, onions or potatoes were grown. Varieties range in pungency from mild to very hot and include All Season (white, Japanese "daikon" type), Chinese Rose Winter (white, med. hot), Round Black Spanish (black skin, white flesh), and White Chinese (also called Celestial, white skin). Sakurajima is a very large type which may grow to 50 pounds. Winter radishes may be harvested and stored similar to other root crops (beets and carrots).

FIG. 6.38. RHUBARB IS A PERENNIAL GROWN FOR ITS LONG PETIOLES

Common Problems.—The cabbage maggot is the only problem most gardeners will encounter. For control, a soil insecticide is worked into the area before planting.

RHUBARB

Rhubarb (*Rheum rhaponticum*) is sometimes called pie plant and is a native to Central Asia, probably Siberia. It was grown extensively in Italy in the sixteenth century and was brought to America from there in the eighteenth century.

Culture.—Rhubarb grows best in areas that have cool, moist summers and winters that freeze the ground several inches. It does not grow well in most parts of the south.

Rhubarb is a perennial and should be planted at one edge of the garden. The area should contain a heavy application of manure or compost which is worked into the soil 12-18 inches. As rhubarb is planted three or four feet apart, each area can be prepared separately. Good drainage is essential for rhubarb.

Crowns from established plants are planted with the crown bud two inches below ground level in early spring as soon as the soil can be worked. Plants are set three or four feet apart in rows three feet apart. Seeds are not recommended as the seedlings vary greatly from the parent plant.

Crowns can be purchased or obtained from established plants. Established plants are dug in early spring and split into pieces with one large bud to each section of crown and roots. Vigorous, healthy plants should be dug and the crowns planted immediately. To maintain vigorous plants that are not overcrowded and producing small petioles, they should be dug and re-established every 8-10 years after planting.

Plants should be fertilized in the spring and mulched with compost or well rotted manure in late fall. Plants require abundant water during the growing season. Under conditions of low fertility, overcrowding or with old plants, seedstalks may form. These should be cut at the base of the plant and discarded so the energy will go into the roots for next year's crop.

Rhubarb varieties with mainly green petioles include German Wine, Sutton's Seedless and Victoria. Varieties that produce red petioles include Canada Red, Crimson Wine, McDonald, Ruby and Valentine.

Harvest.—Rhubarb produces long leafstalks or petioles from the food stored in its fleshy roots from the previous year. The first year after planting, the stalks or petioles should not be picked to allow the roots to enlarge. The second year the petioles may be harvested for two weeks only. The third year after planting, the petioles may be harvested for six weeks or until they become small, indicating that the food reserve is gone. One-third of the petioles or leafstalks should remain on the plant after each harvest.

The stalks are pulled from the plant and the leafblade is removed. Rhubarb leaves contain soluble oxalic acid and the leaves should not be eaten. Leafstalks or petioles from frosted plants should not be eaten as the leaf oxalic acid may have moved into the petiole.

Common Problems.—Rhubarb is relatively free of insect and disease problems. Rhubarb curculio may be a pest in the eastern half of the country. It is a large, usually reddish looking, snout beetle about three fourths of an inch long. The beetle punctures the leafstalks or petioles leaving black spots. The beetle also feeds on curly dock and this weed should be destroyed.

Crown rot also affects rhubarb in the eastern half of the USA. The petiole develops lesions at the base and the entire leafstalk or petiole collapses. There is no effective control and rhubarb should not be grown in the infected area for five years.

SALSIFY

Salsify (*Tragopogon porrifolius*) is also called oyster plant or vegetable oyster due to its faint oyster-like flavor. It originated in the Mediter-

Courtesy of W. Atlee Burpee Seed Co.

FIG. 6.39. SALSIFY IS OFTEN CALLED OYSTER PLANT DUE TO THE FAINT OYSTER-LIKE FLAVOR FOUND IN THE ROOTS

ranean area and is distinct from black salsify and Spanish salsify which are common in Europe.

Culture.—Salsify is a hardy biennial which can be grown in most regions of the USA. It is grown similar to parsnip but needs 150 days to mature from seed. Salsify is more cold tolerant and is planted in the spring as soon as the soil can be worked. The soil should be loose and crumbly at least 18 inches deep so long straight roots will be produced.

Fresh seeds are planted one-half inch deep in rows 18 inches apart. Old seed germinates poorly. Seedlings are thinned to stand three inches apart. Plants should be irrigated until they are established at which time they will withstand some dry conditions.

The only variety listed is Mammoth Sandwich Island. It has few insect or disease problems.

Harvest.—Roots are harvested in the fall after a freeze which improves their flavor. Plants may be left in the ground and harvested as needed. It withstands hard freezing and they can be mulched so roots can be dug during the winter. These plants should be harvested before they begin to grow the following spring or else a long stemmed purple flower will be produced.

SHALLOT

Shallot (*Allium ascalonicum*) is an onion-like plant which originated in western Asia. They were brought to Europe by French knights returning from the Crusades. De Soto brought them to Louisiana in 1532.

Culture.—Shallots can be grown in nearly all parts of the country. They are planted as soon as the ground can be worked in the north and in the fall and winter in the south.

Shallots produce a cluster of bulbs somewhat like garlic. The individual bulbs are planted two inches deep, four inches apart in rows 12 inches apart. They are grown similar to onions (see page 222).

Usually no listed varieties are available. Catalogues simply list "shallot" and bulbs purchased from the produce market or gourmet store may be planted. Once grown, the gardener can save bulbs for next year.

Harvest.—Shallots may be harvested and used similar to green onions. For dry bulbs, plants are harvested when the tops die down. Shallots are hardy and can be left in the ground overwinter. Most types do not produce seed. For best results, the cluster of bulbs should be dug and the small ones planted at the desired time for another crop.

Dry bulbs are stored in a well ventilated, cool, dry area, similar to onions. Shallots are easily stored through the winter.

SOUTHERN PEA AND YARDLONG BEAN

The unqualified word "pea" in the south usually refers to the southern pea (*Vigna unguiculata*) or cowpea. There are three types of Southern pea, each with its own distinct flavor. These types are blackeye pea, cream pea and crowder pea and Southern peas are sometimes referred to by these names. Yardlong bean (*Vigna unguiculata* var. *sesquipedalis*) or asparagus bean is a pole type variety of Southern pea.

The Southern pea is not a pea but a bean and originated in middle Asia. It was then taken to Africa. It was carried to the Spanish settlements in the West Indies by slave traders, where it has become an important food. The Southern pea was then brought to the USA in the 1700's (Meiners and Kraft 1977).

Plant Characteristics.—Southern peas are pole and bush types of short or long season maturity. The bush types mature quickly and are best for gardens outside the deep south. Crowder types have the seeds crowded tightly together in the pod. Cream types produce cream seeds and black-eyed types produce cream seeds with a black embryo area.

The Yardlong bean or Asparagus bean is a pole type. It produces a bean pod which may grow to three feet or more if left on the vine to mature. It

Courtesy of Twilley Seed Co.

FIG. 6.40. PODS OF PINK EYE PURPLE HULL SOUTHERN PEAS

is grown like Southern peas but is less productive than Southern pea varieties.

Culture.—Southern peas are a warm season crop. In the south it can be grown during the summer between the harvest of early spring crops and before planting fall crops. Southern peas are very susceptible to cold and are planted later than snap beans. Southern pea, including Yardlong bean, can be grown in northern climates wherever lima beans can be grown.

Southern peas grow best without a heavy application of nitrogen fertilizer and they are particularly heat and drought tolerant. Excess moisture reduces yield.

Seed should be planted one inch deep, two to four inches apart in the rows. The rows should be two to three feet apart. Pole types, including yardlong bean, will need some type of support, similar to pole snap beans. In the south, successive plantings can be made three weeks apart until mid-summer to provide a continuous supply.

Varieties of Southern pea may be found in garden catalogues under pea, bean, blackeye peas, or southern pea. Varieties include Dixilee (which is tolerant to nematodes), Brown Crowder, California Blackeye (resistant to nematodes), Conch, Colosses, Crowder, Early Ramshorn Black Eye, Knuckle Purple Hull, Lady, Louisiana Purchase, Mississippi Silver, Monarch Blackeye, Pink Eye Purple Hull, White Acre, White Crowder, Texas Purple Hull and Queen Anne.

The Yardlong or Asparagus bean is usually found in garden catalogues listed as such.

Harvest.—Southern peas are harvested as green shell or dry peas. They are harvested when the deep green pod color changes to light yellow, red, purple or silver depending on the variety. This is 55-80 days after planting. The pods should be picked twice each week with the lower pods maturing first. For dry beans, the pods are allowed to remain on the plant and mature. The pods are then picked, the peas removed, dried, and stored for later use.

Yardlong or Asparagus bean can be used like snap beans, green shell, or dry beans. Often they are harvested when the pods are 10-12 inches long, cut into sections and used in Chinese cookery. The pods may be left on the plant and when it begins to change color, the seeds are harvested as green shell peas. The pod can also be left to mature on the plant and the seeds then used like Southern peas.

Common Problems.—Various insects and diseases attack Southern peas. The major pest is the cowpea curculio which feeds on the pods and seeds. Fall planted Southern peas are often attacked by stinkbugs and cornworms. To reduce diseases and nematodes, resistant seed should be used. Purchased seed is more apt to be true to type and carry this resistance than seed saved from the garden.

Courtesy of W. Atlee Burpee Seed Co.

FIG. 6.41. NEW ZEALAND SPINACH IS A WARM SEASON CROP

SPINACH

Spinach (*Spinacia oleracea*) is native to Asia and was used over 2,000 years ago in Iran. It was brought to Spain in 1100 A.D. and taken to America by the early colonists.

Plant Characteristics.—The edible part of spinach is a compact rosette of leaves. Spinach produces a seedstalk easily in response to long days, and hot temperatures further hasten the flowering response. Thus planting times are critical and other leafy vegetables such as New Zealand spinach or Swiss Chard are frequently grown instead of spinach.

Culture.—Spinach is grown in the north as soon as the soil can be worked (five weeks before the last frost) and again in late fall (seven weeks before the first frost). In the south, it can be grown from fall to spring as the plant is a hardy, cool season crop.

Seeds are planted a half inch deep and an inch apart in rows 12 inches apart. Plants are thinned to stand four inches apart before they become crowded in the row. Two or three successive plantings can be made.

Spinach grows well on any fertile, well drained soil. It grows poorly on soils that crust easily. Spinach is shallow rooted and one to one and a half inches of water are needed each week to insure rapid and continuous growth.

Varieties have smooth or thick, dark green savoyed leaves. Spring varieties do not produce seedstalks as rapidly as fall varieties. Spring varieties include America (savoy leaf) and Bloomsdale Long-Standing (savoy leaf). Fall varieties include Chesapeake (savoy leaf, mosaic, mildew resistant), Hybrid No. 7 (savoy leaf, mosaic, mildew resistant), Melody Hybrid (savoy leaf, mosaic, mildew resistant), Viroflay (smooth leaf), Virginia Savoy (savoy leaf, mosaic resistant) and Resistoflay (smooth leaf, mildew resistant).

Harvest.—The entire spinach plant can be cut off just at ground level about 35-45 days after seeding when plants have five or six leaves. An alternate method is to harvest the outer leaves when they are three inches long, leaving the remaining leaves for later harvest. The entire plant should be harvested when a seedstalk begins to form.

Common Problems.—Mosaic and mildew may be a problem and resistant varieties should be used for control. Leaf miners, aphids or cabbage worms may be a problem. (See pages 128 and 132 for control measures.)

SPINACH, NEW ZEALAND

New Zealand spinach (*Tetragonia tetragonioides*) is not a true spinach

Courtesy of Harris

FIG. 6.42. BLOOMSDALE SPINACH

but it is used in the same manner. It is native to New Zealand, Japan and Australia and was introduced to England in the 1700's.

Culture.—New Zealand spinach grows two or more feet tall with a spreading, branching type of growth reaching four to six feet. It is a warm season crop and is planted after all danger of frost is past.

Seeds germinate slowly and seed may be soaked 2 hours in warm water before planting. Seeds are planted one inch deep, four to six inches apart in rows three or four feet apart. Plants are thinned to stand 12 inches apart in the row. Transplants may also be used.

New Zealand spinach is simply listed as such with no named varieties. It has no insect or disease problems of consequence.

Harvest.—Harvest begins about 70 days after seeding by cutting off three inches from the tips of the branches. Leaves and stems are both used. About one-half to two-thirds of the tips may be harvested at any one time. Plants can be harvested until frost.

SQUASH

Squash is native to tropical America and was widely used by the Indians. The male flowers are still eaten as a batter dipped, fried fritter in Latin America.

Plant Characteristics.—Squash plants may be vining, semi-vining or bush types of plants. They have separate male and female flowers on the same plant and belong to three separate species. Thus, squash will cross pollinate with another squash, pumpkin or gourd within the same species (see page 60). They do not cross pollinate with cucumber or watermelon.

Culture.—Squash grows well in practically all regions of the USA. They do not stand frost but in the far south may be grown in winter. Plants may be transplanted (see Plant Growth-pages 42-53) or seeded directly in the garden after all danger of frost is past, and soil temperatures are 60°F or more.

Seeds of vining types of squash are planted two inches deep, four or five seeds per hill. Hills are placed five feet apart in rows eight feet apart. Hills are thinned to two or three plants.

Seeds of semi-vining types are planted two inches deep, four or five seeds per hill. Hills are placed four feet apart in rows six feet apart. Hills are thinned to two plants per hill.

Seeds of bush types are planted two inches deep, 10 inches apart in rows three feet apart. Plants are thinned to stand 30 inches apart in the row.

Squash plants grow best on fertile, well drained soil well supplied with organic matter. Plants should be irrigated during dry weather. Trickle or furrow irrigation is better than sprinkler irrigation as any moisture on the leaves increases the incidence of leaf diseases.

There are many varieties of squash available and page 60 lists some of them.

Courtesy of Harris Seeds

FIG. 6.43. A STRAIGHT NECKED TYPE OF SUMMER SQUASH

Summer squash.—Summer squash is a bush type plant that produces many fruit. The fruit are harvested immature before the rind hardens. Many shapes and colors of fruit are produced by the various varieties. Fruits are usually white, green, or yellow. Fruits may be round and thin (patty pan type); club shaped (Zucchini type); or have a constricted, curved (crookneck type) or straight (straight neck) neck.

Squash fruits should be harvested when they are small and tender. Patty pan types are harvested when they are three or four inches in diameter and other types when they are six to eight inches long and two or three inches in diameter. Larger sized fruit is not of the best quality. All large sized fruit should be picked and discarded to encourage new production. The immature fruits bruise easily and they should be handled with care. Summer squash fruits are best used immediately and should be harvested two or three times a week.

Winter squash.—Winter squash plants are vining, semi-vining or bush types. The fruits vary widely in shape and color. The fruits are harvested when they have become a solid color and the rind is hard. The acorn types are harvested when a yellow-orange color has developed on the fruit in the area where it was in contact with the ground.

Winter squash is usually baked but may be used to make pumpkin pie. Many winter squashes make better pie than some pumpkins.

Winter squash is frequently harvested after a frost has killed the vines but before a hard frost. The fruits are cut from the vines with two inches of stem left on the fruits. Fruits which have been bruised, frost injured or are immature do not store well. They may be stored in a cool, dry place at a temperature of 50-55°F.

Common Problems.—Squash plants have problems similar to cucumber and the cucumber beetle should be controlled from planting onward. Squash may also be attacked by squash bugs and squash vine borer similar to pumpkin. (See pages 128, 132, 197 and 238 for control measures.) If an insecticide is used it should be applied in the late afternoon to prevent damage to bees. Bees are needed for pollination.

SUNFLOWER

Sunflower (*Helianthus annuus*) is native to North America where it grows wild. The giant types can be grown at the edge of the garden to form a screen or windbreak. The seeds of these giant types are eaten for food or used as birdseed.

Culture.—Seeds are planted in early spring, one inch deep and 18-24 inches apart for the giant types. Plants grow best in well drained, fertile

Courtesy of Harris Seeds

FIG. 6.44.   TABLE QUEEN, AN ACORN TYPE OF WINTER SQUASH

FIG. 6.45.   SUNFLOWER PLANTS GROW VERY LARGE

soils in full sunlight. During dry periods they should be irrigated.

Harvest.—Plants take 80-120 days to mature. As the seeds form they attract birds and a paper bag can be placed over them for protection. The head will be brown and the seeds plump at maturity. The head is cut off and the seeds rubbed loose and dried. They can be eaten raw or roasted, similar to pumpkin seeds.

SWEET POTATO

Sweet potato (*Ipomoea batatas*) is native to Central and South America. It was taken to Europe by Columbus and was first recorded as being used in the USA in the early 1600's. There is no evidence to suggest it was used by the North American Indians.

In many African countries, the true yam, which is a different plant (*Dioscorea* spp.), was grown instead of sweet potatoes. When the African blacks were brought to America, they called the sweet potato, a yam (*nyami*), since they grow and are eaten in a similar manner. In the deep south, moist fleshed varieties were grown, while other regions grew dry fleshed varieties, and many people thought of these plants as two different vegetables. Sweet potato and yam are identical species.

Culture.—Sweet potatoes grow best with four or five frost free months but will produce smaller roots under shorter growing seasons. They thrive under the hot conditions of the south but can be grown as far north as southern Michigan, and in the mild climates of the Pacific northwest.

The edible part of sweet potato is a root and plants should be grown in fertile, loose, sandy, crumbly soil. In heavy or wet soils, long and stringy roots are produced. Thus in many areas, sweet potatoes are grown on a ridge of soil 8-15 inches high, and three or four feet apart. This ridge is made before planting.

Sweet potatoes are grown from plants known as "slips." These may be purchased or produced by the gardener. Only disease free plants or roots should be used. To grow slips, disease free roots are placed in a hotbed about one inch apart and covered with three inches of sand or potting soil five or six weeks before transplanting. Soil temperatures should not exceed 85°F and the area should be kept damp but not waterlogged. The slips are removed from the roots by grasping them firmly and rapidly pulling them from the soil. The slips should be planted immediately.

Slips are transplanted one or two weeks after the last frost. They are planted two or three inches deep, 12-16 inches apart on the rigid rows. A starter fertilizer should be used.

Plants are hoed or cultivated to control weeds and prevent the vines from rooting and forming small roots. These roots would prevent the main storage roots from developing rapidly.

Once established, the plants need about three-fourths of an inch of water per week when small and more when growing vigorously. Excessive water after a dry period causes the roots to split. These usually heal with no loss in eating or storage quality. The plants should not be irrigated the last two weeks before harvest.

Common dry fleshed varieties include All Gold, Nemagold, Nugget and Yellow Jersey. Moist fleshed varieties include Centennial, Goldrush and Porto Rico. All these varieties are resistant to several diseases.

Harvest.— Sweet potatoes do not ripen or mature and time of harvest is determined by root size. They should be harvested before the first fall frost but a frost which only damages the vines will not harm the roots if they are dug immediately. Roots bruise easily and should be dug carefully. Roots, removed from the vines, are left to dry on the ground for two or three hours and then cured at 85°F and 85% humidity for ten days. Roots can then be stored at 55°F and high humidity.

Common Problems.—Sweet potatoes have few insect and disease pests in the garden. Various diseases can be controlled by using disease resistant varieties and crop rotation in the garden.

Soil stain or "scurf" causes black spots to appear on the skin of the roots. The roots are still edible once the skin is removed.

Courtesy of Harris Seeds

FIG. 6.46.   JET STAR IS A POPULAR MAIN CROP TYPE OF TOMATO

TOMATO

Tomato (*Lycopersicon esculentum*) is native to the Andes mountains of South America where it was used long before Columbus. It was taken to Europe where it was a popular vegetable by the 1500's. The tomato did not gain wide acceptance in the USA until the mid 1800's. Today it is the most popular vegetable grown in gardens.

Culture.—Tomatoes are a warm season crop and require only a small growing space. They are grown in the extreme south in the winter and the upper south and the north from spring to fall. Tomato does not thrive in cold weather and will not set fruit at temperatures below 58°F. Tomatoes are grown practically everywhere during some part of the growing season.

Tomatoes should be grown where they will receive at least six hours of direct sunlight. They are best started as transplants (see Plant Growth-pages 42-53) and planted after all danger of frost has passed. By using plant protectors during cold periods, the plants may be set out somewhat earlier. The hot, dry, midsummer weather in the south is not favorable for planting tomatoes. Tomatoes do not set fruit above 85°F. Tomato transplants should not have fruit on them when planted, as this stunts their growth and the plants fail to develop sufficiently for a good yield. The transplants should be planted to about the same depth as they were growing indoors. Soil should be pressed firmly around the plant after transplanting and a starter fertilizer added.

Dwarf tomato plants are spaced 12 inches apart in rows three feet apart; wirecaged or uncaged plants are spaced at 24-36 inches in rows four feet apart and staked plants are spaced 18 inches apart in rows three feet apart.

Plants may be allowed to grow on the ground. A mulch should be used under the plants to prevent diseases and conserve water.

Plants may be grown in wire cages to keep the fruits off the ground. This will help control diseases and make cultivation and harvesting easier. A five foot length of six inch mesh, concrete reinforcing wire can be made into a cage 18 inches in diameter (see page 137).

Plants may also be pruned and either staked or trained onto a trellis. Some varieties are not suited for this procedure. The stakes should be pushed two feet into the ground near the plants soon after transplanting. Twine or cloth is tightly tied to the stake, two inches above a leaf stem and then loosely tied around the main stem just below the base of the leaf stem. The plants may also be trained onto a trellis or supported by the side of a building, instead of stakes. Training the plants to a stake or trellis prevents fruit rots and conserves space but increases fruit cracking and blossom end rot. Tomatoes may be produced two weeks earlier by pruning the staked plants, but total yield is reduced. The tomato plants can be pruned to one or two stems. Once a week, the small shoots that appear where the leaf stem joins the main stem are removed. The shoot is bent sharply to one side until it snaps and then pulled off in the opposite direction.

Tomatoes grow best on fertile, well drained soil. Plants can be side dressed when the plants have several fruits. About three pounds of 10-10-10 fertilizer or equivalent per 100 feet of row can be used. During the growing season tomatoes need one inch of water each week and container grown plants will need daily irrigation. However large amounts of water and fertilizer stimulate vegetative growth and the plant may not set fruit.

Varieties.—There are hundreds of tomato varieties available. Fruits come in a number of shapes, sizes and colors. Plants produce an early, main season or late crop and the variety should be adapted to the gardener's growing season. In short growing seasons, early or midseason types may have to be grown. Varieties should also carry resistance to diseases, and in the south and west they should carry nematode resistance. Resistance to verticillium wilt disease, fusarium wilt disease and nematodes is frequently indicated by having the letter V, F, N follow the named variety. In order to grow the variety desired, the plants may have to be grown as transplants by the gardener.

Main Crop Varieties.—The main crop types produce medium to large fruit of various maturities. Most varieties listed are the main crop types. New and more disease resistant varieties are continuously being produced. See your state agricultural experiment station for varieties adapted in your specific location (see Appendix for addresses).

Orange or Yellow Fruit Varieties.—These varieties are frequently considered to be lower in acid but the acid content is similar to main crop varieties. The orange and yellow fruits do have a higher sugar content and taste sweeter. Caro Rich, Golden Boy, Jubilee and Sunray are varieties.

Container Varieties.—Any tomato which can be grown in the garden can also be grown in containers and supported with a trellis. However there are a number of varieties that produce small red fruit under two inches in diameter on plants less than two feet high. Such varieties include Patio, Pixie, Presto, Early Salad, Small Fry VFN (vines three feet high), Tiny Tim, Toy Boy and Tumblin Tom.

Paste Varieties.—These varieties contain less water in the fruits and are eaten fresh or used for paste, catsup or canning whole. Roma VF and San Marzano are varieties.

Salad Tomatoes.—These are often called cherry tomatoes and vary in size up to one and a half inches in diameter. Fruit is yellow or red and

Courtesy of Harris Seeds

FIG. 6.47. ROMA VF IS A PASTE TYPE OF TOMATO

produced on standard type plants. Varieties include Basket Pak (red), Cherry (red), Gardeners Delight (red), Pear (yellow or red), Plum (yellow or red), Red Cherry (red), and Sugar Lump (red).

Harvest.—To obtain the best flavor, tomato fruits should be harvested when they are fully ripe and firm. They ripen best at 68°F. When temperatures are near 90°F, the tomatoes become soft before the color has fully developed. At this time, tomatoes should be picked every other day when the fruits have turned pink and ripened indoors at 60-75°F. Light will increase the color some but it is not required for ripening.

Before frost, green tomatoes can be harvested, wrapped in newspaper and stored at 50-60°F for several months. They will ripen when placed at room temperature. Tomato vines containing the fruit can be hung in a warm shelter to finish ripening for immediate use.

Common Problems.—Insects that attack tomatoes include flea beetle, tomato fruitworms, hornworms, aphids, leafminers, Colorado potato beetles, whitefly and spider mites. (See pages 128 and 132 for control measures.)

The two most common diseases are fusarium and verticillium wilts. Resistant varieties should be grown and crop rotation practiced. Blossom end rot is caused by a calcium deficiency and water stress. This is more common on staked or pruned plants. More uniform irrigation helps.

Sunscald occurs on fruits exposed to high temperatures in direct sunlight. A large, whitish area appears on the exposed fruit and occurs when little foliage is covering the fruit.

Tobacco mosaic virus can be transmitted to tomato by gardeners who use tobacco. Plants should not be handled unless hands and tools are washed and gardeners should not smoke around the plants. The virus is transmitted by direct contact.

Courtesy of Harris Seeds

FIG. 6.48. PURPLE TOP TURNIP

TURNIP AND RUTABAGA

Turnip (*Brassica rapa*) originated in western Asia and grows wild in Siberia. It has been used since prehistoric times. Rutabaga (*Brassica napus* var. *napobrassica*) or Swede turnip was developed in the Middle Ages from a cross between cabbage and turnip.

Plant Characteristics.—The two plants are generally considered as close relatives but they are different plants. Turnip roots are generally white fleshed and become pithy early. Turnip plants grow rapidly and have rough, hairy leaves. Rutabaga roots are generally yellow fleshed, more solid and have a longer storage life. Rutabaga plants have smooth, waxy leaves and need a month longer to develop roots of similar size to turnips.

Culture.—Both plants are cool season vegetables and the most widely adapted root crops in North America. They are grown in the south during fall, winter and spring; and in the north, as a spring or fall crop. Rutabagas grow best in northern regions while turnips grow best in latitudes south of Indianapolis, IN.

Plants are hardy to cold and susceptible to heat and should be planted as late as practical for use in the fall before a hard freeze. Turnips are easily grown in the south during winter and spring. In the north, turnips and rutabagas are best planted for a fall crop after cabbage, peas, early potatoes or sweet corn. If turnips are spring planted, they should be planted as soon as the garden can be worked. However, if they are exposed to temperatures of 40°F for long periods they may flower. Rutabagas are often difficult to grow as a spring crop due to their longer growing season.

Seeds are planted one half inch deep in rows 12-18 inches apart. The area should be irrigated during summer to germinate the seeds and establish the seedlings. Turnip is thinned to stand three inches apart and rutabaga thinned to six inches apart.

Varieties of turnip include Early Purple Top Strap Leaf, Just Right (also for greens), Purple Top White Globe, Shogoin (also called Foliage-also for greens), and Tokyo Cross (also for greens).

Most rutabaga varieties are types of American Purple Top. Laurentian, Purple Top Yellow and Red Chief are also frequently available.

Harvest.—Turnip greens may be harvested a month after seeding. In hot weather turnip roots become bitter and pithy and must be used before warm weather occurs. Fall harvested roots may be two to four inches in diameter for turnips and three or more inches thick for rutabagas. Both turnips and rutabagas may be left in the ground like parsnips and harvested when needed in mild climates. They are hardy to frosts and can be mulched to allow harvest through early winter in northern regions.

Common Problems.—Similar to radish, the cabbage root maggot can be a pest. If a problem exists, an insecticide is needed before the crop is planted.

VEGETABLE SPAGHETTI SQUASH

Vegetable spaghetti squash (*Cucurbita pepo*) is a variety of winter squash which originated along with other squash. Like squash, it has separate male and female flowers on the same plant and it is cross pollinated. It will cross pollinate with any of the other *Cucurbita pepo* listed on page 60.

Culture.—Vegetable spaghetti will grow wherever winter squash is grown and it is grown in a similar manner. Plants may be grown as transplants or seeded directly in the garden after all danger of frost is past.

FIG. 6.49. VEGETABLE SPAGHETTI SQUASH

Four to six seeds are planted one inch deep spaced two inches apart in groups (hills). The hills are three feet apart with rows six to eight feet apart. The hills are thinned to two or three seedlings when the plants begin to crowd each other.

Vegetable spaghetti has disease and insect problems which are similar to squash. Cucumber beetles should be controlled from planting onward.

Vegetable spaghetti is the only variety listed. It may be listed under novelty items or with the fall and winter squash.

Harvest.—Fruits are ready for harvest 100 days after planting when they have turned from green to yellow. Fruits are 8-10 inches long and weigh three to six pounds. Production ends at the first frost which does not harm the fruit. For storage, fruits are harvested with an inch of stem on the fruit and cured in a sunny place outdoors for a week. They are then stored in a cool, dry location.

Vegetable spaghetti may be boiled (30 minutes) or baked (one hour) until the fruit surface yields to pressure. There is less water in the baked spaghetti. The fruit is cut lengthwise, the seeds scooped out and the spaghetti strands removed with a fork. It has few calories and can be used similar to noodles in soups or as spaghetti. Cooked vegetable spaghetti strands can be placed in plastic bags and stored frozen.

WATERMELON

Watermelon (*Citrullus vulgaris*) originated in Africa and was taken to

Courtesy of W. Atlee Burpee Seed Co.

FIG. 6.50.   SUGAR BUSH WATERMELON

Europe in the sixteenth century. Early settlers brought the watermelon with them to America.

The citron (*C. lanatus* var. *citroides*) is a type of watermelon which is used differently. It is not edible when raw and is eaten cooked, pickled or candied. This type of melon was used by the North American Indians before Columbus and is possibly of American origin. (Catalogues list it under watermelon).

Plant Characteristics.—Watermelon requires a lot of space to grow its large vines. Separate male and female flowers occur on the same plant but they do not cross pollinate with cucumbers, squash or pumpkins. The citron melon is grown similar to watermelon.

Culture.—Watermelon can be grown in nearly all regions of the country. It requires more summer heat than muskmelon, but if muskmelon grows well in the area, the small icebox watermelon varieties can be grown. Under short growing seasons, the plants do not produce enough sugar and the melons produced are not sweet. In these areas, early varieties, transplants and mulches should be used.

Watermelons are grown similar to cucumber but require much more space. Transplants (see Plant Growth-pages 42-53) or seeds are planted after all danger of frost is past and are set apart in hills. Seeds are planted one inch deep and thinned to three plants per hill. They may also be planted as single plants, one plant every two or three feet. Rows are spaced six or seven feet apart. For transplants, a starter fertilizer should be used.

Plants grow best on light sandy soils. Watermelon plants are deep rooted and once established will not require irrigation if the soil stores nine inches of water. At this minimum amount of water, yields are increased by irrigation.

There are a number of varieties available which produce red or yellow colored flesh in round, oval or long fruits. Seedless varieties require a standard variety for pollination as they do not produce viable pollen. Seeds of such a variety are generally included when seedless varieties are purchased. Seeds of seedless watermelons are expensive and they are usually started as transplants.

Early varieties or icebox types which mature in 70-75 days with round fruit under 10 pounds include Golden Midget (red flesh-skin turns golden when ripe), New Hampshire Midget (red flesh), Rhode Island Red (red flesh), Sugar Baby (red flesh), and Yellow Baby (yellow flesh). These varieties may be trained onto a trellis.

Main season varieties are red fleshed and mature in 80-90 days. The fruit weighs over 20 pounds. Varieties include Blackstone (oval fruit), Blue Ribbon (long), Charleston Gray (long), Crimson Sweet (oval), Klondike types (long) and Improved Peacock (long).

Red fleshed, oval shaped, seedless varieties which mature in 80-90 days include Triple Sweet and Tri X 313.

Harvest.—A number of indicators can be used to determine if a watermelon is ripe. 1) Fruits have a ground spot where they lay on the soil. This spot becomes light green or yellow as the fruit matures. 2) The curly tendril on the leaf near the stem dries and becomes brown when the melon is ripe. However, in some varieties, the tendril dries up 10 days before the fruit is ripe. 3) The skin becomes rough as they mature. 4) The melon can be rapped with the knuckles. A sharp metalic sound indicates the melon is immature. A dull sound indicates it is mature. This test is best done in early morning as melons thumped in the heat of the day and those that have been picked and stored all sound ripe.

Watermelons are cut off the vine. The rinds may be pickled or candied.

Common Problems.—Insect and disease problems are similar to cucumbers and pumpkins described on page 197. Cucumber beetles need to be controlled from planting onward. Anthracnose disease is a problem in warm moist weather, particularly in the southeast. If this disease is a problem, resistant varieties should be grown; treated seed should be used; the crop rotated in the garden; and all old vines should be removed as the disease overwinters in these vines.

Birds may make holes in the top of the watermelons. The dark skinned varieties, like Sugar Baby, are not as attractive to them.

SELECTED REFERENCES

ANON. 1975. Seed for today. Asgrow Seed Co. Descriptive catalog of vegetable varieties No. *21*.

ADJEI-TWUM, D.C., SPLITTSTOESSER, W.E., and VANDEMARK, J.S. 1976. Use of soybeans as sprouts. HortScience *11*, 235-236.

ANDERSON, E. 1954. Plants, man and life. Andrew Melrose Ltd. London.

BANADYGA, A.A. 1977. Greens or "potherbs"-chard, collards, kale, mustard, spinach, New Zealand spinach. *In* Growing your own vegetables. USDA Bulletin *409*.

BUBEL, N.W. 1977. Vegetables money can't buy but you can grow. David R. Godine Publisher, Boston, Mass.

DOTY, W.L. 1973. All about vegetables. Chevron chemical Co. San Francisco, CA.

GARRISON, S.A., and ELLISON, J.H. 1977. Asparagus starts up slow but goes on and on; rhubarb also takes its own sweet time. *In* Growing your own vegetables. USDA Bulletin *409*.

GIBBONS, E. 1973. Feast on a diabetic diet. David McKay Co. New York.

MEINERS, J.P. and KRAFT, J.M. 1977. Beans and peas are easy to grow and produce a wealth of food. *In* Growing your own vegetables. USDA Bulletin *409*.

METCALF, H.N., and BURNHAM, M. 1977. Miscellany, including celeriac, horseradish, artichoke, peanuts, vegetable soybeans. *In* Growing your own vegetables. USDA Bulletin *409*.

MINGES, P.A. 1977. Play it cool with cole crops (cabbage, etc.); they attain best quality if matured in fall. In Growing your own vegetables. USDA Bulletin *409*.

REYNOLDS, C.W. 1977. The complex art of planting. *In* Growing your own vegetables. USDA Bulletin *409*.

SIMS, W.L., *et al.* 1977. Home vegetable gardening. Univ. Calif. Agri. Sci. Leaflet *2989*.

SPLITTSTOESSER, W.E. 1977. Protein quality and quantity of tropical roots and tubers. HortScience *12*, 294-298.

7

Growing and Preserving Herbs

The botanical definition of an herb is a plant without a permanent woody stem. This would include nearly all plants except trees and shrubs. The popular definition of an herb is a group of plants grown for their flavors, essential oils, and scents. This definition would include sage and rosemary which develop woody stems.

GROWING CONDITIONS

Herbs may be grown in formal or informal gardens, grown with vegetables or grown as an individual plant. The herbs are frequently grown from seed planted indoors. The seeds are planted in individual containers or in a sterile soil mix about ¼ inch deep. The seeds are sown thinly and may remain exposed to the air or covered with a thin layer of sand. The seeds are watered with a fine mist and the container covered with newspaper, glass or damp burlap to prevent the seeds from rapidly drying out. Most herbs germinate best at 70°F or warmer and many seeds are slow and erratic to germinate. Rosemary for example, may take three weeks to germinate. Many herbs such as mint, rosemary, thyme, sage and tarragon are grown from rooted cuttings and mints and chives are grown from divisions of existing plants.

The majority of herbs grow well in any well-drained soil. The soil should be moderately fertile and well supplied with organic matter. If soil drainage is poor, it is preferable to grow herbs in containers or raised beds. If grown in containers, the cold-sensitive herbs may be brought inside during the winter.

The herbs should be mulched to keep leaves clean during heavy rains. The leaves of parsley, for example, can be pushed into the soil during rains and a mulch keeps the leaves and soil separated.

Most herbs grow best with a large amount of sunlight, low humidity, seasonal changes and an average amount of rainfall, evenly distributed. Herbs are grown, therefore, in all locations in the U.S. Herbs generally have few insect and disease problems but parsley is frequented by the caterpillar of the swallowtail butterfly and dill may also have an insect problem.

HARVEST

Most herbs are ready to harvest just before the flowers appear on the plant. At this time they contain the greatest amounts of essential oils and scents. Successive cuttings can be made over the growing season but the lower leaves should be left on annuals to allow them to continue growth. At the end of the season, the entire annual plant can be harvested. Perennials should also be harvested over the growing season. Late harvests should be avoided as the plant needs to regrow and store food in order to survive the winter.

Herbs are best harvested on a clear day in early morning as the essential oils are greatest at this time. The oils diminish as sunlight and temperatures increase during the day. Herbs grown for seed such as dill and caraway may be harvested just before the seeds fall naturally.

DRYING HERBS

The foliage should be washed, the excess water shaken off and dried rapidly. A dark, well-ventilated area where temperatures never exceed 100°F is best for drying. When exposed to open-air, light and high temperatures, the essential oils decline, flavor changes and herb quality rapidly declines. Under proper conditions the total shelf life of most herbs is one or two years.

After the herbs are washed they can be gathered into bunches and placed in a brown paper bag (to prevent them from getting dusty during drying). About one or two inches of stem should be left exposed, the bag tied loosely and hung in a warm, dry location. Seed heads from dill, anise and caraway may also be dried in this manner. The seed heads can be placed in the bag as the seeds are becoming (turning grey or brown) ripe, and the stems cut. Seeds and leaves should be dry in two or three weeks. The leaves can be pulverized by rubbing them between your hands, and the stems excluded.

Herb leaves may be dried on trays. The stems are removed and the washed leaves spread on a tray or window screen. The leaves should be turned to insure uniform drying. If these screens are placed in the oven for fast drying, the temperature should not exceed 100°F, particularly when drying basil. The oven door is left slightly open to allow moisture to escape and the herbs should be dry in three to six hours.

Herbs should be thoroughly dry and stored in airtight containers. If the leaf is stored intact and not pulverized, they usually retain their flavor longer. The leaves can be crushed just before use but storing whole leaves requires more storage space. Dried herbs stored in airtight containers kept in the dark will retain their flavor for one to two years.

FREEZING HERBS

Herbs may be washed, shaken dry and sealed in airtight containers for freezing. They may be chopped or left whole but they should not be blanched before freezing. Frozen herbs should be used without defrosting. Chives, dill, mint, oregano, parsley, sweet marjoram and tarragon freeze well. Caraway, anise and dill seeds may also be stored frozen.

FRESH STORAGE

For fresh storage, the herbs should be harvested and placed in airtight containers. They will keep longer if the foliage is not washed until the herb is ready to be used. Properly stored fresh leaves will retain their quality for two to four months and may be harvested in the fall and stored fresh for use at Thanksgiving.

ANISE

Anise (*Pimpinella anisium*) is an annual plant 18-30 inches high. The plant produces an umbrella-like seed head resembling wild carrot. Both seeds and leaves are used. Anise may be started indoors or planted directly in the garden, one seed per inch about one half inch deep. They should be thinned to three or four plants per foot. Seeds are harvested when they turn brown in late fall and have a sweet, spicy taste. It has a licorice-like flavor used in cakes, cookies and candies. The leaves can be used in cooking or in fruit salads.

BASIL

Basil (*Ocimum basilicum*) is an annual plant which grows 18-24 inches in height. The plants may be either green or purple (opal basil) and are started indoors from seed. They should be transplanted about 10 inches apart. The flowers should be continually removed before the seeds mature to stimulate continual foliage development. Leaves can be harvested until the first frost which kills the plant. The leaves are sensi-

FIG. 7.1. BASIL IS A POPULAR HOME GARDEN HERB

tive to temperature and should be air dried in a shady area. If the leaves are not dry within three days, they should be dried in the oven at 90°F or the leaves will turn brown. Basil may also be grown indoors in a container for fresh use during the winter. Basil is used in soups, stews, omelets, egg dishes and salads.

CARAWAY

Caraway (*Carum carvi*) is a biennial plant usually grown for its seeds. It grows about 18-24 inches high and is planted from seed indoors or directly in the garden. Seeds are planted one half inch deep in rows two feet apart and plants are thinned to six plants per foot or row. The plants should be grown in an area which will not be spaded up the following season as the plants require two years to produce seed. Plants grow the first season, die down when winter comes and regrow the following season. They produce seed stalks the second year. Seed should be harvested when they are brown, and then dried in the sun or shade. Seeds are used in breads, cakes, and with cabbage, cole slaw, carrots, cheese and potatoes. The roots may be prepared and eaten like carrots or turnips. Leaves can be used in soups and stews.

CHIVES

Chive (*Allium schoenoprasum*) is a perennial which grows about one

FIG. 7.2.   CHIVE LEAVES ARE CUT CLOSE TO THE GROUND REGULARLY TO
ENCOURAGE NEW GROWTH. CUT FLOWERS ARE IN THE FOREGROUND.

foot high. It grows in clumps of small, bulbous plants and is usually
propagated by dividing the clumps into five bulblets for transplanting.
The clumps can be planted in the spring or fall and should be divided
every three years to prevent overcrowding. If chives are started from
seed they should be planted one-fourth inch deep as early in the spring as
possible.

Leaves may be harvested throughout the growing season. The plants
should be cut close to the ground regularly to encourage new bulblets to
develop, prevent the leaves from becoming tough, and prevent flower
formation. Flowers are often desirable, however, as an attractive purple
flower is produced in early spring.

The harvested leaves can be used immediately, chopped and frozen for
later use, or dried. They should be dried completely and placed in airtight containers. Any moisture will be absorbed causing the chives to lose
color and flavor.

Chives may be grown inside during the winter and used fresh, but
chives need a rest period to rejuvenate. A clump may be dug in late
January and planted, and grown indoors; or a clump may be planted in a
pot in late summer, the pot sunk into the ground and brought into the
house 90 days after the first killing frost.

Chives have an onion-like flavor and are used in soups, salads, sauces
and with cottage cheese.

Courtesy of Ferry Morse Seeds

FIG. 7.3. THE SEED HEAD OF DILL

DILL

Dill (*Anethum graveolens*) is a hardy annual that grows two or three feet in height. The plant has feathery leaves with an open umbrella-shaped seedhead and resembles wild carrot in appearance. The umbels produce yellow flowers and eventually produce seed. Young dill plants are difficult to transplant and should be planted directly in the garden. They are planted one fourth inch deep and thinned to one plant every 5-10 inches.

Dill leaves, seed heads and seeds are used. Leaves may be harvested eight weeks after seeding by cutting the outer leaves close to the stem. They may be dried or frozen fresh. For pickling, the flowering umbels are used and should be harvested with a few leaves when in full bloom. These may be bagged and dried or used fresh. Seeds should be harvested when they are light brown. The umbels are cut in the early morning when there is less chance of the seeds being shaken loose and lost. The umbels are placed in a bag and when dried the seeds are shaken loose.

Dill easily re-seeds itself for next year and a few plants may be left for this purpose. Frequently new plants will develop from these seeds in late summer or fall. The leaves of these plants are of excellent quality and are harvested before the flower heads appear.

The leaves are used in salads, soups and omelets. The flowering umbels are used in making pickles. Seeds are used in soups and baking.

FIG. 7.4.   OREGANO

MARJORAM AND OREGANO

There are many varieties of these herbs but sweet marjoram (*Origanum majorana*) and Oregano (*Origanum vulgare*) are the most widely grown. The major herb difference between these perennial plants is that oregano is more hardy, but both may not overwinter in cold northern climates. Sweet marjoram is frequently grown as an annual. The plants are grown in a similar manner and both should be heavily mulched during the winter and uncovered in the spring to insure their survival in cold climates.

These herbs are grown from seed, root cuttings or crown divisions. They should be started indoors if grown from seed and transplanted about six inches apart when the soil has warmed. The plants may be dug up in the fall and grown indoors during the winter and planted outdoors the following spring.

Leaves may be harvested throughout the season. When flowers appear the plants should be cut back to about four inches above ground level to stimulate new growth. This second growth is the main crop. The herbs may be cut back two or three times a season.

The harvested plant should be dried rapidly. When dry, the leaves will powder and can be sifted through a screen to remove the woody stems. It may then be stored for later use.

Marjoram and oregano are used with green vegetables, salads, soups, in herb butter, and with various meat and egg dishes.

Courtesy of Harris Seeds

FIG. 7.5. CURLY-LEAVED PARSLEY PRODUCES
THE MOST LEAVES FOR SEASONING

FIG. 7.6. FLAT LEAVED PARSLEY IS USED FOR ITS LEAVES AND ROOTS

PARSLEY

Parsley is a biennial that grows about one foot high. The second year it produces seeds and thus is frequently grown as an annual. There are two distinct types of parsley. The flat leaf or Italian parsley (*Petroselinum hortense*) is used for its leaves and roots. The curly-leaved or triple curled parsley (*Petroselinum crispum*) is used for its leaves.

Parsley is best started from seed indoors but it may be sown directly in the garden in early spring, about one seed per inch and later thinned to stand five inches apart.

Leaves may be harvested throughout the growing season and the plants remain green until early winter. The entire plant is usually harvested and dried in late fall. The leaves should be dried in a short time in the shade and may be finally oven dried. Once dried, parsley leaves are stored in a dry, tight, dark container. When parsley leaves lose color, they also lose flavor.

Parsley is the most widely grown herb used for garnishing and flavoring. It can be blended with other herbs such as basil, marjoram, oregano, rosemary, summer savory and thyme. The combination of these herbs imparts flavor as a unit, rather than as a single herb flavor.

FIG. 7.7. PEPPERMINT IS A RAPIDLY GROWING PERENNIAL

PEPPERMINT

Peppermint (*Mentha piperita*) is a hardy perennial that grows three feet in height and is the most useful of the mints. It is propagated from roots, rooted cuttings or entire plants. Peppermint seed germinates well the first year but the plants produced are often not true to the parent plants. The underground stems spread rapidly and may easily occupy too much garden area. To contain peppermint, a large tile is placed on end buried in the ground with about three inches of tile above ground. The mint is grown in this container which limits its spread.

Peppermint leaves may be harvested throughout the year, with the best quality leaves being produced in late summer. The mint is best harvested when it begins to flower or the lower leaves become yellow. The plant can be cut back to one inch above the ground and all stems and leaves removed to reduce diseases. Peppermint may be completely harvested twice a season. The leaves should be removed and dried in warm shade, and then stored in a sealed container. After the final fall harvest, the plants should be covered with two inches of compost to provide nutrients for the next season and to protect the plants from frost damage.

Peppermint is used in mint jelly and sauce, to flavor tea and other beverages and to put on salads to provide a cooling effect.

ROSEMARY

Rosemary (*Rosmarinus officinalis*) is a perennial evergreen shrub that grows two feet in height. It cannot stand temperature below 27°F, and may be grown as an annual in cold climates, or heavily mulched and covered to protect it during the winter. Plants may be potted and taken indoors for winter use and to produce cuttings.

FIG. 7.8. ROSEMARY GROWING IN A CONTAINER FOR INDOOR WINTER USE

Rosemary can be propagated from seeds, cuttings or layering. Seeds should be started indoors in early spring but frequently only 10-20% of the seeds germinate, and it may take two or three years to produce a cuttable bush.

Cuttings are produced by removing a six inch tip of new growth and placing the lower four inches in sand or vermiculite. To produce a new plant by layering, a lower branch of the bush is buried in the soil. When the roots have formed on the branch, the new plant is cut from the mother plant.

Rosemary should be planted one foot apart and may be trimmed several times each season to harvest the leaves. When the removed stems are thoroughly dry, the leaves are stripped off and stored in a closed container. Rosemary leaves are used as an accent in soups, stews, meats, sauces and leafy greens. It is frequently picked fresh and cuttings laid directly on roasts and poultry. Rosemary may also be added as an ingredient of mixed herbs.

FIG. 7.9.   SAGE IS BOTH AN HERB AND AN ORNAMENTAL PLANT

SAGE

Sage (*Salvia officinalis*) is a shrubby perennial plant which grows 15-38 inches tall. It will withstand most American winters and grows best on well drained soil. The crucial factors in determining how well sage overwinters depends upon when and how many leaves were harvested in the fall. The plant needs some leaves to provide energy for winter survival. The last harvest should occur no later than late summer or early fall and then only leaves and stems high up on the plant should be harvested. The first year of growth only one light harvest is possible if the plant is to survive the winter.

Sage may be propagated from seeds, stem cuttings or divisions of the plant itself (crown divisions). Seeds may be planted indoors a month earlier than planted outside in the garden. The seedlings may be transplanted when they are three inches high and spaced 12-18 inches apart.

Each spring the woody growth should be trimmed back severely to eliminate flowering that prevents vegetative growth. However, some gardeners use little sage and grow the plant as an ornamental. It produces fragrant purple flowers the second and following years.

The top six to eight inches of growth should be harvested at least twice during the growing season. Frequently the leaves and stems are washed, placed in a bag and hung up to dry. The sage is not removed until ready to use. Sage leaves may also be dried in the shade until they are crisp. If the leaves are to be used as a tea, the leaves can be broken up by hand. For seasoning, the leaves should be rubbed through a fine screen.

Sage leaves are used as a tea and for stuffing pork, duck and geese. The powdered leaves are used to flavor cheeses, gravies, sauces and sausages.

SPEARMINT

Spearmint (*Mentha spicata*) is a perennial that grows about three feet tall. It differs from peppermint by having smooth, bright green leaves and its taste is less potent than peppermint. It is grown and harvested similar to peppermint, however.

Spearmint is more popular than peppermint and is the mint most commonly used in julips and other beverages, jellies and sauces.

SUMMER SAVORY

Summer Savory (*Satureia hortensis*) is an annual which grows about 18 inches in height. It grows rapidly and is started from seed either indoors or planted directly in the garden. Seeds should be planted in rows about one fourth inch deep and one inch apart. If the topsoil dries out quickly, the soil should be watered lightly to keep the seeds moist. The plants should be thinned to six or eight inches apart.

Plants are harvested when they are six inches high and harvesting may continue throughout the growing season. This will delay flowering and promote vegetative growth. When the plant finally does flower, the entire plant may be harvested when the flowers open. If the plant is not harvested at this time, the leaves will turn yellow, curl and drop.

The harvested leaves and stems dry rapidly in warm shade. They may be tied into small bundles and dried on paper or fine screens. When dry, the leaves are removed and stored in closed containers.

Summer savory is used in egg, rice and bean dishes; as a tea; in soups, sauces and stuffings; on salads; and nearly all kinds of meat and fowl. It is also used in various herb blends and mixtures.

TARRAGON

French Tarragon (*Artemisia dracunculus*) is a hardy perennial plant which may grow to three feet in height. The desirable variety is French or German tarragon, and seldom has flowers that produce viable seed. The less desirable variety is Russian tarragon which produces large amounts of seed and lacks the essential oils. French tarragon is propagated by cuttings or by splitting the root cluster of a mature plant into two or three new plants (crown divisions) in early spring. These root clusters are planted 12-20 inches apart and should be split into new plants every four years to rejuvenate them.

Tarragon should be mulched to protect the plant over winter. A root cluster may be placed in a 10-inch or larger pot and grown indoors for winter use.

Mature plants can be harvested throughout the growing season and is preferably used fresh. The top growth should be harvested two or three times a season to encourage branching of the stems. Tarragon leaves are sensitive to temperature and should not be dried above 90°F. Leaves should be removed from the stem and dried rapidly in the dark. Tarragon leaves are stored in tight, dry, dark containers.

Tarragon has the sweet aroma of fresh mowed hay. It is often used in herb blends but tarragon flavor can easily overpower other herbs. It is used in sauces, dressings, with green vegetables and in tartar sauce for fish dishes.

Tarragon vinegar is a popular use of this herb. A wide mouth bottle is filled with fresh leaves and stems and the bottle filled with apple or wine vinegar and closed. After a few weeks the tarragon vinegar is ready for use in various salads and sauces.

Thyme

Thyme (*Thymus vulgaris*) is a shrublike perennial that grows 6-12 inches in height. There are many closely related species of thyme which are used as ornamentals and as ground covers. The herb thyme has three varieties which differ principally in the width of the leaves; English (varigated leaves), French (narrow leaves) and German (broad leaves).

Thyme is propagated from seed, cuttings or by dividing the mature plant. Seeds should be planted indoors in early spring and will take about two weeks to germinate at 70°F. When the plants are three inches high,

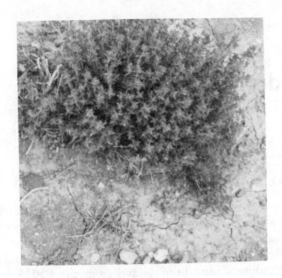

FIG. 7.10. THYME IS A SMALL PLANT WHICH PRODUCES SMALL LEAVES AND THUS IS OFTEN NOT GROWN IN HERB GARDENS

they can be transplanted in the garden about one foot apart. When plants are three or four years old, they should be divided into new plants to prevent the mature plants from becoming excessively woody with a resulting reduction in leaf production. Many gardeners begin new plants from cuttings or seed rather than divide the mature plants.

Thyme should be harvested just before the pink or violet flowers appear. Mature plants can be harvested by cutting the entire plant two inches above the ground. A second crop can be harvested in late summer but only the upper one-third of the plant should be removed. Removing too much foliage may prevent thyme from overwintering, particularly if temperatures fluxuate widely and the plant is not mulched. Thyme is hardy but needs a mulch to overwinter better in cold climates.

Thyme may be blended in with other herbs and many recommend using thyme in practically everything. It is used with meat, poultry, fish, soups, gravies, cheese, chowders, egg dishes and almost all vegetables.

Appendix

ADDITIONAL SOURCES OF INFORMATION

This text covers a wide range of information on producing quality vegetables in a garden. However, some areas are covered only briefly and research is constantly developing new varieties, new techniques and modifying old ones. Additional information on vegetables and a wide variety of other subjects may be obtained from the USDA and the Cooperative Extension Service.

Requests for a list of available publications from the USDA may be obtained from: Office of Communications, U.S. Department of Agriculture, Washington, D.C. 20250. Many such publications can be ordered for a nominal fee from Superintendent of Documents, U.S. Government Printing Office, Washington, D.C., 20402.

The Cooperative Extension Service is a state-wide, service-oriented program with the headquarters located at the state's agricultural experiment station. Nearly every county in the nation has an office, usually located at the county seat. The office is listed in the telephone book under the county government or as the county's Cooperative Extension Service. For example, residents of Champaign County will find the office listed as "Champaign County Cooperative Extension Service." Gardeners may contact these offices for additional information, for help in insect and disease identification, to receive various state publications and be informed of local meetings concerning vegetable gardening. Gardeners may also write directly to the Agriculture Experiment Stations located in their state at the address given in Table A.1.

SEED COMPANIES

The firms listed in Table A.2 represent a partial list of seed-houses. The list indicates the firm's name and address, and a short description of each catalogue. The number of pages devoted to vegetables is listed so

TABLE A.1. AGRICULTURAL EXPERIMENT STATIONS

State	Address
Alabama	Auburn University, Auburn, AL 36830
Alaska	University of Alaska, Fairbanks, AK 99701
Arizona	University of Arizona, Tucson, AZ 85721
Arkansas	University of Arkansas, Fayetteville, AR 72701
California	University of California, 2200 Univ. Ave., Berkeley, CA 94720
Colorado	Colorado State University, Fort Collins, CO 80523
Connecticut	Univ. of Connecticut, Storrs, CT 06268
Delaware	Univ. of Delaware, Newark, DE 18711
District of Columbia	Federal City College, 1424 St. N.W., Washington, D.C. 20005
Florida	Univ. of Florida, Gainesville, FL 32611
Georgia	Univ. of Georgia, Athens, GA 30601
Hawaii	Univ. of Hawaii, Honolulu, HI 96822
Idaho	Univ. of Idaho, Moscow, ID 83843
Illinois	Univ. of Illinois, Urbana, IL 61801
Indiana	Purdue University, West Lafayette, IN 47907
Iowa	Iowa State University, Ames, IA 50010
Kansas	Kansas State Univ., Manhattan, KS 66506
Kentucky	Univ. of Kentucky, Lexington, KY 40506
Louisiana	Louisiana State Univ., Baton Rouge, LA 70803
Maine	University of Maine, Orono, ME 04473
Maryland	Univ. of Maryland, College Park, MD 20742
Massachusetts	Univ. of Massachusetts, Amherst, MA 01002
Michigan	Michigan State University, East Lansing, MI 48824
Minnesota	University of Minnesota, St. Paul, MN 55101
Mississippi	Miss. State University, Mississippi State, MS 39672
Missouri	Univ. of Missouri, Columbia, MO 65201
Montana	Montana State Univ., Bozeman, MT 59715
Nebraska	Univ. of Nebraska, Lincoln, NB 68503
Nevada	Univ. of Nevada, Reno, NV 89507
New Hampshire	Univ. of New Hampshire, Durham, NH 03824
New Jersey	Rutgers Univ., New Brunswick, NJ 08903
New Mexico	N.M. State Univ., Box 3AE, Agriculture Bldg., Las Cruces, NM 88003
New York	Cornell University, Ithaca, NY 14853
North Carolina	N.C. State University, Raleigh, NC 27607
North Dakota	N.D. State University, Fargo, ND 58102
Ohio	Ohio State Univ., 2120 Fyffe Rd., Columbus, OH 43210
Oklahoma	Oklahoma State Univ., Stillwater, OK 74074
Oregon	Oregon State Univ., Corvallis, OR 97331
Pennsylvania	Penn. State Univ., University Park, PA 16802
Rhode Island	Univ. of Rhode Island, Kingston, RI 02881
South Carolina	Clemson University, Clemson, SC 29631
South Dakota	South Dakota State Univ., Brookings, SD 57006
Tennessee	Univ. of Tennesse, Box 1071, Knoxville, TN 37901
Texas	Texas A & M Univ., College Station, TX 77843
Utah	Utah State University, Logan, UT 84321
Vermont	Univ. of Vermont, Burlington, VT 05401
Virginia	Virginia Polytechnic Institute, Blacksburg, VA 24061
Washington	Wash. State University, Pullman, WA 99163
West Virginia	W. Virginia Univ., 294 Coliseum, Morgantown, WV 26506
Wisconsin	Univ. of Wisc., 432 N. Lake St., Madison, WI 53706
Wyoming	Univ. of Wyoming, Box 3354, Laramie, WY 82070

TABLE A.2. SEED COMPANIES

Retail Company	Comments in Catalogue
Abbott and Cobb 4744 Frankford Avenue Philadelphia, PA 19124	20 page catalogue - all vegetables, including open-pollinated varieties.
Alberta Nurseries & Seeds, LTD P.O. Box 29, Bowden Alberta, Canada TOM OKO	14 of 48 pages on vegetables. Listings of short season, hardy types.
Arcnias Seed Store Corp. Box 109 Sedalia, MO 65301	13 of 42 pages on vegetables. Includes flowers, fruits and garden aids.
Burgess Seed & Plant Co. P.O. Box 3000 Galesburg, MI 49053	26 of 44 pages on vegetables. Many unusual items, herbs.
Burnett Brothers, Inc. 92 Chambers St. New York, NY 10007	48 page general catalogue of garden supplies, includes vegetables.
W. Atlee Burpee & Co. Clinton, IA 52732 or Riverside, CA 92502 or Warminster, PA 18974	54 of 182 pages on vegetables. Includes flowers, herbs, general garden supplies.
D. V. Burrell Seed Growers Co. Box 1501 Rocky Ford, CO 81067	97 pages with special emphasis on melons, peppers, tomatoes and varieties for California and the Southwest.
Comstock, Ferre & Co. Wethersfield, CT 06109	11 of 20 pages on vegetables. Includes 40 varieties of herbs.
DeGiorgi Co., Inc. Council Bluffs, IA 51501	112 pages including unusual varieties. Catalogue for sale.
Farmer Seed & Nursery Co. Fairbault, MN 55021	30 of 82 pages on vegetables. Includes midget, unusual and early-maturing varieties; herbs; flowers; fruits.
Henry Field Seed & Nursery Co. 407 Sycamore Street Shenandoah, IA 51601	116 pages for general gardening. Many varieties and suggestions for growing vegetables.
H. G. German Seeds, Inc. Smithport, PA 16749	6 of 46 pages on vegetables. Listing of varieties and price. No descriptions. Includes flowers and vegetable transplants.
Germania Seed Co. 5952 N. Milwaukee Avenue Chicago, IL 60646	8 of 64 pages on vegetables. Lists many varieties including 33 varieties of herbs and 76 of tomatoes.
Glecklers Seedmen Metamora, OH 43540	4 pages of unusual vegetables listed with brief descriptions.
Gurney Seed & Nursery Co. Yankton, SD 57078	22 of 76 pages on vegetables. Many unusual items, hardy plants, and general garden aids.

TABLE A.2. *(Continued)*

Joseph Harris Co., Inc. Moreton Farms Rochester, NY 14624	39 of 92 pages on vegetables. Includes descriptions. Considered authority in many parts of the country.
Charles C. Hart Seed Co. Box 169 Wethersfield, CT 06109	24 pages of vegetables, herbs, flowers, Includes All-America selections.
J. L. Hudson P.O. Box 1058 Redwood City, CA 94604	16 of 112 pages on vegetables. Many unusual vegetables and herbs.
Jackson & Perkins Medford, OR 97501	12 of 40 pages on vegetables. Well-known rose supplier.
La Jardin du Gourmet West Danville, VT 05873	16 pages of hard to find vegetables and herbs.
Johnny's Selected Seeds Albion, ME 04910	28 pages including hard to find Oriental vegetables.
J. W. Jung Seed Co. Station 8 Randolph, WI 53956	18 of 60 pages on vegetables. Many garden aids and newly released varieties.
Lakeland Nurseries Sales Hanover, PA 17331	8 of 64 pages on vegetables, mostly unusual types. Includes general garden aids and wild flowers.
Earl May Seed & Nursery Co. Shenandoah, IA 51603	82 pages of vegetables, flowers, fruits, general garden aids. Many varieties, All-America selections.
Meyer Seed Co. 600 S. Carolina Street Baltimore, MD 21231	23 pages of vegetables. Includes All-America selections.
Nichols Garden Nursery 1190 N. Pacific Highway Albany, OR 97321	64 pages of rare and unusual vegetables, herbs and recipes.
L. L. Olds Seed Co. P.O. Box 1069 Madison, WI 53701	30 of 80 pages on vegetables. Includes All-America selections.
George W. Park Seed Co., Inc. Greenwood, SC 29647	22 of 122 pages on vegetables. Includes midget and unusual vegetables, herbs, flowers, general garden aids.
Porter & Son, Seedsmen Stephenville, TX 76401	14 of 32 pages on vegetables. Includes trickle irrigation systems.
Rocky Mountain Seed Co. 1321-27 15th Street Denver, CO 80217	20 of 64 pages on vegetables. Includes herbs, wild flowers.
Seedway, Inc. Hall, NY 14463	19 of 36 pages on vegetables.

TABLE A.2. *(Continued)*

R. H. Shumway P.O. Box 777 Rockford IL 61101	88 pages. General garden catalogue.
Spring Hill Nurseries Tipp City, OH 45366	8 of 67 pages on vegetables. Includes flowers and fruit trees.
Stokes Seeds Box 548, Main Post Office Buffalo, NY 14240	62 of 158 pages on vegetables. Includes many varieties, unusual vegetables and herbs.
George Taits & Sons, Inc. 900 Tidewater Drive Norfolk, VA 23504	24 of 58 pages of vegetables. Special information for Virginia and North Carolina.
Otis S. Twilley Seed Co. P.O. Box 1817 Salisbury, MD 21801	44 of 64 pages on vegetables. Many varieties for various climates, disease-resistant varieties.

gardeners can determine companies which cover the general gardening area and others which are devoted specifically to vegetables.

NUTRITIVE VALUE OF VEGETABLES

Vegetables play an important role in meeting the needs of humans for vitamins and minerals. Vegetables, particularly potatoes and sweet potatoes, may also make a significant contribution as a source of calories. Leguminous seeds, such as peas and beans are an important source of vegetable protein. Some vegetables also possess laxative qualities. The nutritive value of vegetables is given in Table A.3 and A.4.

By the proper selection and combination of plant proteins it is possible to obtain the necessary supply of essential amino acids required by humans. Essential amino acids are those which the human body cannot make itself and it must obtain these from plant and animal proteins. Vegetable proteins are lacking in several essential amino acids, and to obtain the proper ratio of amino acids, one would need to know the amino acid composition of individual vegetable proteins. If a given protein contains only half the required amount of some essential amino acid, doubling the quantity of protein consumed will not provide optimum growth (but providing the lacking amount of the essential amino acid will). This has been suggested as the reason for the pellagra-like condition of humans who consume meals composed mainly of corn, which is deficient in lysine and tryptophan; even though the quantity of protein

TABLE A.3. NUTRITIONAL VALUE OF THE EDIBLE PART OF VEGETABLES'

Vegetable	Weight (g)	Calories	Protein (g)	Fat (g)	Carbohydrate (mg)	Calcium (mg)	Iron (mg)
Asparagus	145	94	30	3	5	30	0.9
Bean, Dry							
Great Northern	180	210	14	1	38	90	4.9
Navy or Pea	190	225	15	1	40	95	5.1
Lima	190	260	16	1	49	55	5.9
Bean, Fresh							
Lima	170	190	13	1	34	80	4.3
Snap, Green	125	30	2	T	7	63	0.8
Snap, Yellow	125	30	2	T	6	63	0.8
Bean, Mung, sprouts	125	35	4	T	7	21	1.1
Beet	170	55	2	T	12	24	0.9
Beet, greens	145	25	3	1	5	144	2.8
Broccoli	155	40	5	1	7	136	1.2
Brussels sprouts	155	55	7	1	10	50	1.7
Cabbage, raw							
Common varieties	70	15	1	T	4	34	0.3
Red	70	20	1	T	5	29	0.6
Savoy	70	15	2	T	3	47	0.6
Celery or Chinese	75	10	1	T	2	32	0.5
Cabbage, cooked							
Common varieties	145	30	2	T	6	64	0.4
Chinese	170	25	2	T	4	252	1.0
Carrot							
Raw	110	45	1	T	11	41	0.8
Cooked	145	45	1	T	10	48	0.9
Cauliflower	120	25	3	T	5	25	0.8
Celery, raw	100	15	1	T	4	39	0.3
Collard	190	55	5	1	9	289	1.1
Corn, Sweet	140	92	3	1	20	2	0.5
Cucumber, raw, pared							
6-⅛ inch center slices	50	5	T	T	2	8	0.2
Dandelion greens	180	60	4	1	12	252	3.2
Endive, Escarole							
2 ounces	57	10	1	T	2	46	1.0
Kale	110	30	4	1	4	147	1.3
Lettuce, raw							
Butterhead or Boston							
1-head (4 inch)	220	30	3	T	6	77	4.4

TABLE A.3. (Continued)

	Weight (g)	Calories	Protein (g)	Fat (g)	Carbohydrate (mg)	Calcium (mg)	Iron (mg)
Crisphead or Iceburg							
1-head (4-¾ inch)	454	60	4	T	13	91	2.3
Looseleaf-2 large leaves	50	10	1	T	2	34	0.7
Mustard greens	140	35	3	1	6	193	2.5
Okra, 8-3 by ⅝ inch pods	85	25	2	T	5	78	0.4
Onion, raw							
6 young, green-no tops	50	20	1	T	5	20	0.3
1 mature 2-½ inch	110	40	2	T	10	30	0.6
Onion, cooked	210	60	3	T	14	50	0.8
Parsnip	155	100	2	1	23	70	0.9
Pea, English	160	115	9	1	19	37	2.9
Pea, Southern	160	175	13	1	29	38	3.4
Pepper, Sweet							
1 raw, green pod-no stem or seeds	74	15	1	T	4	7	0.5
1 cooked pod	73	15	1	T	3	7	0.4
Potato, medium 5 oz.							
Baked, then peeled	99	90	3	T	21	9	0.7
Boiled, then peeled	136	105	3	T	23	10	0.8
Peeled, then boiled	122	80	2	T	18	7	0.6
Mashed, with milk, 1 cup	195	125	4	1	25	47	0.8
Pumpkin	228	75	2	1	18	57	0.9
Radish, raw, 4 small	40	5	T	T	1	12	0.4
Spinach	180	40	5	1	6	167	4.0
Squash							
Summer	210	30	2	T	7	52	0.8
Winter, baked	205	130	4	1	32	57	1.6
Sweet potato, medium 6 oz.							
Baked, then peeled	110	155	2	1	36	44	1.0
Boiled, then peeled	147	170	2	1	39	47	1.0
Canned	218	235	4	T	54	54	1.7
Tomato							
Raw, 1 medium, 7 oz.	200	40	2	T	9	24	0.9
Juice	243	45	2	T	10	17	2.2
Turnip	155	35	1	T	8	54	0.6
Turnip greens	145	30	3	T	5	252	1.5

¹Unless otherwise stated the vegetable was cooked, drained and 1 cup used. T = trace found. 1,000 mg = 1 g. 1 ounce (oz.) = 28.35 g.
SOURCE: ANON. (1971).

TABLE A.4. VITAMIN CONTENT OF THE EDIBLE PART OF VEGETABLES[1].

Vegetable	Vitamin A (I.U.)	Thiamin (mg)	Riboflavin (mg)	Niacin (mg)	Vitamin C (mg)
Asparagus	1,310	0.23	0.26	2.0	38
Bean, dry					
Great Northern	0	0.25	0.13	1.3	0
Navy or Pea	0	0.27	0.13	1.3	0
Lima	0	0.25	0.11	1.3	2
Bean, fresh					
Lima	480	0.31	0.17	2.2	29
Snap, green	680	0.09	0.11	0.6	15
Snap, yellow	290	0.09	0.11	0.6	16
Bean, Mung, sprouts	30	0.11	0.13	0.9	8
Beet	30	0.05	0.07	0.5	10
Beet, greens	7,400	0.10	0.22	0.4	22
Broccoli	3,880	0.14	0.31	1.2	140
Brussels sprouts	810	0.12	0.22	1.2	135
Cabbage, raw					
Common varieties	90	0.04	0.04	0.2	33
Red	30	0.06	0.04	0.3	43
Savoy	140	0.04	0.06	0.2	39
Celery or Chinese	110	0.04	0.03	0.5	19
Cabbage, cooked					
Common varieties	190	0.06	0.06	0.4	48
Chinese	5,270	0.07	0.14	1.2	26
Carrots					
Raw	12,100	0.06	0.06	0.7	9
Cooked	15,220	0.08	0.07	0.7	9
Cauliflower	70	0.11	0.10	0.7	66
Celery, raw	240	0.03	0.03	0.3	9
Collard	10,260	0.27	0.37	2.4	87
Corn, Sweet					
Yellow Variety	310	0.09	0.08	1.0	7
White Variety	T	0.09	0.08	1.0	7
Cucumbers, raw, pared					
6-⅛ inch center slices	T	0.02	0.02	0.1	6
Dandelion greens	21,060	0.24	0.29	—	32
Endive, Escarole					
2 ounces	1,870	0.04	0.08	0.3	6
Kale	8,140	—	—	—	68
Lettuce, raw					
Butterhead or Boston					
1 head (4 inch)	2,130	0.14	0.13	0.6	18
Crisphead or Iceburg					
1 head (4-¾ inch)	1,500	0.29	0.27	1.3	29
Looseleaf, 2 large leaves	950	0.03	0.04	0.2	9
Mustard greens	8,120	0.11	0.19	0.9	68
Okra, 8-3 by ⅝ inch pods	420	0.11	0.15	0.8	17
Onion, raw					
6 young, green-no tops	T	0.02	0.02	0.2	12
1 mature 2-½ inch	40	0.04	0.04	0.2	11
Onion, cooked	80	0.06	0.06	0.4	14
Parsnip	50	0.11	0.12	0.2	16
Pea, English	860	0.44	0.17	3.7	33
Pea, Southern	560	0.49	0.18	2.3	28
Pepper, Sweet					
1 raw, green pod- no stem or seeds	310	0.06	0.06	0.4	94
1 cooked pod	310	0.05	0.05	0.4	70

TABLE A.4. (Continued)

Vegetable	Vitamin A (I.U.)	Thiamin (mg)	Riboflavin (mg)	Niacin (mg)	Vitamin C (mg)
Potato, medium 5 oz.					
Baked, then peeled	T	0.10	0.04	1.7	20
Boiled, then peeled	T	0.13	0.05	2.0	22
Peeled, then boiled	T	0.11	0.04	1.4	20
Mashed with milk, 1 cup	50	0.16	0.10	2.0	19
Pumpkin	14,590	0.07	0.12	1.3	12
Radish, raw, 4 small	T	0.01	0.01	0.1	10
Spinach	14,580	0.13	0.25	1.0	50
Squash					
Summer	820	0.10	0.16	1.6	21
Winter, baked	8,610	0.10	0.27	1.4	27
Sweet potato, medium, 6 oz.					
Baked, then peeled	8,910	0.10	0.07	0.7	24
Boiled, then peeled	11,610	0.13	0.09	0.9	25
Canned	17,000	0.10	0.10	1.4	30
Tomato					
Raw, 1 medium, 7 oz.	1,640	0.11	0.07	1.3	42
Juice	1,940	0.12	0.07	1.9	39
Turnip	T	0.06	0.08	0.5	34
Turnip greens	8,270	0.15	0.33	0.7	68

[1]Unless otherwise stated the vegetable was cooked, drained and 1 cup used. T = trace found. Dashes in the columns show that no suitable value could be found although a measurable amount of the vitamin may be present. 1,000 mg = 1 g. 1 ounce (oz.) = 28.35 g.

SOURCE: ANON. (1971).

consumed is adequate to supply the required amount of lysine and tryptophan. Thus, vegetable diets are usually supplemented with some meat protein. It is probably a good practice to supply about one-fourth to one-half of the recommended daily protein requirement in the form of animal (or fish) proteins.

Fats provide a convenient and concentrated source of calories. Carbohydrates also provide calories, and they may be converted into fat, or temporarily stored in the liver as glycogen. Much of the sugar (from carbohydrate) absorbed by the body is converted into fat that the muscles use as fuel for mechanical energy. The nervous system also uses considerable amounts of energy to maintain itself in working order and about 20% of the basal metabolism takes place in the brain. The nervous system appears to derive its energy entirely from carbohydrate and seems to have no important stored energy and must depend entirely upon the carbohydrate furnished by the blood stream. Vegetables can provide considerable quantities of fat and carbohydrates.

Vitamin A may be eaten as the vitamin or as one of the carotenoid provitamins (the yellow pigments of most vegetables and fruits). Vitamin A is essential for integrity of epithelial cells, stimulates new cell growth, maintains resistance to infections, increases life, delays senility and is a necessary part of the reactions which occur in the eye for vision. Vegetables, particularly leafy greens, carrots and sweet potatoes are rich in Vitamin A.

Thiamin (Vitamin B_1) is essential for maintaining a good appetite and normal digestion. It is necessary for growth, fertility and lactation. It is required for normal functioning of nervous tissue and heart. The thiamin requirement is related to the calories consumed with large calorie diets requiring more thiamin.

Riboflavin (Vitamin B_2) is involved in numerous functions of cellular metabolism. It is present in eye pigments which are involved in light adaptation. About 0.5 to 3 mg of riboflavin is needed each day.

Niacin is involved in the biochemical machinery of the cells. It is not destroyed in ordinary cooking processes and about 10 times more niacin than thiamin is required each day.

Vitamin C (Ascorbic acid) is essential for good teeth formation, bone formation and repair, and in healing wounds. Scurvy is a result of Vitamin C deficiency and its symptoms usually occur when the body pool of Vitamin C is below 300 mg. The minimum amount of Vitamin C to prevent scurvy is about 10 mg per day but higher amounts (about 30 mg) are recommended to maintain other body functions. Leafy greens, potatoes, sweet potatoes and tomatoes are good sources of Vitamin C.

SELECTED REFERENCES

ANON. 1971. Nutritive value of foods. USDA Home and Garden Bulletin No. 72.

TABLE A.5. METRIC/ENGLISH SYSTEM CONVERSIONS.

METRIC EQUIVALENTS

LENGTH

inch	= 2.54 cm	millimeter	= 0.039 in.
foot	= 0.3048 m	centimeter	= 0.394 in.
yard	= 0.914 m	decimeter	= 3.937 in.
mile	= 1.69 km	meter	= 3.28 ft.
		kilometer	= 0.621 mile

AREA

square inch	= 6.452 cm^2	cm^2	= 0.155 sq in.
square foot	= 0.093 m^2	m^2	= 1.196 sq yd.
square yard	= 0.836 m^2	km^2	= 0.386 sq mile
square mile	= 2.59 km^2	ha	= 2.471 ac
acre	= 0.405 ha		

TABLE A.5. METRIC /ENGLISH SYSTEM CONVERSIONS. (*CONTINUED*)

VOLUME (DRY)

cubic inch	= 16.387 cm³	cm³	=	0.061 cu in.
cubic foot	= 0.028 m³	m³	=	31.338 cu ft
cubic yard	= 0.765 m³	hectolitre	=	2.8 bu
bushel	= 36.368 litres	m³	=	1.308 cu yd
board foot	= 0.0024 m³			

VOLUME (LIQUID)

fluid ounce (Imp)	= 28.412 ml	litre	= 35.2 fluid oz
pint	= 0.568 litre	hectolitre	= 26.418 gal
gallon	= 4.546 litres		

WEIGHT

ounce	= 28.349 g	gram	= 0.035 oz avdp
pound	= 453.592 g	kilogram	= 2.205 lb avdp
hundredweight (Imp)	= 45.359 kg	tonne	= 1.102 short ton
ton	= 0.907 tonne		

PROPORTION

1 gal /acre	= 11.232 litres /ha	1 litre /ha	= 14.24 fluid oz /acre
1 lb /acre	= 1.120 kg /ha	1 kg /ha	= 14.5 oz avdp /acre
1 lb /sq in.	= 0.0702 kg /cm²	1 kg /cm²	= 14.227 lb /sq in.
1 bu /acre	= 0.898 hl /ha	1 hl /ha	= 1.112 bu /acre

Index

Other AVI Books

AGRICULTURAL AND FOOD CHEMISTRY:
PAST, PRESENT, FUTURE   *Teranishi*

BREEDING FIELD CROPS
Poehlman

CITRUS SCIENCE AND TECHNOLOGY
Vols. 1 and 2   *Nagy, Shaw, and Veldhuis*

COMMERCIAL FRUIT PROCESSING
Woodroof and Luh

COMMERCIAL VEGETABLE PROCESSING
Luh and Woodroof

FRUIT AND VEGETABLE JUICE PROCESSING TECHNOLOGY
2nd Edition   *Tressler and Joslyn*

HANDLING, TRANSPORTATION AND STORAGE OF FRUITS AND VEGETABLES
Vol. 1, 2nd Edition   *Ryall and Lipton*
Vol. 2   *Ryall and Pentzer*

HORTICULTURAL REVIEWS
Vol. 1   *Janick*

POSTHARVEST BIOLOGY AND HANDLING OF FRUITS AND VEGETABLES
Haard and Salunkhe

POSTHARVEST PHYSIOLOGY, HANDLING AND UTILIZATION OF TROPICAL AND SUBTROPICAL FRUITS AND VEGETABLES
Pantastico

POTATO PROCESSING
3rd Edition   *Talburt and Smith*

POTATOES: PRODUCTION STORING, PROCESSING
2nd Edition   *Smith*

RICE: PRODUCTION AND UTILIZATION
Luh

SEED PROTEINS
Inglett

SOYBEANS: CHEMISTRY AND TECHNOLOGY
Vol. 1 Revised Second Printing   *Smith and Circle*

SWEET POTATOES: PRODUCTION, PROCESSING, MARKETING
Edmond and Ammerman

TOMATO PRODUCTION, PROCESSING AND QUALITY EVALUATION
Gould